AGE IN SOCIETY 4

scourse Analysis

Th
DO

Language in Society

GENERAL EDITOR
  Peter Trudgill, Reader in Linguistic Science
  University of Reading

ADVISORY EDITORS
  Ralph Fasold, Professor of Linguistics
  Georgetown University
  William Labov, Professor of Linguistics
  University of Pennsylvania

Discourse Analysis

The Sociolinguistic Analysis of Natural Language

MICHAEL STUBBS

BASIL BLACKWELL

1983.

© Michael Stubbs 1983

First published 1983
Reprinted 1985

Basil Blackwell Ltd
108 Cowley Road, Oxford OX4 1JF, UK

British Library Cataloguing in Publication Data

Stubbs, Michael
  Discourse analysis: the sociolinguistic analysis
  of natural language—(Language in Society; no.4)
  1. Discourse analysis
  I. Title   II. Series
  415   P302

ISBN 0-631-10381-3
      0-631-12763-1 Pbk

Typesetting by Unicus Graphics Ltd, Horsham
Printed in Great Britain

Contents

Editor's Preface

Michael Stubbs is an author who has always believed that socio-linguistics should be about language as it is used in everyday life, in conversational situations, by real people. He is also a linguist who has been more concerned than most that the results of linguistic research should be brought to the attention of those involved in the world of education. This book illustrates very clearly both these concerns. Much of the data on which it is based have been obtained by Stubbs himself in genuine, real-life situations; and the theoretical issues debated are accompanied by discussion of their practical implications. The book is one of the very first attempts to give theoretical coherence to a relatively new and hitherto somewhat diffuse and anecdotal field. And, though written from a predominantly linguistic perspective, it also synthesizes, as a result of Stubbs' sensitivity towards and knowledge of these fields, points of view from areas such as sociology and anthropology which have a bearing on the way in which language is used in conversational and other forms of discourse. It is appropriate that a book in this field should look at both language and society: *Discourse Analysis* sheds linguistic light on social process and, through its informed interactional perspective, also advances our understanding of the use of structure of language.

PETER TRUDGILL

Acknowledgements

I owe a major debt to John McH. Sinclair, Professor of Modern English Language at the University of Birmingham. I worked with him briefly on a project on discourse analysis in 1972–73, and was greatly influenced by his approach to linguistic description.

Another major debt is to Margaret Berry, Reader in English Language at the University of Nottingham, who has commented in great detail on drafts of the whole book. She has made so many detailed suggestions, in over a hundred pages of notes, that it would be impossible to acknowledge them individually. I have plundered her notes to an extent that verges on co-authorship. In this way, however, she reserves the right to disagree with me in those places where I have not had the good sense to follow her suggestions. I am very grateful for all her clear and sensible criticisms.

I am also grateful to Margaret Deuchar, Lesley Milroy, Mike McTear, Peter Trudgill, and Henry Widdowson for detailed comments on draft chapters, and to Freda Duckitt and Norma Hazzledine for transforming muddles of typing and handwriting into connected text.

Some of the chapters in this book are revised versions of articles previously published elsewhere, and I am grateful to the publishers for permission to use the material here. Chapter 3 is based on an article first published in M. Stubbs and S. Delamont, eds., *Explorations in Classroom Observation*, John Wiley, 1976. Chapter 7 is based on an article first published in M. Coulthard and M. Montgomery, eds., *Studies in Discourse Analysis*, Routledge and Kegan Paul, 1981. Material in chapter 9 was also first reported by M. Coulthard in chapter 1 of *Studies in Discourse Analysis*. And chapter 10 is based on an article first published in R. Carter and D. Burton, eds., *Literary Text and Language Study*, Edward Arnold, 1982.

Preliminary versions of other chapters were previously circulated in mimeo. Chapter 2 is based on an article co-authored with Deirdre Burton in the *MALS Journal*, Summer 1975. Chapters 4, 5 and 6 are based on an article in the *Belfast Working Papers in Language and Linguistics*, 5, 1981. Material in chapters 8 and 9 is based on sections of *Working Papers in Discourse Analysis*, 5, 1973, English Language Research, University of Birmingham; this research was funded by the Social Science Research Council. Chapter 11 is based on an article in C. Adelman, ed., *Uttering, Muttering*, Mimeo, Bulmershe College of Higher Education, 1976.

In all cases, the material has been extensively rewritten.

Notational Conventions

Single quotation marks ' '
for quotations from other authors.

Double quotation marks " "
for meanings and propositions.

Italics
for short linguistic forms cited in the text.
(Longer forms cited on separate numbered lines have not been italicized.)

Asterisk *
(a) for ungrammatical or semantically anomalous forms;
(b) for forms which are well-formed in isolation, but which create ill-formed discourse in context.

Round brackets ( )
(a) for optional elements of structure;
(b) for comments in transcripts;
(c) for pauses in transcripts, e.g. (2): pause of two seconds;
(d) empty brackets indicate inaudible section on transcript.

Square brackets [ ]
(a) for narrow phonetic transcriptions;
(b) for exchange boundaries (see chapter 7, section 3).

Slanting brackets / /
for broad transcriptions.

$\left\{ \begin{array}{l} A \\ B \end{array} \right.$
system, choose A or B.

Curly brace {
  simultaneous choice.

$$\begin{cases} \{ \begin{matrix} A \\ B \end{matrix} \\ \{ \begin{matrix} C \\ D \end{matrix} \end{cases}$$

choose A or B, and C or D.

1

Discourse Analysis: A Programmatic Introduction

The term *discourse analysis* is very ambiguous. I will use it in this book to refer mainly to the linguistic analysis of naturally occurring connected spoken or written discourse. Roughly speaking, it refers to attempts to study the organization of language above the sentence or above the clause, and therefore to study larger linguistic units, such as conversational exchanges or written texts. It follows that discourse analysis is also concerned with language in use in social contexts, and in particular with interaction or dialogue between speakers. Since the term *discourse analysis* is very ambiguous, I will comment in more detail on this introductory definition towards the end of this chapter. (See section 5.)

1 *Language, action, knowledge and situation*

Much of the fascination of discourse analysis comes from the realization that language, action and knowledge are inseparable. The most essential insight, discussed by J. L. Austin in his 1955 lectures at Harvard University, is that utterances are actions (Austin, 1962). Some actions can be performed only through language (for example, apologizing), whilst others can be performed either verbally or non-verbally (for example, threatening). In addition, as soon as we start to study how language is used in social interaction, it becomes clear that communication is impossible without shared knowledge and assumptions between speakers and hearers.

It follows also that language and situation are inseparable. There is no deterministic relationship, of course, except in highly ritualized situations. In certain games, ceremonies and formal rituals, actual forms of words may be laid down as part of the proceedings, but most everyday uses of language are much more flexible. Given a social situation such as a 'small village shop', it is possible to predict a great deal about the content, functions and style of language used there.

Much of the language will be either local gossip or transactional, concerned with buying and selling. However, I have recently visited a local village shop to perform other speech acts: to *complain* about unsatisfactory newspaper deliveries, and to *ask directions* to a local street. Nevertheless, we often know what kind of language to expect in different situations; and, conversely, given a fragment of language, we can often reconstruct in some detail the social situation which produced it. An easy demonstration of this is to turn the knob on a radio to tune in to different programmes. It usually takes only a few seconds to identify whether we are listening to a sermon, sports commentary, quiz programme, news broadcast, interview, disc jockey, play, or to a programme for young children or school pupils, or whatever. The identifying features include phonology, lexis, syntax and paralinguistic features, such as speed and rhythm. Forms vary according to function: according to the speech event (sermon versus lecture), the speech act (informing versus questioning) and the intended addressee (child versus adult), as well as other factors.

Furthermore, situations can be altered or created by using language in different ways, for example, by selecting the speech act of whispering sweet nothings, rather than nagging, carping, complaining or accusing. Any choice of words creates a mini-world or universe of discourse, and makes predictions about what is also likely to occur in the same context. For example, did the words *nagging* and *carping* earlier in this paragraph imply to you a woman speaker, or can men also nag?

It is obvious enough in a commonsense way, of course, that much language is not to be taken literally, that language is used to perform actions, and that different social situations produce different language. I recently witnessed the aftermath of a minor traffic accident, in which a van ran into two parked cars. It was dark, and the van-driver claimed he had been blinded by oncoming headlights. The two parked cars both belonged to the same man, who was, understandably, annoyed. He questioned whether the van-driver had been drinking, and said that, if the driver did not produce a better excuse for the accident, he would call the police, saying in a paradoxical, self-referential way:

1.1   That's not a threat, it's just a fact.

It was, of course, a threat; and some of the language he later used to perform speech acts such as questioning, complaining and swearing, was also produced rather directly by the situation, and therefore rather predictable. This language was, however, certainly very different from the language he later used to report the accident to his insurance company. The speech acts performed would certainly have been different (for example, reporting and requesting payment, rather than complaining). And the linguistic forms would have been appropriate to a formal written report, rather than to spoken interaction.

Such a view of language as action in context was put forward by Malinowski in the 1920s (Malinowski, 1923), but has not been central to much recent linguistics. (In chapter 8 I discuss other literature on speech acts and provide a more detailed definition of this concept.)

2 The impossibility of discourse analysis?

Such traditional and commonsense insights into the relations between language, action, knowledge and situation mean, of course, that discourse analysis is very difficult. We seem to be dealing with some kind of theory of social action. We certainly cannot restrict our view of meaning and information to matters of logic as many linguists have tried to do. We are not, for example, simply dealing with the truth values of sentences: whether statements are true or false. This is evident, since we often accept as appropriate in every-day conversation utterances which logic would reject as tautological or contradictory. Here are two simple examples I overheard recently in conversation, and which passed unremarked:

1.2   It may rain, or then again it may not.
1.3   It often does, but nine times out of ten it doesn't.

In other words, if we start looking at the everyday use of language, we seem to be involved in different logics, and what is ill-formed from a logical point of view, may be quite normal in conversation, myth or science fiction, which imply different universes of beliefs and different background assumptions.

It may be an overstatement to claim that different logics are involved. A more careful formulation might be that several different factors all interact to determine the acceptability or appropriateness of utterances used in different social contexts: not only their logical or propositional structure, or their truth value, but also knowledge of the rhetorical functions which the utterance may be serving in an argument or casual social conversation. We require knowledge, there-fore, of what speech act is being performed in what speech event. It is because of this complexity in judging acceptability or appropriateness that linguists have often tried to restrict their judgements to grammaticality, or to what seem more straightforward semantic judgements of synonymy (or paraphrase), contradiction, logical entailment, and the like.

However, meaning and truth are not independent of use. Even the truth of a sentence is often dependent on how it is used as an utterance. For example:

1.4   Italy is shaped like a boot and France is hexagonal.

is true in a sense, for certain mnemonic purposes, which might be satisfactory for schoolboys, but not for geographers or touroperators. Truth conditions are not only a question of correspondence between a sentence and the state of the world, but also of different kinds of appropriateness (cf. Austin, 1958: 12).

Furthermore, the concept of truth is in any case applicable only to a narrow range of sentences. Very briefly, only statements can be true or false. But truth or falsity are not applicable to questions, directives, expletives, promises, counterfactuals (e.g. *If Harry was more intelligent, he wouldn't have married Susan*), and other utterances which express probabilities, beliefs or intentions. As well as a view of meaning which deals with truth conditions, we therefore also require to consider the speech acts performed by utterances.

An immediate problem is, then, the depth of indirection which is often involved: the distance from surface linguistic forms to underlying social meanings, from utterances to directives, hints and challenges. Examples of indirect speech acts are very common. For example, a speaker might say:

1.5   Your glass is empty.

And this might mean:

1.6   "I'm offering to buy you a drink."

However, some utterances can be much more indirect. I was in a hospital recently and overheard a consultant surgeon say to a patient:

1.7   Right – a little tiny hole and a fishing expedition – is that it?

What he meant was something like:

1.8   "I am going to operate on you and remove your appendix."

The choice of the very indirect reference was presumably also intended to convey reassurance, by a jocular reference to an every-day operation.

We have, then, the basic problem of how speakers can say one thing and mean another. There is, therefore, also the converse prob-lem of how hearers may perform long strings of interpretation on any utterance they hear. For, however odd the utterance, hearers will do their utmost to make sense of the language they hear, by bringing to bear on it all possible knowledge and interpretation. (I provide more formally analysed examples of such indirection at several points later in this book.) It is well known to linguists that hearers and readers have a powerful urge to make sense out of whatever nonsense is presented to them, and this principle has obvious rele-vance to a practical study of rhetorical devices used in advertising, political manifestos and so forth.

In the face of such obvious difficulties, it is understandable that linguists have often followed the strategy of idealizing their object of study to exclude everything but isolated and decontextualized sentences. For it does seem that beyond the tidy and well-pruned bonsai trees of syntax lies the jungle: menus, road signs, advertise-ments, propaganda, guarantees, recipes, instructions, lectures, speeches, jokes, news bulletins, arguments and the like, not to mention discussions, conversations and novels. However, all is not hopeless. One thing that linguistics has always been particularly good at is developing ways of describing multiple levels or organiza-tion and meaning. Language, situation, knowledge and action are interrelated, but they are not all the same thing, a kind of socio-psychological swamp. There may still be a place for surprisingly autonomous levels of organization. It is plausible, of course, that the organization is not as neat at higher levels. It is perfectly plausible that languages are tightly patterned at the lower levels of phonology, morphology and syntax, and that discourse is more loosely con-structed. Nevertheless, it is quite obvious that menus, stories and conversations have beginnings, middles and ends, and that is already a structural claim.

However, the basic insight about language as action raises another serious problem for analysis. This is the range of different functions which language can serve: promising, asserting, describing, impressing, intimidating, persuading, comforting, gossiping, arguing, complaining, reciting, swearing, protesting, betting, and so on indefinitely. Some functions can be very complex, and may not be acquired as part of communicative competence until relatively late in life: for example, expressing condolences. In many Western cultures, children are protected from social situations in which taboo subjects such as death are discussed. They are often not present at funerals, yet are expected to be able to 'say the right thing' when the occasion arises, without either explicit instruction or informal observation (Saville-Troike, 1982: 233). Further, utterances typically serve more than one function at the same time. However, this kind of unordered list is artificial, for some functions of language are more basic than others. Chomsky has argued that it is futile to study the uses of language, because they might be almost any imaginable. However, as Bennett (1976: 6) argues, one can imagine in principle a community in which language is used only to inform and to enjoin someone to do something, even if we will never come across such a community in sociolinguistic reality. But one cannot even imagine a language used 'for all sorts of purposes', but not to inform and enjoin. And the study of informing, directing and related acts is complex, but imaginably manageable.

Many, if not most linguists, would admit the points I am making. For example, Lyons (1977: 637) writes: 'There is much in the structure of languages that can only be explained on the assumption that they have developed for communication in face-to-face interaction.' However, not all linguists see the need to take the implications of this observation seriously. Lyons himself, in all the 900 pages of the work cited on *Semantics*, does not analyse a single naturally occurring text, written or spoken. Nor, for that matter, does he even study a contrived text.

3   *Discourse analysis and linguistics*

An implication of such points about the uses of language is that much of syntactic theory has to be thoroughly reconsidered. For example, it is arguable that the conveying of factual, propositional information is somehow basic: so basic that it has often not been noticed. (Prague School linguistics is an exception here.) And an increasing number of linguists are starting to suggest that the analysis of sentence structure should be based on an information structure of a given–new or topic–comment kind, according to what is known or taken for granted at a given point in a discourse sequence.

Much of the fascination of discourse analysis derives, in fact, from the realization that the boundaries of linguistics are being redrawn. There is no going back, of course, on the standards of explanation and rigour set by the kind of structural linguistics created principally by Saussure, Bloomfield and Chomsky. However, it has become increasingly clear that a coherent view of language, including syntax, must take account of discourse phenomena. As with any paradigm, transformational grammar carries the hint of its own destruction within it. For as soon as one writes context-sensitive rules of the form 'rewrite *a* as *b* in context *c*', one begins to wonder about the context which acts as the trigger for the rule. It is purely linguistic? Is it within the sentence? Or in the preceding discourse? Or in the act being performed? Or in the social context? Is there any important difference between these triggering contexts?

It follows that the grammatical, structural units of clause or sentence are not necessarily either the most important units for language study, or the biggest, although the clause will probably remain basic as a unit of syntax, of propositional information, and as the potential realization of a speech act. However, there are grounds for arguing that discourse units such as *lecture*, *conversation*, *speech* and *story* are the upper limit of structural organization. Such units are culturally recognizable units, since completeness at this level is recognizable: people say such things as, 'I want to hear how the story ends.' However, larger units are not recognizable in this way. One may talk, admittedly, of a series of lectures. However, the structure discernible over such a series appears to be the structure of, for example, an argument. And such a structure is also recognizable in single lectures or smaller stretches of language.

These are, very briefly, some of the reasons why the study of connected discourse in natural situations is forcing linguistics to reconsider its descriptive categories (cf. chapter 4).

4 *Discourse analysis and sociolinguistics*

It is worthwhile also making explicit the implications of discourse analysis for sociolinguistic theory. Sociolinguistics will ultimately have to be based, at least partly, on analyses of how people actually talk to each other in everyday settings, such as streets, pubs, shops, restaurants, buses, trains, schools, doctor's surgeries, factories and homes. Therefore, sociolinguistics will have to incorporate analyses of how conversation works: that is, how talk between people is organized; what makes it coherent and understandable; how people introduce and change topics; how they interrupt, ask questions, and give or evade answers; and, in general, how the conversational flow is maintained or disrupted. It is principally through conversational interaction, the give-and-take of everyday multi-party discourse, that social 'roles' are recognized and sustained. We can talk about intuitively recognizable social roles such as 'teacher' and 'doctor'. Clearly, in some sense, people *are* teachers or doctors – that is their job. But clearly, also, there is quite specific conversational behaviour attached to being a teacher – as teachers would soon discover if they talked to their families as they do to their pupils. Even in the classroom, a teacher cannot simply *be* a teacher, without *doing* quite specific and describable conversational activities, such as explaining, defining, questioning, and so on. (Chapter 3 develops this point in detail.) 'Roles' have to be acted out in social interaction.

Certainly, sociolinguistics also requires other quite different kinds of analysis. It requires, for example, correlational studies which relate linguistic features to large-scale socio-economic variables, and also general ethnographic description of cultural norms of speech behaviour in as wide a range of situations and cultures as possible. (Saville-Troike, 1982, provides a clear survey of such studies.) However, isolated phonological and grammatical variables, which can be correlated, for example, with the social class stratification, sex or ethnic group of speakers, are plucked out of a conversational context. And ethnographic description is a highly interpretative abstraction from observed conversational interaction, amongst other kinds of data. In one way or another, then, we require analyses of how conversation itself actually works as a partly autonomous system or, more accurately, as a system of systems. More generally, a functional account of language (which I take any sociolinguistic description to be) requires a study of the range of functions served by language from utterances to discourses.

On the one hand, therefore, there is no use of language which is not embedded in the culture; on the other hand, there are no large-scale relationships between language and society which are not realized, at least partly, through verbal interaction. In Goodenough's (1964) famous formulation: '... a society's culture consists of whatever one has to know or believe in order to operate in a manner acceptable to its members, and to do so in any role that they accept for themselves.' Culture is 'what everyone knows', and part of this knowledge is conversational competence. The general vision is of culture as comprising interlocking systems of meaning. And an essential insight here is that one cannot not communicate: staring impassively straight ahead without saying anything still communicates.

From the point of view of both core linguistics and sociolinguistics, Austin's (1962: 147) moral has considerable force: 'The total speech act in the total speech situation is the *only actual* phenomenon which, in the last resort, we are engaged in elucidating' (emphasis in original). However, there are various kinds of idealization which are necessary on the way to this ideal, and in my arguments so far, I have failed to distinguish them clearly. Much of the confusion arises from ambiguities in the term *discourse analysis*.

5   *Terminology*

The terms *text* and *discourse* require some comment, since their use is often ambiguous and confusing. I do not propose to draw any important distinction between the two terms. As they are used in the literature, they often simply imply slight differences in emphasis, on which I do not wish to base any important theoretical distinction. First, one often talks of *written text* versus *spoken discourse*. Or alternatively, *discourse* often implies *interactive discourse*; whereas *text* implies *non-interactive monologue*, whether intended to be spoken aloud or not. For example, one talks of the (written) *text* of a speech. Such ambiguities arise also in everyday terms for discourse. For example, a *lecture* may refer to a whole social event, or only to the main spoken text or its written version. And one can speak of an academic *paper*, meaning what is delivered or read to an audience, or its printed version (Goffman, 1981). A second distinction is that *discourse* implies length, whereas a *text* may be very short. In this usage, complete texts include: 'Exit' or 'No smoking' (cf. Halliday and Hasan, 1976). Some researchers have attempted to draw the distinction in a more interesting way. For example, Widdowson (1979b) distinguishes *textual cohesion*, recognizable in surface lexis, grammar and propositional development, from *discourse coherence* which operates between underlying speech acts. The distinction between surface cohesion between linguistic forms and propositions and underlying functional coherence is an important one, but clearly they can both operate in a given text or discourse. The basic problem is to account for the recognizable unity or connectedness of stretches of language, whether this unity is structural, or semantic or functional. Another theoretically loaded way of drawing a distinction is proposed by Van Dijk (1977). He uses the term *text* to refer to an abstract theoretical construct which is realized in *discourse*. In other words, text is to discourse as sentence is to utterance. Halliday (1978: 40) uses the term *text* to point to the same distinction, but he chooses the opposite term to refer to surface realization, and talks of language being actualized in *text*.

I will also favour the term *discourse analysis* over other terms, more from convenience than for important theoretical reasons. The term *text analysis* could serve equally well, except that it implies work done within a particular European tradition, represented for example by Van Dijk's work. Similarly, the term *conversational analysis* almost always implies an ethnomethodological approach which derives from Sacks' work. Conversation is basic: the commonest use of language, a pervasive phenomenon of everyday life which deserves systematic study on those grounds alone. If only because of its massive occurrence, spontaneous unrehearsed conversation must provide some kind of baseline or norm for the description of language in general. However, the term *conversational analysis* is also too narrow as it appears to cut out the study of more formal spoken language and written language, although there are problems in the analysis of discourse which are common to formal and informal, written and spoken language.

6   *Idealization*

These are largely terminological issues of no real importance. However, there is one confusion which is more important.[1] *Discourse analysis* is used to refer both to the study of language above the sentence (more accurately, above the clause), and also to the study of naturally occurring language. It is sometimes implied that each of these approaches entails the other, but this is clearly not so. Discourse organization may be studied on the basis of intuitive, hypothetical data. Alternatively, naturally occurring data may be studied in terms of phonological or grammatical structure, with no reference to organization above the clause.

In fact, there are three different decisions which have to be made in deciding how much idealization is necessary or justifiable in the study of language. These involve (a) the size of units to be studied: basically smaller or larger than sentences; (b) whether these sequences are to be contrived by the linguist or to be naturally occurring; and

---

[1]   This formulation in section 6 owes a great deal to discussion with Margaret Berry and to an unpublished paper by her.

(c) whether non-linguistic factors of the context are to be studied or not. In practice, a decision to study, say, (a) narratives will often *size of unit* coincide with a decision to record and study (b) naturally occurring stories, and consider (c) the effect of teller and audience on narrative *non-ling.* structure. However, in principle, the decisions are independent. (Lyons, 1977: 586ff, 633ff, further distinguishes other kinds of idealization.)

This is a substantial point of confusion. It leads to the terminological confusion that any study which is not dealing with (a) single sentences, (b) contrived by the linguist (c) out of context, may be called *discourse analysis.* Surprisingly, even some studies of (a) isolated, (b) contrived, (c) decontextualized sentences manage to squeeze into discourse analysis. For example, most of the substantial literature on speech act theory falls under this description. This literature is often discussed as part of discourse analysis, since it provides an essential basis for a functional view of language as action; and an essential basis for reclassifying syntactic units as functional units. Thus something which is syntactically declarative, say:

1.9   I wish you'd stop doing that.

may have to be reclassified, not as a statement, but as a speech act of request. And such a reclassification may be necessary before sequences of utterances can be analysed. (See chapter 8.)

7   The state of the art

This short introductory chapter has set out, in rather programmatic terms, some of the main problems for discourse analysis. It is tempting to formulate the pseudo-naive question: is the study of real connected discourse not simply linguistics? And to argue, as Labov (1972c) has done, that there is something trivial about a study of language that cannot describe and explain the ways in which people use language to talk to their friends, shout at their children, conduct business in shops and restaurants, and all the rest. To answer fully such pseudo-naive questions, requires not only a full discussion of the place of idealization in any academic study, but also an account of the changing relationship between linguistics and other academic disciplines, including literary criticism, anthropology and philosophy.

There is not even one single definable development which has led to the current avalanche of relevant work on discourse. Rather, there has been a gathering consensus, particularly since the mid-1960s, that some of the basic assumptions of Saussurean–Bloomfieldean–Chomskyan linguistics must be questioned. As I have indicated briefly already, this consensus has come about due to work in different disciplines. Some of the main contributing scholars have been from: anthropology, in particular ethnography (Gumperz, Hymes); sociology (Goffman) and in particular ethnomethodology (Sacks, Schegloff); philosophy (Austin, Searle); artificial intelligence (Winograd); and sociolinguistics (Labov); as well as substantive areas which themselves span linguistics, psychology and sociology, such as child language (Ervin-Tripp, Ochs Keenan). All of these scholars have contributed to the growing consensus that much contemporary linguistics is artificially and unnecessarily limited in its data and methods, and have made important contributions to studying how language is used.

I am particularly conscious that there are other important areas of study (for example, social psychology) and important aspects of spoken interaction (for example, intonation and kinesics) that I have hardly mentioned. I have also not discussed in this book the wide range of applications of discourse analysis, although I have discussed this elsewhere (Stubbs, in press). I can only point out that no one is in a position to write a comprehensive account of discourse analysis. The subject is at once too vast, and too lacking in focus and consensus. Imagine the rather comparable task of writing a book simply entitled *Grammar* in, say, the 1920s. Anything at all that is written on discourse analysis is partial and controversial.

I do not wish to argue, therefore, that linguistics *is* discourse analysis, nor do I wish to argue that discourse analysis should be a separate sub-branch of linguistics. Such a separation of disciplines and branches of disciplines is often useful until it has been established that there is an interesting set of phenomena, previously ignored, which should be studied. However, a more important argument is that a coherent view of language must take account of its everyday use in connected discourse.

I hereby conclude this chapter, then, by performing a complex of self-referential and multi-functional acts: apologizing, complaining, defining, warning and offering a caveat. However, I also hereby admit that there is something rather unsatisfactory about such meta-acts; complaining about the difficulties of discourse analysis, rather than doing it. In the next chapter, I will therefore begin to analyse naturally occurring conversational data.

8   *The organization of the book*

The rest of this book is organized in the following way. Chapters 2, 3 and 4 introduce three different approaches to discourse analysis, which have considerable plausibility and which can give considerable insights into written and spoken discourse. Chapter 2 takes a particular extract of transcribed conversational data and examines it closely: this can reveal many features of spoken discourse of great potential interest to linguistic description. On the other hand, it has the inevitable limitations of any study which is restricted to a single text. Chapter 3 focuses on language use in a particular social setting. It is based on field-work observations of the functions served by utterances in a particular type of speech event: classroom teaching. Again, this can give insights of both practical and theoretical interest, but has the limitations of any such observational and ethnographic work. Such discussions, which begin from different kinds of conversational data, are often a good introduction to discourse analysis for students. Students generally have to examine for themselves a considerable amount of linguistic data, before they discover the kinds of regularities and patterns which linguists take for granted. Chapter 4 discusses more directly some limitations in traditional linguistic descriptions of language, which are restricted to the semantics and syntax of sentences. Again, this may be a useful introduction for students familiar with the most basic concepts of descriptive linguistics. It provides also a further discussion of a different kind of data, and more explicit discussion of the kinds of argument which can be based on data. Together chapters 2, 3 and 4 raise many of the descriptive and theoretical problems which discourse analysis must tackle, with as many detailed examples as possible.

Chapters 5, 6 and 7 are rather more abstract. They discuss more directly the nature of the descriptive model which is applicable to discourse, and in particular how far the concepts which have been developed in linguistic theory are useful in discourse analysis. For example, is discourse analysable in terms of systems and structures, in the way that phonological and syntactic organization are? It is this combination of the description of the details of naturally occurring language (chapters 2, 3 and 4), with the use of linguistic descriptive concepts (chapters 5, 6 and 7), which defines discourse analysis, as I use the term in this book; and which distinguishes discourse analysis from related studies in sociology, social psychology, anthropology and other disciplines.

Chapters 8 and 9 discuss a central problem in the analysis of natural language: the depth of indirection involved in many utterances. This problem has received much attention from speech act theorists, and therefore allows also a discussion of some aspects of speech act theory and its relation to discourse analysis. From the point of view of the analyst, the problem can be formulated as: how far is discourse organization observable in the surface features of texts? Chapter 10 then takes a single whole text (of a short story) and discusses how such concepts of indirection can contribute to its interpretation.

Finally, chapter 11 discusses theoretical and practical problems in collecting data for discourse analysis, and provides a large number of ideas for students and researchers who are involved in analysing natural language.

Several arguments are maintained throughout the book, and on the whole the earlier chapters are easier reading than the later ones. On the other hand, the chapters are relatively self-contained, and can be read largely independently by someone who already has some knowledge of the field.

2

On Speaking Terms: Inspecting Conversational Data

It is easy to get the impression that discourse analysis is at least a foolhardy, if not a quite impossible undertaking, and that expanding the narrow range of phenomena that linguists study to include natural language in use causes all hell to break loose. Certainly, the task is daunting. However, the chaos can be contained in various ways, and, in fact, only some hell breaks loose.

One way of preventing panic and mental paralysis in the face of problems which have so far defeated linguists, sociologists and philosophers, is to study in detail a particular transcript of conversational data. After a few introductory points, I will do so in this chapter. This will provide an opportunity for a detailed informal introduction to the kinds of phenomena which discourse analysis has to explain, and the kinds of discourse phenomena which recent linguistics has typically ignored. It will provide some initial arguments that such conversational data are, after all, manageable and amenable in principle to systematic analysis. Alongside some commentary on data, there will also be, however, brief glimpses into the theoretical chasms over which we are precariously suspended.

1 Discourse organization

It has sometimes been maintained that there is no linguistic organization above sentence level. However, I suspect that some people believe this because they have never looked for such organization. To maintain this would be to maintain the odd position that conversation or written text consists of unordered strings of utterances. Connected discourse is clearly not random. People are quite able to distinguish between a random list of sentences and a coherent text, and it is the principles which underlie this recognition of coherence which are the topic of study for discourse analysts.

There are several other ways of demonstrating informally that discourse is organized. First, conversationalists themselves frequently refer to discourse structure in the course of conversation, by utterances such as: *oh, by the way* ...; *anyway, as I was saying* ...; *before I answer that* ...; or *that reminds me* .... In everyday situations, conversationalists are aware that not anything can follow anything: some utterances require to be prefaced by such an excuse or a claim of relevance. (Cf. Schegloff and Sacks, 1973.) This insertion of such metatext, pointing to the organization of the text itself, is particularly common in certain discourse styles, such as lecturing, and it occurs in written as well as spoken discourse. However, it is also perfectly normal in casual conversation. This ability to jump out of the system and comment on it makes discourse organization significantly different from sentence organization. It is possible, of course, to have isolated self-referential sentences. Common examples are provided by sentences which include explicit performative verbs (such as *ask*, *tell*, *promise*):

2.1   I'm *asking* you who you were with last night.

But in the course of conversation, it is quite usual, and passes unnoticed, for an utterance to step outside the conversation, comment on its progress, and propose a re-orientation:

2.2   Look, let's consider this in another way.

And there is no analogue to this in syntactic organization. More accurately, such utterances are simultaneously conversational acts *in* the linear sequence of discourse and also acts at a higher metalevel, which comment on the lower level. The routine nature of such utterances has been taken as an argument that such comments from conversationalists give interesting access to the way they themselves understand the conversation, and therefore should have privileged status as data (cf. Schegloff and Sacks, 1973). I discuss such metatext at more length in chapter 3.

Second, there are many jokes which depend on our ability to recognize faulty discourse sequences. The simplest possible type is:

2.3   A: Yes, I can.
       B: Can you see into the future?

At the risk of being tedious, this joke depends on two things: the recognition that the question–answer sequence has been reversed; and that the grammatical cohesion has been disrupted. *Yes, I can* is elliptic and only interpretable via the following, instead of the preceding, utterance.

On the same model is the joke about the man who goes into a chemist's shop. The exchange goes:

2.4   Customer: Good morning. Do you have anything to treat complete loss of voice?
       Shopkeeper: Good morning, sir. And what can I do for you?

In this case, the shopkeeper's utterance occurs in the wrong structural position. It occurs second, although it is strongly marked as an opening conversational move: by the greeting, the address term, the content and form of the question.

Such examples demonstrate immediately our discourse competence to recognize that utterances can occur in some sequences but not others. Therefore, discourse should in principle be analysable in terms of syntagmatic constraints on possible sequences of utterances. Such examples therefore provide one quick and informal answer to the often-repeated claim that in conversation 'anything can follow anything'. This objection does, however, require a much more detailed and formal response, and I give such a response in chapter 5.

For the present, I simply wish to point out that deviant sequences are recognizable as such. Some discourse sequences are impossible, or at least highly improbable. Consider this example (based on an example by Labov):

2.5   I approach a stranger in the street.
       *Excuse me. My name's Mike Stubbs. Can you tell me the way to the station?

The sequence of speech acts is ill-formed:

2.6   *apology + identification + request for directions.

There appear to be two ways of explaining why 2.6 is ill-formed. Either the sequence of acts is itself ill-formed: there are co-occurrence restrictions on the sequence. Or alternatively the combination of speech acts and social situation is ill-formed: speakers do not identify or introduce themselves to strangers in the street. A plausible rule is that *identification* is unclear only if speakers predict further interaction on a later occasion. Thus speakers are likely to introduce themselves to people they meet at a party, but not in a railway carriage. (Berry, 1980a, discusses such constraints on the use of the act identification in much more detail.) I am not sure how one could distinguish between these two claims: that the constraint is on the sequence of acts, or that it is between an act and a situation. However, the example has already shown: (a) that although the individual sentences in 2.5 are well-formed, the whole sequence is not; (b) that traditional grammatical descriptions are therefore unlikely to have any useful explanation to offer, since they are restricted to within sentence boundaries.

It is more difficult to find comparable deviance across two speakers' utterances, for our ability to contextualize almost anything readily copes with odd sequences. But deviant sequences do occur:

2.7   A: Goodbye!
        B: Hi!

The oddity of this particular sequence is explicable via B's participant knowledge that the exchange occurred after A and B had approached each other down a long corridor. The greeting was prepared in advance of the actual encounter, and the split-second timing of the exchange itself meant that A's contribution was interpreted only after B had spoken.

Examples like the following are similarly recognizably odd, but not difficult to contextualize:

2.8   A: What's the time?
        B: Oh no!

B's response might be paraphrasable as "Oh no, I've left a cake in the oven" or, in general, "I've just remembered something important enough to supersede your question." The possibilities of interpretation are indefinitely large. What is important is not only finding or constructing impossible or non-contextualizable sequences, but the ease with which such incongruity may be recognized. It is both apt and significant that in the Theatre of the Absurd there are many examples of odd juxtaposition. These occur at the syntactic level (cf. N. F. Simpson's plays *A Resounding Tinkle* or *The One-Way Pendulum*); but also at the level of discourse. Consider this example from Samuel Beckett's *Endgame*:

2.9   Hamm: Why don't you kill me?
        Clov: I don't know the combination of the larder.

It is not difficult to find an implicit linking proposition. One possibility is: "If I kill you, I will starve to death." However, it is our awareness of such conversationally odd exchanges, amidst the situational and artistic absurdities, that gives a further clear indication that conversation is not random. So, in everyday situations, for a conversation to be unmarked, there are constraints on possible sequences of utterances.

Not much is known about such constraints on discourse sequences. They are not entirely analogous, for example, to constraints on syntactic ordering. Some of the differences between the concept of *well-formedness* as it applies to sentences and to discourse, are discussed at length in chapter 5. For the present, it is sufficient to note that there are constraints, and therefore discourse is structured. Such constraints are linguistic. They are not simply reducible, for example, to some form of topical organization. They are constraints on the occurrence of certain conversational acts in certain orders, as well as on the sequencing of propositions and of surface lexical and syntactic cohesion.

2   Inspecting transcribed data

My general purpose in this chapter is simply to convince the reader that spontaneous conversation, although it may look chaotic when closely transcribed, is, in fact, highly ordered. It is not, however, ordered in the same ways as written texts. I will argue that conversation is polysystemic; that is, its coherence depends on several quite different types of mechanisms, such as repetition of words and phrases, structural markers, fine synchronization in time, and an underlying hierarchic structure relating sequences of discourse acts.

We can make almost no progress without data in the form of a close transcript of audio-recorded natural conversation. This is the least we can get away with. As I have to present a printed transcript to the reader, I will restrict my comments to features easily represented in this form, although I am very aware that important cohesive features are to be found in systems of intonation, in paralinguistic features such as tempo, rhythm and voice quality, and in non-verbal kinesic systems. I like to use the spelling *cohearence* as a reminder that many of the linking mechanisms of conversation require to be heard to be appreciated. (Brazil, 1975, and G. Brown *et al.*, 1980, discuss in detail functions of intonation in discourse. Birdwhistell, 1970: 237ff, discusses the structuring functions of gestural systems: kinesic juncture.)

We require closely transcribed data for several reasons. First, intuitions (introspective data) are notoriously unreliable in this area.

Second, most people are simply unfamiliar with what such material looks like. Third, given these two points, a close transcript of conversation can allow us to see ways in which conversation is ordered which we would never imagine just by thinking about it, as a sentence grammarian might be tempted to do. Formulating this point in another way, we can say that such data characteristically *look* odd in transcript – but the corresponding audio-recording does not *sound* odd. Transcribing conversation into the visual medium is a useful estrangement device, which can show up complex aspects of conversational coherence which pass us by as real-time conversationalists or observers, and 'through which the strangeness of an obstinately familiar world can be detected' (Garfinkel, 1967: 38).

People are, in general, unused to studying close transcripts of conversational data. When they do look at such materials, they tend to see them as chaotic or unordered: relative to written texts or to the highly idealized sentences which are data for the grammarian. Conversational data therefore tend to be characterized in terms of their putative defects. At a recent seminar of linguists, staff and postgraduates, which was discussing the data analysed below, the following characterizations of the data were offered:

> There is no beginning; there is a lack of official stages; the turn-taking is disrupted and fairly random; the speakers don't seem to link things up; one of the speakers is excluded and consciously ignored by the others; and so on.

Some of these comments are factually wrong: the turn-taking is not random. Some are unperceptive: the links and boundaries are there if one knows what to look for. However, any such implicitly prescriptive comments, which characterize language in terms of putative defects instead of searching for the order underlying surface anomalies, run entirely counter to one of the most fundamental principles of linguistics as a scientific discipline. If we cannot discover the inherent organization of linguistic data, then this is a defect in us as analysts, not in the data.

3   Some observations on the data

The data, an extract from an interview recorded in an Edinburgh school, are presented in the appendix to this chapter, section 11, prefaced by a brief contextual note. Utterances (1) to (24) are included to give the reader the immediate conversational context, including the first reference (17) to the haunted house, which becomes a major topic. Most of my comments are restricted to utterances after (24).

The interviewer, MS, was the author, but the interview was not recorded with conversational analysis in mind. This talk was an unplanned interlude after the main business of the interview was over. It will be clear from some comments below that MS was, in any case, in no position to manipulate the talk, as he lacked the conversational competence to do much more than occasionally disrupt the conversational flow by clumsy expressions of attention and interest. The two boys, G and M, being close friends, were on close speaking terms, and MS was only partly competent in their dialect and style of talk.

Here then are some observations on the data, intended not to provide an exhaustive analysis, but to give detailed examples of different types of conversational organization which the reader may then observe in other data. My comments will probably make little sense unless the reader has now read through the data appendix.

An initial obvious but important point is that conversation is a *joint production*. One immediate implication of this is that speakers constantly take account of their audience by designing their talk for their hearers. This implies much more than saying that speakers shift their style of language to suit the context. It means that speakers must understand their audience: they must have some idea what the audience already knows and what they want to know, and therefore of how to select and present information. For example, G corrects himself as follows:

(32)   somebody you told me when I was about five or six ...

G (re)designs his talk so that M is brought into the story, and M knows immediately what it is that he has told G: see (34). He knows 'what G is talking about' before G has said it. The use of the second person *you*, instead of the potential choice of *he*, marks a sharp change in addressee. G is not only bringing M into the story, which is primarily directed at MS, but is switching to M as temporary addressee and presenting him with a conversational role to which M immediately responds (34). Throughout the data, concessions are made to MS as a stranger: e.g. (14–16), (26), (29–30). It is interesting how at (32) G begins his utterance with a lexical choice designed for MS, an auditor without 'common understanding' (cf. Garfinkel, 1967): that is, *somebody* is a term that anyone can understand as meaning "a person that you don't know but whose identity is unimportant for the point of my story". G then realizes the inappropriateness of this choice for his other hearer, who shares background information with him, and he quickly modifies his utterance. It is a useful exercise simply to consider how the discourse might differ if MS was absent, and M and G were reminiscing to each other about the haunted house.

Further, conversation is a joint production composed in real time. Consider (32–35):

(32)   G: somebody you told me when I was about
(33)   five – ⌈or six   there was m –
(34)   M: ⌊there was money there
(35)   G: money hidden there

M knows what G is going to say, what G has in mind as we often put it, even before G has said it. (34) correctly predicts (35). Conversationalists have the technical competence to make such predictions and interpretations, and to analyse the implications of utterances, in a fraction of a second. This is real joint production. M has a completion ready which proves that he has understood G. That is, (34) is a proof of communication, a proof that the speakers are on the same wavelength. Jefferson (1973) discusses the functions of split-second timing in proving understanding between speakers, and speakers' capacity to place talk with precision by, for example, coming in at just the right moment with a sentence-completion.

What we are concerned with here, then, are ways in which speakers can check on whether their hearers are following, ways in which speakers provide feedback to keep the talk going, and ways in which hearers can claim or prove their understanding. (These are Sacks' terms, see Sacks, 1970.) Some feedback items display only that the conversationalist is in touch with the rhythm of the talk: for example, *mm* (65, 82), *uhuh* (71). Some prove that at least part of the point of the preceding talk has been understood: for example, *not much good* (42), or more elaborate endorsements of preceding utterances. Thus in

(60)   aye there was only about that much left of the stair

M both acknowledges a valid contribution to the discourse (*aye*) and paraphrases part of (58–9). Compare how (56–8) endorses (53–5) through the formally recognizable criteria of the linker *as well*, and the choice of words, across two utterances, from a well-defined semantic field: *knocking down, ripped away, tore away, smashed in, tugged, fell in.* Such lexical cohesion could be systematically analysed in the way proposed by Halliday and Hasan (1976).

Insertions like *you know* (47, 67, 70, 76, 80, 83), as well as serving a feedback and sympathetic circularity function, are one literal mechanism for taking account of what other conversationalists do know. In casual conversation it is often possible to be cavalier about supplying information which can be filled in by hearers. Thus cover-words like *thingummy* or *what-d'you-call-it* can often be used. G. Brown (1977: 107ff) discusses the use of such items in conversation. In the present data, there is an example at

(66)   only about – that much of a support you know for – thing

There are more elaborate ways of telling hearers that they have had enough information. I will comment further on these below.

So far, I have given brief examples of several formally recognizable mechanisms of discourse cohesion: shifts in addressee, synchronization in time and lexical repetition. By emphasizing some specific mechanisms by which conversation is sustained as a joint production composed and interpreted in real time, I am emphasizing how discourse analysis can study interaction.

4   *Narrative organization*

I turn now to the overall structure of the talk. It is possible to show that long chunks of apparently casual conversation, stretching over several minutes, have overall structural organization. There is a very simple structural claim which is very relevant here: stories have beginnings, middles and ends. For example, jokes and stories told in conversation do not just start. They are often introduced by one of a relatively small number of prefaces such as *guess what?* ...; *y'know what?* ...; *that reminds me* .... When M says *you shoulda seen me once* (9), he is making an offer to tell a story with a preface functionally equivalent to: "Do you want to hear (I'm going to tell you anyway) what happened to me once." (See Sacks' perceptive work, 1970, on the organization of stories in conversation, and on the concept of prefaces which were the original inspiration for some of my remarks here. See also Turner, 1972, on the achievement of beginnings: starting is done.)

Similarly, stories do not just stop: they are ended. It is clear for the present data that all three speakers recognize a boundary after

(85). There is a two-second pause, followed by a sharp change in topic to procedural matters, expressed in two tight exchanges of quite different sequential structure to the previous talk. We can label these two exchanges roughly as:

(86)   MS: question ⎫
(87)   G: answer   ⎬
(88)   MS: accept   ⎭
(89)   G: question ⎫
(90)   MS: answer   ⎬

If we accept the claim that stories must be brought to a close, and not just stopped, then we may be able to find utterances which serve this function by looking closely at the talk before this boundary, which is clearly marked by several independent criteria.

One way to signal the end of a story in casual conversation is to use a cliché-cum-proverb with little informational content, of the type: *Still, that's life*; *Well, that's the way it goes*; *But something may turn up – you never know*; *Still, we may as well hope for the best.* G uses a cluster of such expressions between (74) and (81):

> it might have been something . . . you know – that might have
> been something . . . it makes you think

Such utterances with little significant propositional content, provide no new information which can serve as a resource for further talk, and can therefore serve as endings. Repetition of whole phrases is also a marker of endings. MS probably misinterprets (76–7) as requiring a show of interest to keep the talk going, and blunders in with a request for further details (78). But G refuses to treat the wh-interrogative (78) as a question: he simply repeats what he has already said (79–81).

(78)   MS: what you think it coulda been
(79)   G: well s pieces of bone about the size and you c –
(80)   you know just – wee bits of bone and it makes you
               think

Similarly repetition introduces no new propositional content. The vagueness of G's utterance is probably also intentional: again, his utterances are probably intended as formal markers of the end of the story, and not as resources for further talk. By (86) even MS has realized that the story is over.

The utterances I have glossed, on loose semantic criteria, as cliché-cum-proverbs without much informational content are, however, also formally marked by almost the only complex tenses in the data; *might have been* (74, 76) and *keep thinking* (75); and by a number of simple present tenses, *you know* (76, 80), *makes* (80). (I am taking *keep* to be a catenative which forms complex verbal groups: cf. Palmer, 1974.) These contrast with the predominantly simple past tenses of the story from (32) onwards. Significantly, the only other complex tenses in the data occur at other boundary points. I have already identified *you shoulda seen me once* (9) as a recognizable story beginning: we now see that this boundary is formally marked by *should have seen*. Note two further examples of this discourse function of tense-selection. At (32) G begins his predominantly simple past tense narrative about smashing up the house. This has been prefaced at (29–31) by M who uses the present tense *folk just go up there and muck about there*. Also, G's other use of *might have been* (45) not only co-occurs with *I was too young to understand then* (49), which is at least potentially a generalization-cum-ending. But also, and more significantly, M chooses this point (51) to begin his longest continuous utterance in the data. Thus G seems to have come to a temporary halt and M seems to recognize this. Note that we thus have evidence that the participants themselves recognized and responded to the boundaries we have identified on independent formal criteria. The boundaries are not merely imposed by us as analysts, but take account of the turn-taking within the discourse.

There are two points here, then. One is descriptive: stories in conversation are structured – they have recognizable and describable beginnings and endings. And one is methodological: once we have candidate categories for structural markers, such as story endings, then we may be able to find candidate exponents of such markers in data where none are immediately apparent. That is, rather than dismiss G's utterances as defective, for example as vague or repetitious, we may be able to discover their positive structural function. Birdwhistell (1970: 107) makes this point in a more general form:

> ... apparent redundancy is often an agent of reinforcement which serves ... to tie together stretches of discourse ... behaviour which appears merely repetitive at one level of analysis ... always seems to be of special social and cultural significance at other levels.

Note briefly, also, the general implications of these comments on the discourse functions of tense selection. Tense has long been an embarrassment within sentence grammars of English. There is a striking lack of correspondence between tense and reference to time; time references are made by many devices other than tense; and there are problems over the distinction between tense and aspect. Within sentence grammars little more can be done than to point to these complications and to suggest an ad hoc list of functions which tense-selection may have: such as, marking an utterance for politeness or formality, suggesting that an event is unlikely or unreal, expressing tentativeness or certainty, or expressing the present relevance of past events (e.g. see Sinclair, 1972: 182ff; Palmer, 1974: ch. 3). If it can be shown that tense-selection has specific discourse functions, then some of the problems may be solved. Sentence grammars can concentrate on what they are designed to do best: describing the formal aspects of tense-formation (for example, the recursive generation of complex tense forms), and discussion of the functions of tense can be 'lifted out' of sentence grammar to be formally handled at the level of discourse. Sinclair and Coulthard (1975) make similar comments on the ceiling effect in grammar and related remarks on the discourse functions of tense.

A slightly different way of summarizing one of my main points is as follows. In some ways, the transcribed talk may look chaotic. But on closer study, the boys turn out to be telling a story which is highly constrained, conventionalized and ritualized in two senses. First, in terms of content, it has many stock ingredients of a traditional mystery story: a haunted house, hidden money, old paintings, bloodstains and splinters of bone – *I keep thinking in the night ... it makes you think* (75, 80). Second, there is its standard story format and structure: stories do not just emerge from events – they have to be constructed. Incidents have to be made into talk, by being appropriately prefaced, told and ended in conventional, rule-governed ways. Events have to be translated into speaking terms. Or, as Labov (1972d) puts it, experience has to be transformed into narratives. (See below.) We can develop this point by further considering other systems of organization in the data.

The effect of the narrative as an archetypical adventure or mystery story is achieved mainly by the lexical choices made by the two story tellers, who draw on a common store of semantically related terms. For example, the nouns most frequently used, and therefore made prominent for the listener, refer firstly to the physical environment of the story: the *haunted house* (17, 23, 29, 69, 85), anaphoric references to it (29, 30, 32, 34, 35, 52), and references to its *rafters* (31, 73), *walls* (36, 53, 58, 59, 83) and *stairs* (56, 58, 61, 63). This thematic emphasis on the strange environment of the house gives feasibility to the boys' unlikely discoveries. The shift of scene from the familiar and domestic to the strange and remote is a device common to both adults' and children's adventure or fantasy literature, and is found in Medieval Romance (Auerbach, 1946), classic novels, science fiction, popular adventures and fairy tales. Note particularly the sharp shift at (29) from discussion of the boys' school, their real everyday environment. I have already identified (29) as a stereotypical story-opening of its kind marked by present tense selection. A second set of nouns refer to the items found by the boys. Again these present prominent information due to their frequency: *money* (34, 35), *crutches* (38, 38, 62, 62, 75, 85), *paintings* (41, 44), and *bone* (68, 70, 79, 80). Collectively, these referents are also reminiscent of traditional trove in treasure and adventure stories. Note also the frequent, conventionalized *it/that/there/they* + copula, which is common to much narrative description (33, 34, 44, 51, 60, 64, 66, 68, 83). (In chapter 10 I give a much more detailed analysis of the functions of this construction in narrative.)

The two boys are clearly marking their roles as story tellers and are making appropriate stylistic choices for the task. One final example: an interesting structure in G's (58–9) *I tugged and I tugged and the stairs fell in.* This is conspicuously reminiscent of the story of the wolf and the three little pigs, and of the wolf's repeated threat, *I'll huff and I'll puff and I'll blow your house down.* Whether or not G's choice of utterance is conscious, it seems as explicit indication that he is aware that he is telling a story. Stories do not just happen: they are constructed in rule-governed ways.

We can also study repeated elements on a syntagmatic axis, by noting various features of lexical repetition. First, repetition of lexical items may simply mark cohesion within single utterances of one speaker. See, for example (29–31, 38–9, 83–4). Second, repetition may mark cohesion in an individual speaker's utterances across a dialogue sequence. That is, a speaker repeats his own lexical items, but these are not necessarily taken up by other speakers. For examples in M's talk, note the repetition of *go up, went up* and *came up* in (30, 40, 42, 46, 52). From (29) to (50) M is in competition for the floor, and there is little shared lexis with G. But when conversational harmony is restored, shared lexis is used as a cohesive mechanism in the dialogue. Third, then, repetition may be continued across two or more speakers' utterances. I mentioned briefly above that such repetition may be a formal marker of joint production, which can function to show one speaker endorsing another's utterance. See, for example, the repetition of *wall*, *stairs* and *found* across (53–63). Fourth, cohesion across sequences of dialogue may be maintained by the frequent use of lexical items from a well-defined semantic field. Cohesion across (29–85) is marked by items from the semantic fields of destructive action and seeking and finding, that is, simple repetition of near synonyms: *smashed* (32, 35, 45, 57), *burst* (36), *knocking down* (52, 52), *burnt out* (29), *ripped* (54), *tugged* (58, 58), *tore* (56); and *find/found* (37, 38, 39, 41, 53, 59), *hid* (35, 85), *looking* (36), *see/saw* (44, 54), *scattered* (69, 84). As well as typifying the action of the story, these items provide the talk with close lexical cohesion.

Consider also the superficially neat lexical patterning between G and MS at (35–8), where there is one of the few question–answer exchanges in the data. We have the following surface lexical repetition and patterns:

(35–6) G: I   looking   it (= money)
(37)   MS: you find   it (= money)
(38)   G: I   found   (crutches)

But note that, whilst the surface form of G's response (38) is a satisfactory lexical and syntactic fit to (37), G is not, in fact, answering MS's question, but using the question as an entry into another related topic. That is, a fully fitting answer to (37) would be *yes (I found it)* or *no (I didn't find it)*.

A general point follows from these observations. Lexical repetition formally marks discourse cohesion and provides a conversational mechanism by which a polite surface consensus may be maintained. Lack of such cohesion probably marks lack of convergence and orientation between speakers (Sinclair and Coulthard, 1975). But such surface fit may function merely to maintain solidarity in constructing the discourse itself, whilst speakers express different underlying positions. That is, such cohesive devices provide a marker of ritual equilibrium (Goffman, 1955) in conversation.

5 *Interactional roles*

The observation above about social roles such as story-teller can be developed as follows. It is an empirical finding that some discourse types can be usefully represented as variations on recursive two-part question–answer (QA) exchanges or three-part question–answer–feedback exchanges. I use *exchange* to mean the minimal unit of interactive discourse. For example, Sinclair and Coulthard (1975) propose that teacher–pupil talk is often characterized by an underlying exchange structure:

Teacher:	initiation	I
Pupil:	response	R
Teacher:	feedback	F

A hypothetical dialogue might proceed:

Teacher:	what's the capital of France?	I
Pupil:	Paris	R
Teacher:	right	F
Teacher:	and Germany?	I
Pupil:	Bonn	R
Teacher:	good	F

Similarly, Coulthard and Ashby (1975) propose for doctor–patient talk, a three-part exchange structure of:

Doctor:	initiation	e.g. you've only had one attack?
Patient:	response	well, as far as I know
Doctor:	follow-up	yeah

These are clearly not the only exchange types possible in these situations, but they are characteristic; and they provide a way of formalizing a mechanism by which one speaker, teacher or doctor, retains the conversational initiative.

It is intuitively clear that some types of interview (speech event) might be structured largely by such QA pairs or IRF triplets, with the interviewer filling the first and third slots in each exchange. However, this type of exchange structure does not hold for the present data. The conversational initiative does not return to MS after each of the boys' utterances. On the contrary, MS makes only a few follow-up utterances (42, 65, 71, 82) and two follow-up questions (37, 78) which are closely tied to something G has said. Thus, it would be of no help whatsoever to approach the present data with the notion that it is an interview and that the conversational roles are interviewer and interviewee. Such roles do not exist in the abstract. They have to be realized and sustained through particular discourse strategies. Roles such as *teacher*, *doctor*, *pupil* or *interviewer* cannot be abstracted from the interactional activities which constitute them.

The exchange structure in the present data might usefully be represented as an initiation (I) by one speaker followed up by some kind of supportive item. If we take conversational support to be one kind of feedback (F), we can propose an exchange structure IF. Exponents of F are the types of acknowledgement, endorsement, claims and proofs of understanding discussed above. This structural formulation permits a close study of the general observation that listeners in two-party or multi-party discourse are primarily expected to provide audience appreciation and ritual support to the speaker. Lack of such conversational support on the telephone, for example, quickly leads to a breakdown in communication and to *Hello! Are you still there? I thought you'd hung up.*

6   Discourse analysis and interaction

One important implication of discourse analysis is as follows. One of the biggest linguistic conundrums of all is: how do we understand what someone is talking about? Traditional linguistics has little directly to say about this. However, I have shown here that conversational analysis can answer an answerable version of this question, namely: how do speakers show that they understand each other? I have suggested several mechanisms by which conversationalists can show that they are in conversational touch. Sacks (1970) proposes the concepts of claiming and proving understanding, which I have used above; Sinclair and Coulthard (1975) talk of speakers' orientation to each other; McIntosh (1973) talks of markers of involvement; Bernstein (1971a) talks of sociocentric sequences. And these concepts are all ways of making more precise Malinowski's concept of phatic communion (cf. Laver, 1974). In chapter 3, I develop further the metaphor of speakers keeping in touch with each other. It is clear that, whereas linguistics studies language, discourse analysis can study the actual mechanisms by which communication, understanding and interaction are maintained. Language (static structures and systems) and communication (dynamic processes) are by no means parallel concepts.

Expressed more generally, this means that discourse analysis must be concerned with ways in which information is selected, formulated and conveyed between speakers; or alternatively assumed to be known and shared knowledge, taken for granted, and not selected at all. It is therefore concerned, not just with whether statements are true or false, but with states of information, and differential access to information. Part of a speaker's task is to understand his hearers, what they know already, and what they expect and want to hear. Such points immediately make clear the importance of concepts such as information focus, and given and new information. (Such concepts have been made particularly explicit in work in artificial intelligence which has succeeded in setting up computer question answering systems, cf. Winograd, 1972.)

However, if we recognize this view of meanings being negotiated between speakers, we are left with a very general problem which has been called the co-ordination problem (Bennett, 1976: 186–7). How is such co-ordination possible? Speaker and hearer always have different problems. And there is no pre-existing fact to which they both have access, and to which they can refer. The speaker wants to convey X, and makes a guess about what the hearer knows already. The hearer wants to make sense of this, taking into account what he thinks the speaker is assuming. And so on. It is not at all obvious what has to be co-ordinated with what. This problem of negotiating mutual understanding when speaker and hearer inevitably have different perspectives gives a glimpse of one particular theoretical void over which discourse analysis is suspended.

7 Narrative structure

My analysis in this chapter has, admittedly, been informal, although it has been quite detailed; and I have indicated how it could easily be made more systematic, for example, by using Halliday and Hasan's (1976) method of analysing textual cohesion. Another way of making some of my observations more systematic is to analyse the narrative in ways proposed by Labov and Waletsky (1967) and Labov (1972d). Their structural analysis of narratives of personal experience allows me to draw together several points I have made in this chapter.

Labov (1972d) defines a minimal narrative as a sequence of two clauses which are temporally ordered: a change in their sequence results in a change in the sequence of the narrative events. For example, the following tell two different stories under a normal interpretation:

2.10   I hit John and John hit me.
2.11   John hit me and I hit John.

Although neither temporal sequence nor cause and effect are explicitly mentioned, we would normally assume that a different person started the fight in each case. (Chapter 4 discusses such uses of *and* in more detail.)

Such *narrative clauses* are also characterized syntactically by (a) simple past tense, and (b) unmarked word order, namely subject–predicate–complement–adjunct (SPCA). The skeleton of the narrative told by G can therefore be identified from such clauses, for example (56–9):

S	P	C	A
I	got	a rope	
	smashed in		at the side of the wall
I	tugged		
I	tugged		
the stairs	fell in		

As I suggested above, clauses with other tense forms and other possibly more complex syntactic structure have functions other than sustaining the narrative action. Thus most stories contain at or near the beginning some identification of the time, place or persons of the story. A syntactic marker of such *orientation clauses* is past progressive tense, for example, at

(2)   I used to go along there when I was much younger.

Orientation clauses are also characterized by the fact that their place in a longer sequence can be altered without necessarily altering their interpretation.

Labov's analysis of the ways in which personal experience is transformed into narrative form is much more complex than I can show here. However, my brief comments should indicate how an overall structural analysis of such data is possible on the basis of formal features of the language. These include the discourse function of different syntactic structures and tense selection; and the function of a shift away from basic simple narrative syntax (cf. Wolfson, 1979).

The complete structure which Labov proposes for narratives of personal experience include the following structural elements:

Abstract: providing a summary or encapsulation of the story.
Orientation: identifying the time, place, persons, activities and situations; usually marked by past progressive tense.
Evaluations: indicating the point or interest of the story.

Narrative	
clauses:	as defined above.
Result:	saying what finally happened.
Coda:	signalling the end.

The only obligatory element is at least two narrative clauses. Narrative clauses also differ from other elements in that their relative sequence is fixed, although the abstract and orientation will tend to occur near the beginning. I do not have the space here to analyse the whole story in this way, but it should be clear in general terms how my observations could be reorganized in such a way.

In the remainder of this chapter I will make explicit the general interest of such analyses of conversation for an understanding of language.

8   *Natural conversation*

An important general notion which I have used several times, without proper definition, is the concept of *natural* conversation. In fact, I have used, without distinction, several roughly synonymous terms, and other terms are found in the literature. For *natural* conversation, one finds terms such as *spontaneous*, *unplanned* and *casual*. And these terms are opposed to terms such as *artificial*, *contrived*, *invented*, *introspective*, *intuitive* and *hypothetical*. I may even appear to have argued myself into a contradiction, for I have talked of the boys' conversation as being both spontaneous and also as highly organized. This objection is easily answered: behaviour may be automatic, unselfconscious, and in that sense spontaneous, yet nevertheless deeply organized in ways that are generally unrecognized by users. Indeed, this is true of much linguistic behaviour. However, the concept of spontaneous discourse requires more explicit discussion than I have given it so far.

Although many such terms are used more or less synonymously in the literature, they disguise two rather different distinctions. The first distinction is between (a) language which occurs naturally without any intervention from the linguist; and (b) language which is elicited by the linguist as part of some experiment. Type (b) includes data which are the linguist's own introspections or intuitions: data which he has elicited from himself. A second distinction is between (c) language which is spontaneous in the sense of unplanned, and which is composed in real time in response to immediate situational demands; and (d) language which is deliberately planned, rehearsed, thought about, altered and edited. Type (c) characterizes most spoken language, including everyday conversation, whereas type (d) characterizes most formal written language. It might be argued that normal conversation is, by definition, unplanned and unplanable, and that it is relatively unpredictable, except sometimes in the short term. Types (b) and (d) often coincide. That is, introspective data is often highly self-conscious and mulled over at great length with reference to a particular theoretical problem, and this constitutes a major limitation in using such data as representative of normal language use (cf. Labov, 1975a). It means that many examples used in linguistic arguments are stylistically closer to written than to spoken language because both written language and well-considered introspective data are heavily edited and revised. This is a problem with much data in transformational grammar, despite the fact that it claims to study language, independently of particular varieties of language (cf. Crystal, 1980). There is confusion, therefore, over the object of study: characteristics of English or characteristics of restricted styles of English, for example.

There are therefore at least two dimensions along which data can lie, and examples are as follows:

	Naturally occurring	Planned
Everyday conversation	+	—
Much written language	+	+
Introspective data	—	+

Ochs (1979) provides a very useful discussion of the distinction between planned and unplanned discourse, and of many formal linguistic features which characterize speech which is unplanned and relatively unpredictable. She defines unplanned discourse as talk which is not thought out prior to its expression (1979: 55), and has not been prepared, but points out that much discourse falls some-where between the two extremes of planned and unplanned. It may well be, for example, that, in the data used in this chapter, G has told his story about the haunted house before. The narrative may have been planned and rehearsed overall, but it has clearly not been rehearsed in all its details, since it is locally managed, utterance-by-utterance, to take account of the demands of social interaction.

I have already given examples of many of the features which Ochs lists as characteristic of unplanned speech in general: frequent repetition; simple active sentences with unmarked SPCA word order; the joint construction of propositions over two speakers' utterances. Other features which Ochs notes can also be illustrated from the data, a tendency to string together co-ordinate clauses, often linked by *and*, rather than to use subordinate clauses; the juxtaposition of clauses with no explicit link at all, e.g. (72–4); arguments and predicates not syntactically linked, e.g. (78–80); the deletion of referents, including subjects of clauses, e.g. (41), (52); the use of deictic modifiers (e.g. *this*) rather than definite articles, e.g. (29); left-dislocated syntactic structures, in which the subject noun phrase is followed by a co-referential pronoun, e.g. (29). Taken together, several of these characteristics mean that semantic relations between propositions or between parts of propositions (e.g. subject and predicate) are often not explicitly marked. Mere juxtaposition may be used, or an element of information may be deleted altogether. In addition, it means that topic–comment structures are prominent.

These points do not imply that the speakers' language is 'ungrammatical'. However, they do imply that the syntax is significantly different from the syntax of most formal written language. In addition they imply that the unit of *sentence* is not always applicable to conversational English. There is no difficulty in dividing the transcript into clauses with a basic SPCA structure. However, any attempt to divide the transcript into sentences involves making arbitrary decisions about sentence boundaries, due to the large number of clauses coordinated with *and*, and a few other items such as *but* and *then*. Rather than sentences, we have loosely coordinated clause complexes (cf. Crystal, 1980: 159).

These observations are of central importance to the linguistic description of English, which has tended to be almost exclusively based on styles towards the more formal and planned end of the stylistic continuum. Linguistic description has therefore tended to overemphasize certain syntactic devices, and has often failed to study the function of different syntactic choices.

9   Native speaker fluency

The concept of unplanned discourse raises one other issue of very general importance for linguistics, although it is not often discussed. This is the question of what constitutes native speaker *fluency* in a language. When the concept has been discussed, it has generally been from the point of view of language teaching (Crystal and Davy,

1975; Leeson, 1975) or language pathology (Dalton and Hardcastle, 1977).

A commonsense observation is that native ability in a language involves *speaking* it *fluently*. One would not normally regard someone as having native competence if he was able only to understand written language, however perfectly. The whole of Chomskyan linguistics is, of course, an explicit attempt to characterize the concept of a native speaker's competence in a language. However, the notion of fluency plays no part in this concept of competence. The Chomskyan view is static. Linguistic competence involves the ability to do syntactic and semantic manipulations on isolated sentences or pairs of sentences: for example, the ability to recognize ambiguous sentences, or whether one sentence entails another, or is synonymous with another. This current Chomskyan view therefore ignores two things which are central to the commonsense view of linguistic competence, and also to the view of discourse competence which underlies my discussion here: the ability to handle connected discourse, and the ability to do this in real time without prior rehearsal. In other words, the native speaker can improvise, maintain continuity in speech and comprehension, respond immediately to unexpected utterances, make rapid changes of topic and speaker, and so on. The native speaker has therefore the ability to use language under the communicative stress (cf. Givón, 1979: 105) of real time processing. These points hold even given the generally recognized normal non-fluencies (cf. Crystal and Davy, 1969), in unplanned discourse: that is, normal hesitation phenomena, filled pauses, repetitions, false starts, and the like.

There are two main points at issue. First, the kinds of discourse phenomena discussed in this chapter are important to a balanced concept of native speaker competence in a language. Second, the commonsense concept of fluency is clearly a cover-term for a complex of factors, but is worth consideration alongside the linguist's concept of competence, which is normally very highly idealized.

The implication that syntactic and linguistic organization in general should be studied from the point of view of perceptual and processing strategies is an interesting issue, but has not been studied in detail by linguists. (Newmeyer, 1980: 219–23 summarizes some exceptions to this claim within Chomskyan linguistics.)

10 *Conclusions*

My presentation in this chapter has been relatively informal and
introductory, although I have commented in detail on several formal
linguistic features of the data. I have shown that spoken discourse is
open to analysis. The analysis as it stands is illustrative, rather than
systematic: I have not, for example, proposed an analysis which gives
a comprehensive description of the data; although I have indicated
briefly how one could move further in the direction of such rigorous
and comprehensive description. I have also shown that much traditional linguistic description neglects intuitively important aspects of
linguistic competence, because it neglects a close study of naturally
occurring conversational language. Discourse analysis therefore
appears to be both possible and interesting, despite the glimpse into
several theoretical chasms along the way.

11 *Data appendix*

This is an extract from an interview with two boys, G and M, aged 12.
They are talking about New Haven, the district of Edinburgh where
they live. MS is the interviewer (the author).

```
G:   there's quite a lot of they old fishermen's houses –        (1)
     I used to go along there when I was much younger but         (2)
     they've demolished most of the Haveners –                    (3)
M:   ⌐aye (        )                                               (4)
G:   Lhardly anything left except the ⌐harbour                     (5)
M:                                    L(                 )          (6)
G:   and the old primary – that – that dates back – that's        (7)
     a hundred and twenty seven years old                         (8)
M:   you shoulda seen me once –⌐(          )                       (9)
G:                             Lall the old houses are             (10)
     knocked down                                                  (11)
M:   we were mucking about in the playground –                    (12)
     (several seconds inaudible)                                   (13)
G:   I I climbed – the roof of the: – what's that height          (14)
     from one roof – you climb onto the one roof and right        (15)
     up the drainpipes about sixty seventy feet isn't it Mike     (16)
M:   what the haunted ⌐house                                       (17)
G:                    L(        ) – no – at the – school           (18)
     once you've got onto that wee roof where the ball goes       (19)
     up – right onto the top on the top s – near the spire –      (20)
```

```
           's about seventy feet — isn't it — it's roughly that —        (21)
           I climbed ┌ up that                                           (22)
M:                   └ (        brother) up the top of the haunted       (23)
           house — and then on top of that                               (24)
G:         I went up the top of the school and I was on                  (25)
           the spire and this — the school in the centre's got a         (26)
           big huge skylight I just about fell through                   (27)
           ┌ that                                                        (28)
M:         └ this haunted house it was burnt out — an' er — folk just    (29)
           go up there and — muck about there and muck about             (30)
           ┌ in the rafters                                              (31)
G:         └ I smashed the place up somebody you told me when I          (32)
           was about five —┌ or six                    there was m —     (33)
M:                         └ there was money there                       (34)
G:         money hidden there and I smashed the place in I ju —          (35)
           looking for it I burst down every wall and everything —       (36)
MS:        d'you find it  (1)                                            (37)
G:         I found t two pair o' crutches — old crutches                 (38)
           bloodstained but that was all I found hhh                     (39)
M:         I went up ┌ (              )                                   (40)
G:                   └ found a couple of old ┌ paintings                  (41)
MS:                                          └ not much good              (42)
M:         I went ┌ and                ┌ I went up with                   (43)
G:                └ but I di I d I just saw └ they were old paints so     (44)
           I smashed them in they might ┌ have been something            (45)
M:                                      └ I went up with my pal —         (46)
           ┌ y'know — my pal and myself                                  (47)
G:         └ (    )    (      )                                           (48)
           ┌ I was too young to understand then                          (49)
M:         └ (                 )                                          (50)
           there was nothing — to do in the afternoon so he just         (51)
           came up there — started knocking the knocking the             (52)
           walls down — never found a thing — all the walls are          (53)
           ripped away — and all you could see is the — (out)            (54)
           the frames o' them                                            (55)
G:         I tore the stairs away as well and I got —                    (56)
           a rope and I smashed in at the side of the                    (57)
           wall and I — tugged and I tugged and the stairs               (58)
           ┌ fell in — and then the wall that was where I found          (59)
M:         └ aye there was only about that much (left                    (60)
           of the) stair                                                 (61)
```

```
G:   a pair of crutches —  ⌈bloodstained crutches            (62)
M:                          ⌊these stairs only about that     (63)
     size⌈      — and it's                                     (64)
MS:      ⌊mm                                                   (65)
M:   just no support there's only about — that much of a      (66)
     support y'know for — thing                               (67)
G:   there was wee bits of what looked like bone —            (68)
     scattered all over the house — but — I just — sharpened  (69)
     it up you know you can sharpen up bone —                 (70)
MS:  uhuh —                                                   (71)
G:   I just ⌈— used it for anything —                         (72)
M:          ⌊the rafters                                      (73)
G:   it might have been something —                           (74)
     they bloodstained crutches I — I keep thinking in my     (75)
     the night you know — that that might have been           (76)
     something —                                              (77)
MS:  what you think it coulda been —                          (78)
G:   well s pieces of bone about that size and you c —        (79)
     y'know just — wee bits of bone and it makes you          (80)
     think —                                                  (81)
MS:  mm —                                                     (82)
G:   cos they were in the wall you know — somebody            (83)
     might have been had — scattered the bits all over the    (84)
     house and hid the crutches and that  (2)                 (85)
MS:  what time does this period end is it ⌈ten                (86)
G:                                         ⌊quarter past      (87)
MS:  quarter past oh that's all ⌈right                        (88)
G:                               ⌊what time is it             (89)
MS:  ten past ...                                             (90)
```

3

On the Same Wavelength:
Analysing Ethnographic Data

> *... this conversation is going on a little too fast: let's go back to the last remark but one.*
> *(Lewis Carroll* Through the Looking Glass, *1872)*

In the last chapter I focused attention on the details of a particular transcript. In this chapter I will propose a different approach to understanding spoken interaction: studying a particular speech event in a particular social setting. This approach could be called ethnographic: it studies patterns of observed and recorded communicative behaviour. Saville-Troike (1982) provides a good introduction to work on the ethnography of communication. In order to be specific, I have to concentrate on one type of speech event (a school lesson). The same methods of observation and analysis can be applied to other events, although school lessons are a good place to start naturalistic observation of spoken interaction, since they are highly organized in some rather obvious ways. As in the last chapter, my general argument will be that this approach has considerable insights to offer, but also limitations.

1 Some initial observations

Consider the following fragment of field note data collected during a period of observation in a secondary school. At the start of one English class which I observed, the teacher, after talking quietly to some pupils at the front of the room, turned and said to the whole class:

3.1   Right! Fags out please!

No pupils were smoking. So the teacher did not mean his words to be taken literally. I interpret his remark as having the primary function of attracting the pupils' attention, of warning them of messages still to come – in short, of opening the communication channels. The remark had a contact function of putting the teacher in touch with the pupils. (*Contact* is Hymes', 1962, term: see section 6.)

The problems of analysing language-use of this kind are not trivial, and yet they have not received much detailed consideration by linguists. For example, how did the the pupils know that the teacher did 'not really mean' that they had to extinguish their non-existent cigarettes? What shared knowledge and expectations concerning appropriate speech behaviour did they draw on in order to interpret successfully what the teacher actually meant? How could the teacher say one thing, yet mean another? Readers will be able to think up many other meanings the utterance might have in other contexts.

In this chapter, I begin by discussing various concepts which can begin to answer these questions, and then take these concepts as a basis for isolating the particularly striking contact features of teachers' talk. The general concepts are therefore introduced in order to show how teaching can be considered as a particular kind of speech event and thus compared with other situations in which people speak to each other. The concepts and descriptive framework are illustrated by samples of teacher–pupil interaction collected in tape-recordings and field-notes during periods of classroom observation.

I hope, incidentally, that the title of this chapter and these opening paragraphs have themselves performed a *contact* function of preparing the reader for what I want to discuss and thereby putting us both on the same wavelength.

2   *Data collection*

The data on which this chapter is based were collected by observation and note-taking, and by audio-recording. The classroom observation was done over a period of about six weeks in an Edinburgh secondary school. I attended English lessons with two teachers, mainly with pupils aged 12 to 13 and 16 to 17 years. During the periods of observation I was simply concerned to write down as much as I could of what the teacher said, concentrating mainly on noting ways in which the teacher controlled or organized the lesson. Otherwise, in order to provide as much context as possible for the teacher's talk, my field notes included as many other details of pupils' responses and other classroom events as I could write down in longhand. The tape-recordings are of small group lessons at a summer school. I recorded small groups from a purely practical point of view of obtaining higher quality recordings than is often possible in a normal classroom with its echoing walls and thirty to forty children. As I was interested primarily in how to describe the teachers' speech behaviour, I was not too concerned that this behaviour might be different with small groups and large classes. I estimated that the direct observation in a more typical classroom situation would in any case provide an informal check that the samples of data were not too incompatible for my present purposes. Below, I quote data from both sources so that readers can judge for themselves.

Prospective researchers should be aware that it is often possible to write down in a field notebook a great deal of useful data, even on use of language, especially when they know what sort of behaviour they are looking for. They should also be aware that a tape-recorder, whilst providing more objective and detailed data, is undiscriminating and may well provide too much data, unless the data are collected with a specific aim in mind. Five minutes of conversation may take over an hour to transcribe if the recording is clear, and correspondingly much longer for a poor recording.

3   *Problems of perception*

A general problem in discourse analysis is that students look at data, and 'don't know what to say'. There are so many things which might be commented on: a great range of phonological, lexical or syntactic features, as well as paralinguistic and non-verbal behaviour, all of which can contribute to conversational organization. When almost anything might be relevant, we need some way of focusing the attention. In the last chapter, I discussed one such research strategy: concentrating on a particular transcript of conversational data, and inspecting it to see what organizational features we might be able to find. In this chapter, I will discuss a different strategy: considering some specific functions which utterances can serve in conversation, and then studying data to see whether we can identify utterances with those functions.

In chapter 11, I will discuss such methodological questions much more fully. However, note immediately some dangers in the proposed way of approaching data. It assumes that school classrooms are familiar, and that readers have a stereotype of classrooms to which I can refer. A danger of such commonsense stereotypes is that they can be a barrier to analysis, and can prevent us from seeing what is really going on. Of course, teachers and pupils themselves also have very strong expectations about what normal classrooms are like. There is no way of escaping from such taken-for-granted cultural knowledge, but although we have to start from this assumed competence, the aim is to make the competence explicit. Linguists have long known that a grammar of a language can be set up only by a researcher with intuitive access to the system. And yet, the grammar aims to model that intuitive knowledge. Similarly, the organization of discourse can be studied only from within. Phrased slightly differently, we all have expectations about teacher–pupil discourse, but such expectations do not transform themselves magically into a script for a classroom dialogue. It is the task of discourse analysis to study how the script is constructed, and how general taken-for-granted stereotypes of teacher and pupil behaviour are related to the detailed utterance-by-utterance organization of classroom discourse. (P. Atkinson, 1981, provides a very clear discussion of this point.)

4   Communicative problems in the classroom

Starting then from our commonsense stereotypes of school classrooms, consider some communicative problems which teachers have in classrooms, and some of the communicative functions which their language must therefore serve in both teaching and classroom management.

Teachers have to devote a great deal of time and effort simply to keeping in touch with their pupils – not only because of the far-from-ideal communication conditions in the average school classroom, but also because of the very nature of teaching. They have to attract and hold their pupils' attention, get them to speak or be quiet, to be more precise in what they say or write, and to try and keep some check on whether at least most of the pupils follow what is going on. Teachers' talk is therefore very different from preachers' talk. Trying to control and teach a class full of children for forty minutes is very different from delivering a monologue to the converted. It is also very different from commentators' talk: for example, describing on the radio, as it happens, to people who cannot see it, thirty horses riding by, or thirty men playing rugby. Such different kinds of discourse differ greatly, for example, in the kind of information transmitted. Teachers' talk is characterized by a high percentage of utterances which perform certain speech acts including: informing, explaining, defining, questioning, correcting, prompting, ordering, requesting. It is also characterized by discourse sequences which have few, if any, parallels outside teaching, including: drills around the class, dictation to the class, group answers, and the like.

Another major part of our commonsense knowledge of classrooms is that teachers have more power and control than pupils, and this should also be identifiable in their language. Much classroom talk is characterized by the extent to which one speaker, the teacher, has conversational control over the topic, over the relevance or correctness of what pupils say, and even over when and how much pupils may speak. In the traditional chalk-and-talk classrooms, pupils have correspondingly few conversational privileges. This has often been pointed out by educationalists (e.g. Barnes *et al.*, 1969; Flanders, 1970), but the range of verbal strategies actually employed by teachers to control classroom talk has yet to be fully described. Also the topic has rarely been discussed in the context of what is a central concern of the sociolinguistics of face-to-face interaction: how talk is heard by speakers to be organized and coherent in various ways, and therefore how it is heard to be appropriate to different social situations and encounters.

A study of classroom data might therefore be expected to have two aims. First, it might enable us to define a certain characteristic discourse style. Is teachers' talk definably different from other such styles? There are, after all, other social situations in which one participant has significantly more control than others. Consider, for example, doctors versus patients (cf. Coulthard and Ashby, 1975) or magistrates versus defendants (cf. S. Harris, 1980). Second, since it seems intuitively clear that teachers' talk is particularly characterized by utterances which serve particular functions, this may enable us to collect and analyse a rich source of data on this range of speech acts.

5   Sociolinguistics and language variation

Sociolinguistics covers a wide range of studies of how language is used in its social contexts, but all the studies have one thing in common: they deal with language variation. They emphasize how malleable language is and how its form and function change across different cultures and across different social situations within one culture. The aim is, of course, to find systematic patterning within the variation.

Various social factors determine the individual speaker's use of language. All speakers are multidialectal or multistylistic, in the sense that they adapt their style of speaking to suit the social situation in which they find themselves. Such style-shifting demands constant judgements, yet speakers are not normally conscious of making such judgements until they find themselves in a problematic situation for which they do not know the conventions, or for which the criteria for speaking in a certain way clash. On the other hand, it is intuitively clear that a teacher, for example, does not speak in the same way to his wife, his mother-in-law, his colleagues in the staff room, his headmaster, a student teacher, or his pupils. His way of talking to his pupils will also change according to the matter to hand: teaching an academic subject, organizing the school concert, or handing out punishments. People therefore adapt their speech according to the person they are talking to and the point behind the talk. These are social, rather than purely linguistic, constraints.

6 *Language functions*

One way of analysing such variation in language behaviour, which has been developed since the early 1960s, is to isolate various *factors* in the social situation which influence or interact with the kind of language used, and to discuss associated *functions* which language fills in different situations.

Language does not play a constant role across different social situations – it is revealing to consider how unimportant language may be in certain contexts! Yet many people still assume that language has at most two general functions of referring to the external world and communicating explicit messages (a referential–cognitive function) and of expressing feelings (an emotive function). This distinction may hold as an initial classification, but it is quite inadequate as a detailed analysis. It is now something of a commonplace in sociolinguistics to say that language can have many functions. For example, in a lecture or a BBC Third Programme talk, or in this book, language may have as its primary function the task of getting a message across and of persuading the addressee of some point of view. But cocktail party chat, talk about the weather, reminiscing about old friends, a headmaster's address to the school, or pupils' avid discussion of last night's football match, may have the primary function of establishing or maintaining social relationships and solidarity: very little new propositional information may be communicated. Other functions of language include: organizing social effort; reliving experiences; releasing tension or 'getting something off one's chest'; crystallizing ideas or 'putting things in a nutshell'; remembering things (a mnemonic function); measuring time; or simply filling embarrassing silences.

In the same way, brief utterances within longer stretches of discourse may also have different primary functions. It is important to realize that the function of an utterance may be quite distinct from its traditional grammatical description. For example, a teacher may say:

3.2   Come down to the front.

This is a clear imperative. But he may also say:

3.3   Stevie, I don't think it's a good idea for you to sit beside anybody else, do you?

Although it does not have imperative syntax, 3.3 has the clear function of getting the pupil to move: surface syntactic forms must be distinguished from speech act functions, such as request or order.

The type of functional approach to language which I am proposing here derives largely from work by Hymes on the ethnography of communication. Hymes (1962, following Jakobson, 1960) proposes seven 'broad types' of function which language in use serves:

1   expressive/emotive
2   directive/conative/persuasive
3   poetic
4   contact (physical or psychological)
5   metalinguistic (focusing on meaning)
6   referential
7   contextual/situational

He argues that these seven functions correspond, in general terms, but not neatly, to various factors to which speakers attend in speech situations. Appropriate language may depend on different combinations of:

1   sender
2   receiver
3   message form
4   channel (e.g. speech versus writing)
5   code (e.g. dialect, language or jargon)

6 topic
7 setting or situation

Hymes (1972) gives a much fuller list of components of speech than the 1962 article, but the changes do not affect the points I am making here. (The papers in Cazden *et al.*, eds., 1972, apply some of Hymes' ideas on the ethnography of communication to the classroom setting, but few of the papers analyse specific tape-recorded data.)

The speech functions which Hymes calls *metalinguistic*, contact and poetic are particularly relevant to a teacher's communicative concern in the classroom. Hymes shows that, among the many functions which language may serve in different situations, it may do the work of focusing back on language itself: on its forms, or on some aspect of the communication situation. According to Hymes' analysis, language with a *metalinguistic* function focuses on the underlying code. Thus a speaker might focus on the meaning of language used by saying, for example: *Go and look it up in the dictionary!* Language with a *contact* function focuses on the channels of communication, as when a speaker says: *Can you hear me?* And language with a *poetic* function focuses on the message form, as in: *What oft was thought, but n'er so well expressed.* Hymes is therefore discussing various ways in which speakers refer to talk, in the course of talk. Hymes' examples (cited above) are useful, although they are not entirely clear: *Go and look it up in the dictionary!* certainly focuses on language, but it is also a directive; it tells someone to do something. All utterances are multi-functional.

Hymes himself, and others using his concepts of language functions, have worked almost exclusively at the level of general cultural patterns of speech behaviour, and have not generally used the concepts to analyse specific interactions observed and recorded in specific social contexts. Although the concepts are helpful in thinking about specific interactions, they turn out to dissolve into a wide range of different but related conversational strategies. I will demonstrate this in detail below with references to language functions in teachers' talk. On the one hand, then, the reader should bear in mind that Hymes is quite explicitly claiming to propose a generalized scheme, and not a model to be applied to the analysis of actual discourse. On the other hand, I would propose, as a principle for sociolinguistics, that any analysis of language in use will ultimately stand or fall on its success in analysing what people actually say to each other in real social situations.

Another aspect of language which Jakobson (1960) and Hymes (1962) only hint at without exploring systematically, is the network of relations between different language functions. It is clear initially that checks or controls on meaning, on language form, and on the channels of communication are closely connected. They all involve communication about features of the communication itself. I therefore propose to regroup the contact, metalinguistic and poetic functions of language, under the label of *metacommunication* – they are all communication about communication – and to investigate utterances which serve this broad function in teaching situations.

This concept of metacommunication is also close to Goffman's (1964) concept of a social situation as being 'an environment of mutual monitoring possibilities'. People are constantly monitoring each other's behaviour, interpreting it, reading between the lines, and so on. Goffman is vague, however, about what people actually *do* in order to carry out such monitoring. I will try to analyse the concepts of language functions and monitoring into specific kinds of speech acts, in order to show some of the verbal strategies which speakers have for keeping in touch with other speakers; and therefore try to show how aspects of Hymes' and Goffman's concepts can be closely grounded in conversational data.

7   Metacommunicative acts

I use the term metacommunication then, to refer to verbal monitoring of the speech situation. Such a definition turns out to be rather wide. Initially metacommunication seems to include: messages about the channels of communication, checks on whether they are open and working; messages which serve to keep communication ticking over smoothly; control over who speaks and how much, and cues for speakers to stop talking or to interrupt (e.g. cues for turn-taking); checks on whether messages have been received and understood; and control over the content of acceptable communication. In a sense, all speech has some metacommunicative function. For example, by simply continuing to speak, a speaker is signalling, among other things, that he wants the channels to remain open and that he wants to be listened to. However, all utterances have many functions, and I am assuming here that it is possible to distinguish utterances which serve a primarily metacommunicative function.

Paradigm examples of utterances with a pure metacommunicative function of checking and oiling the communication channels themselves, are found in situations in which speakers cannot see each other and therefore have no normal visual feedback. Typical (hypothetical) examples are:

3.4   Hello! Can you hear me? Oh, you're still there. I thought you'd hung up.

3.5   Come in Z-Victor One! Do you read me?

3.6   Roger! Out!

These examples refer to the physical communication channels, in this instance, telephone and radio. But in addition, many metacommunicative metaphors, or common expressions in use in everyday English refer to checks that the meaning of a message has been correctly conveyed: *I couldn't get through to him*; *I managed to get the idea across*; *Do you follow me?*; *We don't seem to be on the same wavelength*; *I'm sure he didn't mean what he said*; or *He never says what he means.* It is often useful to look at common idioms connected with speech and communication. In this case they illustrate that the speech functions which I have been discussing are not abstruse concepts coined by linguists, but functions which language is commonly felt to have by its speakers.

A particular kind of metacommunication is metalanguage: language about language, language which refers to itself. Again this is not something which has been dreamed up by theoretical linguists. Consider some more commonly heard expressions: *How dare you talk to me like that!*; *She said it with such feeling*; *He likes nothing better than to hear the sound of his own voice*; *He always knows what to leave unsaid*; *Who are you to talk?*; *Who do you think you're talking to?*; *Don't use that tone of voice with me!* All these common expressions draw attention to the constant gap between what is said and what is meant, and therefore to the need to do constant interpretative work on speech.

In general, everyday talk about language is rich in terms and expressions for meanings and language functions, but poor in terms for language forms. Austin (1962: 149) pointed out the very large number of terms in English for speech acts, and a systematic study of such everyday built-in metalanguage has often been proposed. For example, Hymes (1962), Hoenigswald (1966), Fishman (1971) and Longacre (1976) all propose doing a semantic field analysis of linguistic metaterms in English or other languages. However, I have not come across such a study.

I do not wish to imply that such everyday terms have any privileged status for analysts. It is clear, in fact, that many everyday metaphors present a misleading view of language as consisting of bits of information which are parcelled up by a speaker and sent down a tube or along a channel to a hearer, possibly past some barrier or other, who may or may not 'grasp' the meaning. The idea that meanings are 'in' words and sentences, and can be sent around in such containers which are opened up at the other end, is an obviously inadequate view of language and meaning. It ignores the effect of context on meaning and the negotiation of meaning between speakers. (Cf. G. Lakoff and Johnson, 1981, for discussion of such everyday metaphors about language.) Nevertheless, such everyday ideas are worth critical consideration, as data, not as definitive analyses.

8   *Monitoring classroom talk*

One social situation in which at least one of the participants takes particularly active steps to monitor the communication system is school teaching. Such monitoring may actually comprise teaching or at least a major part of it. Teachers constantly check up to see if they are on the same wavelength as their pupils, if at least most of their pupils are following what they are saying, in addition to actively monitoring, editing and correcting the actual language which pupils use. Teachers therefore constantly exert different kinds of control over the on-going state of talk in the classroom.

Consider the following more detailed examples of the kind of metacommunication which characterizes teacher-talk. The examples are taken from notes made during observation of English lessons in an Edinburgh secondary school. They are the actual words spoken by teachers. For illustration, I have chosen examples which, even out of context, have a clear metacommunicative function, but the context must be taken into account in interpreting the function of utterances in this way. The different kinds of metacommunication which I illustrate here can, without much adjustment, be further formalized into a category system which would therefore comprise one possible coding scheme for classifying tape-recorded samples of teacher–pupil interaction.

Attracting or showing attention. A teacher constantly makes remarks primarily to attract or hold the attention of the pupils, and therefore merely to prepare them for the message still to come. Compare 3.1 above.

3.7   Now, don't start now, just listen.
3.8   Yeah, well, come on now, you guys!
3.9   Eh, wait a minute, let's get the facts.
3.10   (The teacher claps his hands several times.) Right, right, right, right, right!
3.11   ... you pair of budgies at the back!

or he may say something to show his own continued attention to the pupils when they are speaking.

3.12   Yeah. Mmhm. Uhuh.

Controlling the amount of speech. Teachers frequently exert control simply over whether pupils speak or not. This may take the form of an order to a pupil to say something, or a request (usually an order) not to speak.

3.13   Do you want to say something at this point?
3.14   Brenda? ... (Long pause.) Morag?
3.15   Anything else you can say about it?
3.16   I could do with a bit of silence.
3.17   I don't like this chattering away.
3.18   Look, I'd prefer it if you belted up.
3.19   Who's that shouting and screaming?
3.20   Eh, some of you are not joining in the studious silence we're trying to develop.

Checking or confirming understanding. Teachers may check whether they have understood a pupil, or confirm that they have understood.

3.21   A very serious what? I didn't catch you.
3.22   I see.

And they may try and check whether their pupils are following.

3.23   Do you understand, Stevie?

Summarizing. Teachers often summarize something that has been said or read, or summarize the situation reached in a discussion or lesson; or they may ask a pupil to give a summary of something that has been said or read.

3.24   The rest all seem to disagree with you.
3.25   Well, what I'm trying to say is ...

Defining. A teacher may offer a definition or reformulation of something that has been said or read.

3.26   *Incarnate* – that means "in the flesh".
3.27   Well, these are words suggesting disapproval.
3.28   *Sonsie* is just "well stacked".
3.29   *Whore* – (the word occurred in a poem) – now you don't want to get too technical about that word – it's just a girl.

Or the teacher may ask a pupil to give a definition, or to clarify something.

3.30   Well, Brenda, does that mean anything to you?
3.31   What's *glaikit*?
3.32   David, what's the meaning of *hurdies*?
3.33   Can anybody put that in a different way?

(*Sonsie*, *glaikit* and *hurdies* are Scots words, meaning respectively "attractive" or "buxom", "stupid" and "buttocks" or "hips".)

Editing. He may comment on something a pupil has said or written, implying a criticism or value judgement of some kind.

3.34   I take it you're exaggerating.
3.35   That's a good point.
3.36   That's getting nearer it.
3.37   No, no, we don't want any silly remarks.

Correcting. Or he may actually correct or alter something a pupil has said or written, either explicitly or by repeating the 'correct' version.

3.38   Teacher: David, what's the meaning of *paramount*?
        Pupil: Important.
        Teacher: Yes, more than that, all-important.
3.39   (The teacher is correcting a pupil's essay with him.) The expression *less well endowed* might be the expression you're wanting – men don't usually pursue women because they're *well-built*.

Specifying topic. Finally, the teacher may focus on a topic of discussion or place some limits on the relevance of what may be said.

3.40   I'm not sure what subject to take.
3.41   You see, we're really getting onto the subject now.
3.42   Now, we were talking about structures and all that.

3.43   Now, before I ask you to write something about it, we'll talk about it.

3.44   Well, that's another big subject.

Note first that the definitions of the utterances are consistently functional. I am concerned here with the kinds of things that teachers do, and not directly with the style of language in which they do it. A teacher may ask his pupils to *develop a studious silence* or to *belt up*. On my analysis. both these requests fulfil the same function of controlling the amount of talk in the classroom. Clearly, at least some of the remarks I quote also perform other functions simultaneously. For example, a remark that some pupils are *not joining in the studious silence we are trying to develop* might perform the function of being sarcastic. I am directly concerned in this chapter with only one level of language functions.

Second, the way in which I have described the speech functions means that some functions are automatically subcategories of others. For example, if a teacher defines something that has been said, then he is also performing the function of checking that his pupils understand something, as well as attracting their attention. Similarly, if the teacher requests a pupil to define something, he is again checking whether he and the pupils are on the same wavelength, as well as requesting the pupil to speak and also attracting attention. It is for this reason that I have been careful all along to speak of utterances having a primary or main function. For it is a characteristic of speech that utterances typically fulfil several distinct functions simultaneously, although it is often possible to rank them in order of importance.

My first claim is, then, that the examples I have given of teacher-talk all have a primarily metacommunicative function of monitoring the working of the communication channels, clarifying and reformulating the language used. My second claim is that such metacommunication is highly characteristic of teacher-talk, not only because it comprises a high percentage of what teachers do spend their time saying to their pupils, but also in the sense that its use is radically asymmetrical. Speakers hold quite specific expectations that it is the teacher who uses it. It is almost never used by the pupils; and, when it is, it is a sign that an atypical teaching situation has arisen.

As a more extended example of this kind of analysis of teachers' use of language, consider the following extract from the beginning of a tape-recorded discussion between a young native English-speaking teacher and two French boys, P1 and P2, aged twelve. The communication is problematic in some of the ways I discussed above. The teacher has been asked to discuss a specific subject, capital punishment, with the pupils. Initiating a discussion is typically more problematic than continuing it once it is under way. Consider the difficulty sometimes caused by having to initiate social contacts and 'break the ice' with strangers, and how offering cigarettes and other ruses are often used to oil the embarrassing first moments. However, here the teacher has the added problem of explaining to pupils, who do not speak very good English, exactly what is required of them. Almost all his effort is therefore devoted to coaxing along the communication process itself: proposing a topic of discussion, checking if his pupils are following, defining terms, inviting the pupils to speak, editing and correcting their language. In other words, the various different kinds of communicative stress which the teacher is under seem to have led to a very high degree of explicit monitoring of the discourse. There is almost nothing he says in this short extract which does not fall into one of the categories of metacommunication as defined above. The primarily metacommunicative functions of the teacher's language are glossed down the right-hand side of the page.

	Transcript of tape-recording	*Metacommunicative functions*
T1:	right, –	Attracts pupils' attention
	as I was saying – –	Attracts pupils' attention
	the subject of the discussion	
	is capital punishment –	Specifies topic of discussion
	now –	Attracts pupils' attention
	you don't understand what	
	this means	Checks pupils' understanding
	capital punishment – is when	
	– a murderer	Defines a term
	do you know what a	Checks pupils' understanding
	murderer is –	
	a murderer	Repeats to check
		understanding
P1:	yes	
T1:	if a man kills another man	
P1:	ah yes yes	
T1:	he is a murderer –	Defines a word
	then – when – a murderer is	
	arrested – and he has a trial –	
	then what happens to him	
	afterwards –	

	what happens after that	Reformulates to check understanding
P1:	he has a punishment	
T1:	yes he is punished	Corrects pupil's language
P1:	punished	
T1:	now –	Attracts pupils' attention
	what punishment do you think he should get?	
P2:	prison	
T1:	prison	Checks his own understanding or shows attention
P2:	(makes strangling gesture)	
T1:	can you tell what – explain	Explicitly controls amount of speech
P2:	they put a rot	
T1:	a rope	Corrects pupil's language
P2:	a rope – around his neck	
T1:	yes	Shows attention
P2:	and hang him	
T1:	and hang him	Repeats to check his own understanding or show attention
	so ah we've got two different ideas here	Summarizes

In this fairly extreme, and for that reason all the more revealing, example, one can see very clearly some of the strategies which a native speaker of English employs to try and keep in touch with a foreign speaker and which a teacher employs to keep in touch with pupils. Very few studies have explored what speakers actually do in order to communicate across this kind of language barrier in particular dialogues. However, Ferguson (e.g. 1977) in a series of very useful papers has proposed studying the strategies which native speakers use in problematic communication with foreigners, babies, deaf people, and so on. (On foreigner-talk, see also Ferguson, 1975; Krakowian and Corder, 1978.) These studies have looked mainly at phonological, lexical and syntactic simplification, rather than at the kinds of language functions discussed here.

Now contrast the example of teacher–pupil discussion above with the following extract between another young native English-speaking teacher and two older French pupils, P3 and P4, aged seventeen. The main point to be noted about the following extract is that the pupils use language which has clear metacommunicative functions: in other words they use language which is normally restricted to the teacher. The teacher still uses language to try and direct the discussion, although he lets some mistakes go without comment. However, the pupils are also spontaneously using language which refers back to things they have previously said, defines terms they have used, sums up their own position, questions the teacher's summary of what they have said and questions his right to ask certain questions. This means that the teaching situation is more like a genuine discussion with the participants on an equal footing. On the other hand, the teacher's position is threatened to some extent and this is reflected in the way he has lost his casualness. He hesitates, repeats words and phrases, and makes a lot of false starts. A discussion on corporal punishment has been under way for about ten minutes.

T2: you don't think corporal punishment is er – in a school – you think corporal punishment is all right at home – but er – but not in a school

P3: no I don't say that I said until a certain level the cane I am against

T2: 'Until a certain level' I don't understand you

P3: ah yes I explained ten minutes ago

T2: well – I still don't – 'until a certain level' I don't – I don't quite understand what you mean

P3: the cane I am against slaps I am for

T2: oh – yeah – I see

P4: I can't agree – if er a smack can do nothing

T2: a slap

P4: a slap can do nothing if er – I don't know – a text to learn by heart do nothing

T2: you think that a text is just the same thing – thing to give er – something like er – lines – to write out or to learn – it's just the same thing

P4: it's not the same thing – I don't say that – it has no more effect

T2: it has no more effect

(The discussion continued with P4 telling a story about a friend of a friend who had committed suicide after being corporally punished at school.) The teacher brought the discussion to a close as follows:

T2: would you like to eh say – sum up what you think about – corporal punishment in general
P3: in general
T2: like to sum up yeah – what you think now after this discussion – in a few words to say – what you think
P3: I am always of the same opinion I am against
T2: you're against corporal punishment
P3: yes
T2: and er –
P3: there are we have too many bad consequences in the future for –
P4: but I keep the same opinion as the er –
T2: you have the same opinion
P4: yes because what you said – what you said – what you told us it's nothing I have destroyed – for me I think that – it seems for me that with the last example that I give you all your opinions are com – all your er –
T2: arguments
P4: arguments are completely destroyed
T2: for you
P4: yes I think
T2: well I think we'll leave it at that

The discussion ended at this point. Having provided the pupil with the word he needs to complete his attack, the teacher simply breaks off discussion with a conventional phrase. The loss of casualness throughout the teacher's speech indicates a break in the routines. As Hymes (1962) says: 'In general, instance of the breaking off of communication or uneasiness in it, are good evidence of a rule or expectation about speaking . . .' If people feel uneasy when one thing happens, then they had expectations that something else could have, or should have, happened in its place. So the extract illustrates another way in which the study of miscommunication is fruitful. A useful way of working out what rules hold in a situation, if there is no direct way to observe them, is to study what happens when they are broken. (Cf. chapter 11.) Speakers have systematic ways of adapting to the problematic, but these ways are restricted. Some measures of speakers' rigidity or flexibility in adapting to breaks in the routines can probably be developed. One could study for example whether different teachers make different use of the meta-communicative functions listed above.

9   *Two descriptive rules of language use*

What can be called the systems-management aspect of speech events, has two sides to it: first, the effort which goes into simply making the interaction continue smoothly: second, the expression of values which underlies this.

I have already pointed out the radically asymmetrical situation of talk which typically holds in a school classroom. One can go further and say that many forms of language which a teacher uses frequently with his pupils would simply not be tolerated in other situations in which different expectations hold about the rights which the various speakers have. For example, a typical teacher-question is *What do you mean?* Pupils are frequently asked to define more precisely what they are talking about. However, Garfinkel (1967: 42ff) describes experiments in which people were asked to clarify the meaning of commonsense remarks made in the course of different everyday conversations and small talk about the weather, the speaker's health, activities they were engaged in, and so forth. When students asked unsuspecting friends and spouses to clarify what they meant by remarks which would ordinarily have passed unnoticed, initial bewilderment sometimes developed into violent reactions of the *What do you mean, 'What do I mean?'?* type. Having described several incidents of this kind, Garfinkel does not make clear, however, that only specific social situations where specific role relations hold between speakers will permit explicit monitoring of the other's speech in this way.

The quite specific expectations which speakers hold about what constitutes appropriate monitoring behaviour for other participants can be formulated as a descriptive rule as follows (cf. Labov and Fanshel, 1977). Suppose there are two speakers, A and B:

> If A makes repeated and unmitigated statements about B's speech, or asks repeated and unmitigated questions about B's understanding of A, B will accept these statements or questions as legitimate and appropriate only if B believes that A has the right to make such statements or ask such questions; and this right is inherent in only a limited number of role relationships of which the paradigm example is teacher–pupil, where A fills the role of teacher.

The various qualifications in the rule as I have formulated it, cover various cases. A pupil may sometimes be permitted to ask mitigated metaquestions of a teacher, such as *I don't quite see what you mean* (hypothetical example). Similarly, I specify 'repeated' since a pupil may get away with an occasional example, but only a teacher can do it frequently. This is a case of particular difficulty in describing speech behaviour, namely that there are often no absolutes which can be isolated. A feature of speech may express no particular social information about the speaker if present in low proportion, but will give significant information in high percentages. For example, little information about the social relationships of speaker and hearer is available from the fact that metacommunication occurs. I gave examples above of everyday metacommunicative statements, and said that states of talk are always propped up and coaxed along in this way to some extent. But a high percentage of utterances with a metacommunicative function, all used by one speaker, would probably indicate a teaching situation.

A related and very general interpretative rule is:

> Explicit metacomments on anyone's speech are heard as evaluative in any social context (unless they are heard as doing the legitimate, practical work of checking on understanding or on whether the audience can hear clearly, etc.).

If hearers have no interpretative rule of this form, it is difficult to account for the coherence of conversational exchanges such as this example from my field notes. A student has joined two workmen in a pub, and they have bought him a drink, although they do not already know him. (It is Christmas Eve!) The two workmen have been talking for some minutes, the student listening. Then the conversation went:

3.45   W: You're not saying much.
        S: (Pause.) I'm just enjoying my Guinness.

The problem for discourse analysis is to specify how these two utterances are heard as coherent: how S's remark is heard as an appropriate and relevant response to W's remark. Why does S say that? The linguistic links between the two utterances are minimal and precarious. There is a *you–I* sequence, and the *just* might refer back to something, but this is hardly enough to explain the coherence.

One way to interpret the sequence is as follows: W's remark is a metacomment, and is therefore heard as evaluative, as drawing attention to a situation which should be righted, as complaining that S is not contributing to the conversation, and further, as more or less demanding that S does contribute. This interpretation is justified by the rule formulated above. (Possibly W felt he had the right to demand conversation from S since he had bought him a drink.) S clearly does not take W's remark as an informative, although its grammatical form is a statement. An appropriate response to an informative utterance would have been, *No* or *That's true.* To reply in this vein would, in turn, probably be heard as insolent. Rather, we hear S's response as an excuse or an account for his silence. This interpretation might in turn be backed up by an interpretative rule of the form: if one utterance is heard as a complaint, then try and hear the following utterance as an excuse (cf. Turner, 1970). There are other cues in S's response which make the interpretation of an excuse a likely one. S's response is not only appropriate in so far as it provides a reasonable excuse for not talking. It also skilfully turns a complaint into an occasion for reiterating thanks, by referring with appreciation to the drink which W has bought.

Note also the kind of concepts which are used in the formulation of these rules of speech behaviour. The rules include explicitly sociological concepts such as 'right' and 'role relationships'. Some problems of linguistic description can only be solved in socio-linguistic terms: notions of variety-shifting require concepts of 'appropriateness' and 'language function' to deal with them. So it seems also that some aspects of sociolinguistic description can only be formulated in sociological terms.

One of the general implications of the view of verbal interaction put forward in this chapter is that any situation of talk is a micro-cosm of basic social and personal relationships. The kind of language used by speakers reflects who is talking to whom, and what the point of the talk is. By the very way in which a teacher talks to his pupils, he inevitably communicates to them his definition of the situation and the form of teacher–pupil relationship which he considers appro-priate. The teacher's values, concerning, for example, who has the right to control talk in the classroom, as well as basic sociocultural values and status relationships, are put into effect linguistically. I have indicated one way in which the social order of the classroom can be studied through the language used.

It is not difficult to collect other data which illustrate the way in which adults comment on children's language. One convenient source of data is radio phone-in programmes, where it is easy to compare how the 'experts' on the air respond differently to questions from adults and children. It is common, for example, for the expert to comment explicitly on a child's question, and to evaluate it, before giving an answer. Thus an astrologer prefaced her answer to a twelve-year-old boy's question (about whether animals' lives were influenced by the stars) with:

3.46   That's a nice question. I think that's a really nice question.

Similarly, a government spokesman on education explicitly invited a question announced from a nine-year-old girl, by saying:

3.47   OK, Susan, let's have it.

Questions from adults were not commented on in this way. By adding explicit metacomments into the question–answer exchange, the speaker can convey a view of other speakers' conversational rights and competence.

10   Limitations on the analysis

Although the analysis I have proposed here is interesting in the ways I have suggested, there are nevertheless several rather severe limitations on this type of analysis.

Sinclair and Coulthard (1975: 15–17) have proposed four criteria of adequacy which they say should be met by any description of discourse, and these criteria provide a good way of drawing attention to the nature of the description developed in this chapter. (a) The descriptive categories should be finite in number, otherwise there is only the illusion of classification. (b) The descriptive categories should be precisely relatable to their exponents in the data, otherwise the classification will not be replicable. (c) The descriptive system should give comprehensive coverage of the data, otherwise it is possible to ignore the inconvenient facts. (d) The description should place constraints on possible combinations of symbols, otherwise no structural claims are being made.

It is clear that the kind of description which I have provided in this chapter does not meet these criteria. Let us consider them briefly in turn. (a) I proposed several categories for classifying teachers' talk, but it is clear that other related categories could also be proposed. This is a general problem in a functional classification of language (cf. chapter 1, section 2): there is no obvious limit to the functions which language may serve. (b) By concentrating on the functions of utterances, I have failed to give any precise description of the linguistic forms (mainly lexical and syntactic) which realize the functions. In other words, I have assumed that readers can recognize the kinds of utterance I have discussed, and I have not specified recognition criteria. The analysis is therefore inexplicit, although it may well be precise enough to be applied to data in practice. (c) By picking out only utterances with certain functions, I have been very selective in the description of the data. Since I have not imposed a criterion of comprehensive coverage of data on the description, I have left open the possibility that I have described only utterances which it is easy or convenient to describe, and have ignored awkward examples. In fact, the field-note data were collected in a form which precludes any comprehensive description. (d) I have largely described the function of utterances in isolation, independently of the discourse sequences in which they occurred. Again this is partly a limitation imposed by the fragmentary nature of the field-note data. It might be felt that the attempt to code utterances as isolated acts is therefore only a preliminary to discourse analysis, as it does not tackle directly the problem of analysing connected sequences of discourse.

These four criteria provide a useful framework for evaluating any description of language: they can also be applied to the textual commentary in chapter 2, for example. On the other hand, criteria of adequacy are themselves open to discussion. For example, criterion (c), comprehensive coverage of data, would be rejected by many linguists as a secondary consideration. It may be more interesting to investigate some characteristic of English in depth, rather than to give a possibly superficial categorization of the whole of particular texts. Thus, in this chapter, I have been concerned with particular kinds of speech acts, rather than describing everything that teachers say.

In addition, if the criteria show how the description proposed in this chapter is not yet quite discourse analysis, they do show also how it is a genuine preliminary to discourse analysis. They show very precisely, in fact, how the description can be developed. Consider again the example with which I began the chapter. Readers will have noted that I still have not said exactly how I do know that the remark *Fags out, please!* (3.1) has a metacommunicative contact function. Roughly, I would propose that we interpret the remark in this way because of its position in a conversational sequence: (1) at the opening of the speech event 'school lesson', (2) immediately after *Right*, which more obviously functions to attract attention, and (3), referring back to my field notes, before the utterances, *People who want to do some language stuff come down to the front*, and *Come on then, will you get on then!* In other words, we 'know what it

means' because of where it occurs in a string of other utterances
which serve the general function of getting the class organized and
getting the lesson under way. The interpretation of utterances
depends crucially on their position of occurrence in a discourse
sequence. This is relevant to criterion (d) and shows that discourse
analysis must study such sequences.

Although there are these rather severe limitations to the kind of
ethnographic approach to spoken discourse which I have proposed
in this chapter, this by no means implies that such work is worthless.
On the contrary, as long as we are aware of its limitations, it can give
considerable insights into both applied and theoretical concerns, and
I will conclude this chapter with one example of each. After all, any
description at all has inherent limitations. The only solution is to
make those limitations explicit, and to combine different kinds of
description, which have different biases. (Cf. chapter 11.) No single
description can account for the wide range of linguistic, pragmatic
and social factors which contribute to the coherence of discourse.

11   *The hidden curriculum or medium as message*

I will start with discussion of the applied educational interest which
such a description may have.

Writers on the classroom have emphasized how regularly the
teacher defines and redefines the situation. Jackson (1968) reminds
us that children spend over 1,000 hours a year in school, which
comes to at least 10,000 hours by the time they leave. And for most
of that time the teacher is talking! Flanders (1970) estimates that for
70 per cent of the lesson someone is talking, and for 70 per cent of
this time the teacher is talking. This average is based on thousands of
hours of observed lessons in many subjects. Also, classrooms tend to
be rather standardized and routine places: a constant, ritualized,
stylized environment. It would be strange indeed if the very organization of all this teacher-talk did not hammer home, time after time,
taken-for-granted assumptions concerning appropriate teacher and
pupil behaviour. The medium has ten thousand hours to convey its
message. What are some of the messages cumulatively conveyed by
the detailed organization of teacher-talk at the level of speech acts?

I have said that utterances with a metacommunicative function do
a particular kind of work: namely, smooth out periods of talk, guide
messages, and generally prop up and coax along the communication
process. Such utterances are therefore in some sense basic to inter-

action. They have to do with the structure of discourse itself, and without them, talk would grind to a halt. However, such talk is basic to teaching in another way. It works to organize the transmission of knowledge, and to convey a conception of how knowledge should be transmitted. Clearly, one would expect this function also to be central in a coding scheme which claimed to identify characteristic features of teacher-talk. The categories in the coding scheme have to do with explaining, summarizing, correcting, editing, evaluating, defining topics, and so on. Simply to list such speech acts makes explicit many assumptions about what it is to teach somebody something. Assumptions, for example: that only the teacher knows what is relevant to a subject being taught; that teachers assume they know when a pupil is paying attention, and therefore when learning is going on; that teaching the names of phenomena is valuable in itself; that it is valuable to explain phenomena verbally; that there is always a correct answer to teachers' questions; and, of course, that the appropriate pupil response is passivity, and that it is the teacher's job alone to organize teaching situations.

In other words, the coding scheme provides one way in which to study in detail, at the level of speech acts, how the 'hidden curriculum' (Snyder, 1971) is transmitted to students, how students learn, without being told in so many words, but through thousands of hours' of exposure to teacher-talk, what is appropriate pupil behaviour, and how they will be evaluated at the end of the day. Underlying the coding scheme is therefore a conception of what teaching *is* (cf. Stubbs, 1976: ch. 7).

The transmission of knowledge in the classroom could also be discussed with reference to Bernstein's (1971b) concept of the 'framing' of educational knowledge. Framing concerns the form in which knowledge is transmitted; not only what is transmitted, but the boundary between what may be taught and what may not. Bernstein's analysis in this paper is elegant, but highly abstract, and not grounded in speech data. (On this last point, see my comments on Hymes' and Goffman's work above.)

12 *Object language and metalanguage*

The ability of language to refer to itself has long been a topic of study in linguistics, philosophy and artificial intelligence, and the data discussed in this chapter therefore also provide a way of approaching a topic of central theoretical importance.

It is usual to distinguish between an *object language* which can refer to a specific domain, and a *metalanguage* which can refer to the object language. Alternatively, linguists often distinguish between the *use* and *mention* of a linguistic expression. If I say:

3.48   Who's that man over there?

then I am using the expression *that man* to refer to something in the world. Alternatively, if I say:

3.49   *That man* is a noun phrase.

then I am mentioning the expression *that man* and making a meta-linguistic statement. *Noun phrase* is an expression in the metalanguage.

Usually, the distinction is clear, but sometimes an expression is used and mentioned at the same time. If I say:

3.50   That's all I have to say, period.

then I am both mentioning the metalinguistic term *period*, and also using it to try and close the topic (cf. Hofstadter, 1979: 703). The blur occurs here because the term is used to organize the discourse itself. This is precisely the kind of blur which I have illustrated at length above. Metacommunicative utterances are both utterances in the sequence of discourse and comments on the discourse.

The phenomenon that I have discussed here under the label of metacommunication, has also been discussed in general terms by Garfinkel and Sacks (1970), who talk of *formulating* a conversation as a feature of that conversation:

A member may treat some part of the conversation as an occasion to describe that conversation, to explain it, or characterize it, or explicate, or translate, or summarize, or furnish the gist of it, or take note of its accordance with rules, or remark on its departure from rules. That is to say, a member may use some part of the conversation as an occasion to *formulate* the conversation ...

A more systematic account of such phenomena would have to distinguish more clearly than I have done so far, between the different kinds of entity to which utterances can refer in a universe of discourse. Lyons (1977: 667ff) has pointed out that deictic expressions (*it*, *this*, *that*, etc.) can refer to linguistic entities of various kinds in the co-text of utterance: forms, parts of forms, propositions and speech acts. If for example a teacher says:

3.51   (=3.32) David, what's the meaning of *hurdies*?

then he is referring to a lexical item. If he says:

3.52   (=3.33) Can anybody put that in a different way?

the *that* refers not to a linguistic form but to a proposition. If he says:

3.53   (=3.43) Now, before I ask you to write something about it, we'll talk about it.

he is referring explicitly to the speech act being performed.

Thus, the data I have cited in this chapter could be re-analysed in this way to investigate how speakers refer to linguistic entities in the universe of discourse. Goffman (1981: 280ff) has proposed another rich source of data on such metacommunication: the ways in which radio announcers correct and comment on what they have said.

Sperber and Wilson (1981) have also pointed out a very general interest of the use–mention distinction. They argue that the distinction can provide an explanation of irony and parody. Irony may be the implicit mention of propositions; and parody is the mention of linguistic expressions. One general concept involved here is intertextuality: the understanding of one text may depend on knowledge of other texts.

Generally, in both linguistics and philosophy, questions of use and mention have been discussed in the abstract. I have shown in this chapter that it is possible to collect a large amount of everyday conversational data to throw light on the ways in which we can talk about talk.

4

On a Different Level:
Particles, Adverbs and Connectors

'Well, . . . '
'What's the use of a well with no water in it?'
        (Traditional, cited by Opie and Opie, 1959; 50)

In chapters 2 and 3, I have discussed two possible approaches to discourse analysis. One is to take a transcript of conversational data and to inspect it carefully for the kinds of surface organization and patterns it shows. A second possibility is to take an ethnographic approach: to collect data by recording and observation, to neglect the surface form of utterances, but to pay particular attention to their underlying functions. These two approaches take their inspiration from different academic disciplines. The close inspection of texts has traditionally been the province of literary criticism, whereas the ethnography of communication has developed from anthropology.

A third way of identifying the kinds of phenomena which discourse analysis has to explain is to pay particular attention to aspects of language which syntax and semantics have had difficulties in explaining. This third approach would, therefore, draw its inspiration predominantly from linguistics: if only from difficulties within linguistics. There is a growing realization that there is a range of linguistic phenomena which do not fit neatly into the syntactic and semantic categories of contemporary linguistics. Despite great developments in linguistics over the past 75 years, and particularly since the mid 1950s, linguistic description is still firmly based on traditional parts of speech and on the view that the clause or sentence is the basic linguistic unit. In fact, linguists often exaggerate how innovatory linguistics is, although units such as *noun, verb, sentence* and the like, have been central in the description of language for over two thousand years, and still are.

Three areas of English, which are based on this view of language, and which have resisted traditional treatment in grammar, concern adverbs, co-ordinating conjunctions, and the range of items often classified as particles (including *well*, *now*, *right*, and so on, especially when they are utterance-initial or occur on their own as complete utterances).

I have room here for only these three examples. Note, however, that many of the most interesting problems in contemporary syntax and semantics, including those discussed here, appear to cluster at the rank of clause or sentence, the largest unit traditionally defined by syntax. Thus the clause or sentence has to act as the most relevant formal unit for intonation, propositional information (including entailments and presuppositions), illocutionary force, and many aspects of sociolinguistic sensitivity to context. These are all highly controversial aspects of linguistics with no general consensus about how to describe them. This is pointed out by Sinclair and Coulthard (1975: 121), who argue that this is prima facie evidence that an artificial ceiling has been reached in syntax, and that this pressure from below is an argument for establishing structural units above the sentence.

1   *Well* ...

One type of item about which syntax and semantics have little to say is represented by *well*. Other such items include, especially when utterance-initial or complete utterances, *now*, *right*, *OK*, *anyway*, *you know*, *I see*, *hello*, *byebye*. Syntax has little to say about them, since they make no syntactic predictions. Most, if not all, have uses in which they are potentially complete utterances. Nor does semantics have much to say about such items, since when they are not used in their literal meanings, they have no property of thesis: that is, they have no propositional content. For this reason, they are common at the closing of conversations, where they can be used without introducing new topics (Schegloff and Sacks, 1973). This transaction-management function relates them to summonses such as *hey!* or *John!* and to greetings and farewells in general. Further, such items are purely performative and have no truth value: to say hello to someone *is* to greet them. The other main fact about such items is that they are essentially interactive, and almost all are restricted to spoken language. When utterance-initial, the function of items such as *well*, *now*, and *right* is to relate utterances to each other, or to mark a boundary in the discourse. Some (e.g. *now*, *anyway*) may be used to mark initial boundaries of units of written or spoken language, and they are therefore immediate indications that continuous discourse is analysable into units larger than the sentence. Bublitz (1978) discusses such items in English, and also comparable modal particles in German, such as *bloss, mal, wohl, schon, ja, doch*. Longacre (1978) discusses such particles in various non-Indo-European languages.

Some of the main points about such items can be made in a discussion of *well*. The lexical item *well* has several different functions and meanings. As an adjective, it can contrast with *ill*. (*He was ill, but is well again now*.) As an adverb it can modify a following item. (*He is well qualified*.) However, when *well* occurs utterance-initially, it does not generally have what might be referred to as these literal interpretations. In utterance-initial position, there is little agreement about what part of speech it is. If we are restricted to traditional part of speech categories, then it is presumably an adverb. However, it has also been labelled *interjection, filler, initiator*, or has been given 'the suitably vague and central term *particle*' (Svartvik, 1980: 168).

In its use as an utterance-initial particle, it is almost entirely restricted to spoken English, where it is very common. In this function, it is notoriously difficult to translate into foreign languages, and it is notoriously poorly explained in dictionaries. This is because it has no propositional content, and also because dictionaries are mainly based on written data. Utterance-initially, it usually has one of two functions. It may have a rather general introductory function (*Well, what shall we do?*). In such positions, it may be more or less synonymous with *now, so, OK, right, anyway*, and may function as a disjunction marker (Schegloff and Sacks, 1973) indicating a break with what has gone immediately before, and the initial boundary of a new section of discourse. Sinclair and Coulthard (1975) refer to this function as a *frame*. Alternatively, if *well* occurs utterance-initially after a question, it indicates an indirect answer, claiming relevance although admitting a shift in topic. Labov and Fanshel (1977: 156) call such items discourse markers. As R. Lakoff (1973) points out, *well* cannot preface a direct answer to an information question:

4.1   Q. What time is it?   A: *Well, two o'clock.

In other words, *well* can indicate a break in the discourse, a shift in the topic, either as a preface to modifying some assumptions in what has gone before, or as a preface to closing the topic and potentially the whole conversation.

These few observations about *well* and related items already indicate several important points. Such items are not well accounted for by traditional linguistic categories. They are largely restricted to spoken language, due to their largely interactional functions. And the fact that one of their main functions is to act as boundary markers is an immediate indication that they are the boundaries of units of discourse larger than clauses or sentences. These points and others can be developed by a more detailed look at various adverbs.

2 *Adverbs*

It is usually admitted that adverbs are a heterogeneous class. This is tantamount to admitting that they have no satisfactory and natural explanation within sentence grammar. Some adverbs have clear discourse functions, in that they make metareferences to the discourse itself, and indicate its structure to hearers or readers. (Cf. chapter 3.) Examples include *firstly*, *finally* and *furthermore*. Often the same discourse function may be served by items in different syntactic classes such as prepositional phrases, infinitival phrases or whole clauses: *in the first place*, *to conclude* or *one might add*. Other adverbs do not appear to be items in the syntactic structure of the clause or sentence, so much as indications of the speaker's attitude to the proposition being conveyed. This interpretation is characteristic if the adverb occurs in initial position, possibly separated by a pause and/or uttered as a separate tone group. For example:

4.2   Admittedly/frankly/fortunately, I can't see anything.

Such items are usually called sentence adverbs. To show that they cannot be accounted for satisfactorily by syntactic explanations, one would have to show that their distribution is constrained not only by syntactic facts, but also by pragmatic or discourse facts. There are, in fact, co-occurrence restrictions between sentence adverbials and the speech act being performed, and I discuss these below.

As well as problems over adverbs, there are problems, more generally, with adverbial phrases. Crystal (1980) has pointed out that adverbials have been neglected in much linguistic description for another reason. From a syntactic point of view, adverbials are always considered an optional element in clause structure. However, they are very common in casual conversation. Crystal cites spoken data in which adverbials occur in 59 per cent of clauses, or 66 per cent if clauses are excluded in which adverbials would be impossible or unlikely. Conversely, noun phrases account for a relatively small amount (28 per cent) of clause exponence. Pronouns and adverbials together account for 57 per cent.

3   *Please*

Several of the main arguments about the problematic nature of adverbs can be illustrated in a particularly clear way with *please*, which is often regarded as a sentence adverb (e.g. by Strang, 1962: 166–7). The distribution of *please* cannot be explained entirely on syntactic grounds, but only by stating co-occurrence restrictions between *please* and functional categories of speech acts (cf. Sadock, 1974). The basic aim of descriptive linguistics is to predict correctly the surface distribution of morphemes. If such distributions can be stated by stating co-occurrence restrictions between grammatical and lexical categories, then this is an argument against the need for discourse as a level of linguistic description. If, on the other hand, distributional statements require reference to functional discourse units, then this is an argument in favour of redrawing the boundaries of linguistic description.

It is clear, in fact, that traditional grammars cannot deal with *please* at all, since by all syntactic tests it is unique. In terms of a traditional part of speech analysis, it is presumably an adverb, given that this is already an ill-defined, heterogeneous category. Its distribution in syntactic frames is at least comparable to other items which are more obviously adverbs, for example, *quickly, elegantly*. There are some clear syntactic constraints on its distribution within clauses. Thus *please* can occur in the bracketed positions in the following clauses, but not elsewhere:

4.3   (please) $\left\{ \begin{array}{l} \text{will you} \\ \text{tell him} \end{array} \right\}$ (please) $\left\{ \begin{array}{l} \text{open the door} \\ \text{to come at once} \end{array} \right\}$ (please)

However, its distribution is not entirely identical to any other item. One simple difference is that it allows no submodification, although other adverbs do: *very quickly, very kindly, most easily, most kindly, *very please, *most please*. Quirk *et al.* (1972: 470) almost admit that it is a unique item by setting up a class of formulaic adjunct for a small class of adverbs which are used as markers of courtesy: *please, kindly, graciously*.

Syntactically, then, *please* is almost unique. Second, it appears only marginally to be a syntactic item at all, since it makes no syntactic predictions about what may follow it. It is, in fact, potentially complete, since it may be a sentence substitute:

4.4   A: Would you like some tea?   B: Please.

Third, it is a functional item, in that its only function is as a marker of politeness or mitigation. It has no property of thesis: it is not 'about' anything. There is, therefore, nothing to be said about *please* in a semantic account of English. Fourth, it is therefore also essentially interactive: its essential function is to get someone else to do something, and it is, therefore, largely restricted to spoken language.

There are no constraints on the co-occurrence of *please* with different surface syntactic structures. Thus it can co-occur with declarative, interrogative, imperative and moodless clauses:

4.5   I'd like some more pudding, please.
4.6   Can I have some more pudding, please.
4.7   Give me some more pudding, please.
4.8   More pudding, please.

However, there is a restriction on the speech act that *please* may co-occur with. It can co-occur only with a sentence which is interpretable as a request, but cannot co-occur with statements, promises, offers, invitations, threats, and so on.

4.9   *He ate more pudding, please.
4.10   *I promise you can have more pudding, please.
4.11   *Would you like more pudding, please?
4.12   *Do you want to come to a party, please?
4.13   *Give me more pudding or I'll hit you, please.

Notice in 4.13 that, conversely, *please* cannot co-occur with even an imperative surface form, if this form is not a realization of a request. I am assuming in these cases that the sentences are spoken as single tone groups. If *please* is utterance-initial, spoken as a separate tone group and followed by a pause, it is easier to interpret such utterances as requests. Even here, however, some co-occurrences are ruled out; or require very elaborate contexts to force an interpretation as a request (cf. Ross, 1975: 238):

4.14   *Please, Napoleon was a Corsican.

In fact, as Butler (1982) argues, there is a gradient of restriction on the distribution of *please*, according to the directness or opacity of the speech act performed. In clear-cut, transparent requests (including surface imperatives), *please* can occur in all positions: utterance-initially, with or without a break in the intonation contour, before the main verb, or utterance-finally. The most opaque cases may allow *please* only utterance-initially before a break.

Related distributional facts allow *please* to occur in an utterance after an offer, but not after a compliment, question, request, and so on.

4.15   A: Would you like some tea?   B: Please.
4.16   A: That's a nice hairdo.
4.17   A: Have you got the time?   } B: *Please.
4.18   A: Will you open the door?

I am assuming here that *please* is expandable into the request – for example, *I would like some tea, please*; but not *I will open the door, please*. And I am assuming, therefore, that it is not being used to challenge a precondition of an utterance, and to mean, say, "Please, I'm busy, don't disturb me."

Other related distributional facts permit the occurrence of *thanks* in the next utterance:

4.19   A: Can you be a little more quiet, please.
        B: (Stops making noise.)
        A: Thanks.

In summary, there are several distributional facts about *please* and related items such as *thanks*, which cannot be explained by reference to the syntax and semantics of single sentences. We have to look, rather, at the syntagmatic chaining of whole clauses or sentences. And furthermore, these syntactic units have to be reclassified as functional speech acts.

4   Tests for speech acts

My argument so far has been that such distributional constraints can be established on the basis of introspective judgements about discourse sequences. Such distributional statements make predictions which require to be checked against naturally occurring discourse, in a search for counter-examples. However, let us assume for the present that we have confidence in our statements of distributional constraints, and take the argument one step further. If we have confidence in our statements about *please*, then these statements may in turn be used as a test for speech acts.

Consider how the distribution of *please* may be used as a test for requests. Searle (1975a), in his well known article on indirect speech acts, proposes categories of sentences which are 'conventionally used in the performance of indirect directives'. These categories (pp. 65–6) include sentences concerned with:

(a)   H's ability to perform an action
(b)   S's wish that H will perform an action

    (c)   H's doing of an action
    (d)   H's desire to do an action
    (e)   reasons for doing an action

These categories are clearly semantically based, although in many cases lexical items can be used to provide formal recognition criteria. Searle claims (p. 68) that most of his examples take *please*, either at the end of a sentence, or before the verb, but this is true only of categories (a) to (d):

4.20   (a)   Can you (please) be a little more quiet (please).
4.21   (b)   I hope you'll (*please) do it (please).
4.22   (c)   Aren't you (please) going to eat your cereal (please).
4.23   (d)   Would you mind (please) not making so much noise (please).

However, *please* cannot co-occur with Searle's category (e) items, assuming that the sentence is uttered with a single tone group.

4.24   *Ought you to eat quite so much spaghetti, please?
4.25   *Why not stop here, please?
4.26   *It would be a good idea if you left town, please.

This is evidence that such items are not primarily requests or directives, but are hints or suggestions whose directive force is only interpretable by inference. At least the test captures the fact that category (e) items are less central requests than (a) to (d).

The basic aim of such tests, then, is to try to distinguish between what is centrally semantic, and what is not conveyed by propositional meaning but has to be inferred from context. More generally there is a closed class of items which can be used for such tests. These include: *OK, thanks, I see, I guess so, oh!* These items are all non-initial and essentially discourse items which can only occur in response to another utterance. Also, they are not interchangeable: they are, at least partly, in complementary distribution. I argue similarly in chapter 6 that *yes* and *no* are not always in contrastive distribution, and that these items can therefore also be used as tests of the illocutionary force of the preceding utterance. Note also that since the class of such items is closed, this automatically provides a control on the number of preceding categories of utterance which they can classify. Recall that a basic problem in discourse analysis is to provide some principled limit on the proliferation of functional categories (cf. chapter 3, section 10). We seem to have here one solution to the problem. Note that the solution is discourse-based.

Utterances are classified according to a closed class of items which can follow them in a syntagmatic chain.

The identification of speech acts is not normally regarded as an empirical and testable matter. Illocutionary force is normally pursued by traditional introspective methods, including judgements about synonymy, paraphrase and other semantic intuitions. And illocutionary force clearly does have to do with the preconditions and commitments involved in making promises, offers, requests, warnings, and so on. However, illocutionary force can be tested, and one basic procedure of testing and classification is to study the discourse consequences of candidate speech acts. The kinds of tests I am proposing here are still based on introspective judgements, but I am proposing tests based on possible syntagmatic sequences: discussion of illocutionary force has usually been based entirely on discussions of isolated sentences, not in a discourse sequence (cf. chapter 8). Martin (1981) also discusses syntagmatic constraints between utterances as tests of illocutionary force.

Consider some further examples. If *yes* and *OK* are considered in isolation, they may appear to be synonymous. However, they are not always interchangeable. *OK* may occur after requests for action, commands, offers and invitations, but not after questions:

4.27   A: Do you want to come?   B: OK/Yes.
4.28   A: Does he want to come?   B: *OK/Yes.

A rather obvious, but crucial, factor in interpreting possible illocutionary force is first versus second or third person reference: contrast 4.27 and 4.28. First person reference is usually a precondition of conveying certain illocutionary forces (e.g. promise), just as second person is a precondition of others (e.g. request), whereas questions are less restricted.

OK, *sure* and *all right* can be used on their own as a verbal response to direct requests, but not to opaque hints and suggestions. Thus:

4.29   A: Will you shut the door (please).
        B: OK/Sure/All right.
4.30   A: It's draughty in here (*please).
        B: *OK/*Sure/*All right.

Such occurrences as 4.30 would at least require co-occurring sighs and other markers of resignation, and probably also a following comment, as in: *(Sighs.) Oh, OK, I'm just going to shut the door.*

Similarly, *thanks* can occur after utterances which may be construed as offers, invitations or compliments, but not after requests for information, despite their possible similarity in syntactic form (cf. 4.27, 4.28):

4.31   A: Do you want me to come?   B: Thanks.
4.32   A: Do you want him to come?   B: *Thanks.

Only if a context can be found which will allow 4.32 to be construed as an offer, is *thanks* possible. One such possible context is if the speaker has authority over *him*, and can speak on his behalf. Such factors complicate the usual preconditions for personal reference in speech acts, and mean that independent tests such as I am proposing here are useful, although, as with any introspective judgements, they are open to errors. Or consider a guest speaking to a hostess:

4.33   A: I could eat all that pie myself.   B: Thanks.
4.34   A: I could eat a horse.   B: *Thanks.

where 4.33 could be construed as a compliment about the cooking, but 4.34 can only be interpreted to mean that A is hungry. In this case there is nothing in the syntax, for example the modal verbs or the person reference, which distinguishes the two sentences.

The observations about *please* and *thanks* can be related in exchanges such as:

4.35   A: Would you like some tea?
        B: Please.
        A: (Pours out tea.)
        B: Thanks.

As an elliptical request, *please* is a response to the offer. *Thanks* is also a response. Hence elliptical exchanges, such as:

4.36   A: Would you like some tea?
        B: Thanks.
        A: (Pours out tea.)

A response of *oh!* marks a preceding utterance as an inform which conveys previously unknown information. That is, it indicates something about the speaker's state of knowledge before and after the utterance. *Yes* after the same inform indicates that the information is already known:

4.37   A: Harry's died.   B: Oh!/Yes.

Some informs will also allow a following utterance with *so* as a dummy item, as in *I guess so* or *So he is, So he has*, and so on.

4.38   A: It's raining again.   B: Oh!/Yes./So it is.
4.39   A: Why is it always raining?   B: *So it is./*I guess so.

I am unable to formulate exactly the conditions under which *so* may
be used in such elliptical responses, but it seems to be partly dependent on whether the information is verifiable in the immediate context of utterance. There is, therefore, an interaction between the
syntactic form and the degree of certainty of the proposition or at
least the nature of the knowledge involved. (Hopi is not the only
language to distinguish in its grammar between statements whose
truth is immediately observable, known through hearsay, and so on:
pace Benjamin Lee Whorf. See also chapter 6, section 8.)[1]

None of these tests is watertight, but then it is not usual to find
single tests which distinguish grammatical categories from each other.
Typically, different tests have to be combined. Thus the use of *please*
as a test for requests can be combined with the *thanks* test.

5   Pragmatic connectors

Adverbs, then, and certain items in particular, provide problems for
sentence based grammars, but are of great interest in a study of
discourse sequences, since their functions are largely to do with the
organization of connected discourse, and with the interpretation of
functional categories of speech acts. Another set of items which have
not received any natural treatment within grammar are items known
variously as conjunctions, connectives or connectors, and in particular
the co-ordinating conjunction *and*.

It is a commonplace of philosophical logic, as Grice (1975: 41)
and others have pointed out, that there is only a superficial and
apparent equivalence between operators in the propositional calculus
such as &, V and →, and natural language items such as *and*, *or* and *if*.
In fact, the behaviour of natural language connectors such as these,
and also *but*, *since* and *because*, cannot be explained in either logical
or purely syntactic terms, and they can be shown to have pragmatic
functions. (Gazdar, 1980, provides a useful short review of some of
the issues.) One of the main issues concerns what kinds of units are
connected by such items. Logical operators connect propositions,
simple and compound: $(p \& q) \rightarrow r$. Natural language connectors
may connect syntactic units such as words, groups or clauses, but
they may also relate speech acts.

---

[1]   I am grateful to Margaret Deuchar for her observation on this point.

It is obvious enough in a commonsense way that logical operators are not equivalent to natural language connectors. For one thing, the propositional calculus has no axioms: it only has rules. In other words, the rules operate on unanalysed atomic propositions, p, q, and so on, with no reference to their content. So the following strings are all well-formed:

4.40 $(p \& q) \rightarrow (q \& p)$.
4.41   If p and q, then q and p.
4.42   If Henry is a monk and pigs have silk ears, then this implies that pigs have silk ears and Henry is a monk.

And so on, with any such gibberish. The system merely manipulates the proposition symbols automatically or typographically, without interpreting them in any way. (Cf. Hofstadter, 1979: ch. 7.)

Almost by definition, conjunctions cannot be fully dealt with within syntax, since they are not really part of the structure of syntactic units. They have rather a sequencing function of relating syntactic units and fitting them into a textual or discourse context. Part of the confusion may arise because conjunctions normally fall under the same intonation contour as the following clause. It has been evident from the early days of Immediate Constituent analysis that co-ordinating conjunctions cannot easily be handled within grammar. Thus IC analysis demands that sentences be divided into immediate and ultimate constituents on the basis of successive two-way cuts. But there is no obvious way to decide between two analyses such as:

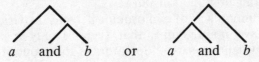

where *a* and *b* are words, groups or clauses. Much more obvious is:

but such a three-way analysis attacks this basic premise of IC analysis. Co-ordination has also proved a problem for more recent grammatical models.

Further, it is clear that English *and* has a much wider range of functions than logical *&*. Logical conjunction with *&* is symmetrical:

p & q = q & p. However, logicians have generally assumed that English *and* is ambiguous between a symmetrical sense, and an asymmetrical, temporally consecutive sense. Natural language *and* may be used for a symmetrical relation, so that these two sentences may be used synonymously:

4.43   He plays the flute and she plays the clarinet.
4.44   She plays the clarinet and he plays the flute.

However, it is easy enough to think up a narrative context in which 4.43 and 4.44 could imply a temporal sequence: consider them, for example, as being in the historic present tense.

With many examples, however, the only likely interpretation is a temporal one. Therefore, changing the sequence of the clauses related by *and* will change the meaning. These two sentences tell different stories:

4.45   He got drunk and crashed the car.
4.46   He crashed the car and got drunk.

A basic interpretative principle is that if *and* can be interpreted temporally, as *and then*, it will be; and if, further, it can be interpreted causally, it will be. Schmerling (1975) argues that such temporal and causal interpretations are implicatures and not logical entailments, since they can be cancelled, for example by *both*. (Grice, 1975, proposes such cancellation as a test for conversational implicatures.) This test is not entirely convincing. It would be a dangerous discourse tactic to state to a policeman:

4.47   I both got drunk and crashed my car.

Adding some phrases such as *But not in that order* would, however, cancel the implied sequence and not make the sentence logically contradictory. Other uses of *and* do not permit reversal at all.

4.48   I asked him and he'll come.
4.49   *He'll come and I asked him.
4.50   Do that again and I'll hit you.
4.51   *I'll hit you and do that again.

Or, as used on news broadcasts:

4.52   Afghanistan, and Soviet troops have occupied Kabul.
4.53   *Soviet troops have occupied Kabul, and Afghanistan.

Schmerling (1975) discusses a large number of such examples, but she reaches few conclusions except that there are a large number of uses for *and* and that 'it is not a unitary phenomenon'. In other words, she can provide no explanation for the range of phenomena. See also Sacks (1972) for a detailed discussion of inferences from the sequence of clauses in a narrative; and Labov (1972d) on the linking of narrative clauses in a temporal sequence. (Cf. chapter 2, section 7.)

There is a comparable range of phenomena for English *if*, which clearly has uses not equivalent to logical →. Haiman (1978) discusses examples such as:

4.54   If Max comes, we'll play poker.
4.55   If you're so smart, why aren't you rich?
4.56   If you're hungry, there's food in the fridge.
4.57   If I was a bad carpenter, I was a worse tailor.
4.58   She's fifty, if she's a day.

Haiman starts from the view that a similarity in syntax is likely to reflect a similarity in meaning. He argues that the *if*-clauses are topics: that is, old information, or what is being talked about. And he points out that often *given that* can be substituted for *if*. In other words, he relates the function of the *if*-clauses to the current state of knowledge of the speakers. This explanation appears also to hold for the sentence-initial clauses followed by *and* in the examples above which do not permit reversal. It is clearest in the news broadcast example 4.52, which is only usable if Afghanistan is currently known to be in the news.

Van Dijk (1979) and McTear (1980) have argued that what are usually termed conjunctions may on occasion relate not syntactic units such as words or groups, or semantic propositions, but speech acts, and therefore be pragmatic connectors. Van Dijk gives examples such as:

4.59   Do you want a sandwich? *Or* aren't you hungry?
4.60   A: Let's eat!   B: *But* I'm not hungry.

where the connectors appear to query the conditions for an appropriate offer or suggestion. McTear (1980), Davison (1975: 162–3) and Morreal (1979) argue similarly that *because* can often function to mark a justification for the preceding speech act, giving grounds for believing a proposition to be true or a reason for making the utterance. McTear (1980) usefully summarizes several syntactic tests which distinguish sentences such as 4.61 below which have a possible syntactic or semantic interpretation of *because*, and 4.62 where only a pragmatic interpretation is possible.

4.61   He was drowned because he fell off the pier.
4.62   He was drunk, because he fell off the pier.

Sentences like 4.61, but not 4.62, will permit reversal of the clauses, with or without clefting of the *because*-clause, and yes–no interrogation of the whole sentence:

4.63   *Because he fell off the pier, he was drunk.
4.64   *It is because he fell off the pier that he was drunk.
4.65   *Was he drunk because he fell off the pier?

Sentences such as 4.61 have a structure such as *effect + cause*, whereas 4.62 is *assertion + justification*. (I am assuming that examples like 4.65 are spoken as a single tone group.)

Such pragmatic uses are particularly common in spoken language, where *because* is often phonologically reduced to *'cos*. But written examples also occur. Here are two related examples using *for* and *since* from Le Carré (1979: 7) and from the last line of a letter.

4.66   On one of these August days – the fourth, and at twelve
        o'clock exactly, *for* a church bell was striking and a factory
        bell had just preceded it ...
4.67   ... if you will let me know what time your train arrives, I will
        meet you at the station. My home number is Sheffield 123456,
        since we are temporarily without a secretary in the
        department.

Another problem in discussing the functions of such connectors is again the comparative neglect of conversational data. In formal written English, a wide range of connectors is normal: *and, but, if, since, because, whereas, however, nevertheless*, and so on. However, a much narrower range accounts for most occurrences in conversational English: *and, but* and *if* are the commonest, and they therefore have a wide range of functions.

There is an important issue in applied sociolinguistics here. Bernstein (1971a: 47ff, 157ff) has argued that a characteristic of restricted code is that it relies on a small group of conjunctions, such that an approximate term is constantly substituted for a more exact logical distinction. However, Bernstein has confused a stylistic characteristic of spoken versus written English with a logical matter. In any case, the number of connectors used does not determine the logical power of the system. The propositional calculus generally uses five operators for: *not, and, or, if*, and *if and only if*. However, it is possible to set up a system using only *and* and *or* which has the same

logical power. Bernstein has confused two things: (a) logical power
and a question of lexical synonymy – there is no logical difference
between synonyms such as *but*, *however*, *nevertheless* and so on; and
(b) logical power and stylistic preferences between spoken and
written English – written English uses a wider range of lexical synonyms. This second point is true of written English in general, incidentally, not just of so-called logical connectives. (Gazdar, 1979,
discusses these logical points in Bernstein's work; and for further
discussion of Bernstein's neglect of the distinctions between spoken
and written English, see Stubbs, 1980: 111–12.) Many such con-
fusions arise simply from the lack of descriptions of naturally occurring conversational English.

6   *Conclusions*

As I emphasize at several places in this book, even if individual
arguments in this area are correctly formulated and understood, it
is often by no means obvious what should be concluded from them.
I have given examples of various lexical and syntactic characteristics
of English which cannot be accounted for within sentence grammars.
It is now widely recognized that recent linguistics has been based on
a restricted range of linguistic data. The data have often been simplified, throughout the last two thousand years of grammatical study,
by being drawn from written language or from introspection. In
addition, since conversational language has not been systematically
described, it is in any case easier to focus attention on permanently
recorded written languages, and introspective judgements have
themselves been unduly influenced by written language. (Cf. chapter 2,
section 8.)

It is now also widely recognized that extra-sentential phenomena
are relevant to phenomena within the clause. It is probably no longer
in serious dispute that what are optional rules from a purely syntactic
or semantic point of view have pragmatic effects. It is therefore now
obvious in a general way that many details of linguistic organization
will be missed, if language in use in connected discourse is ignored.
An impressive variety of phenomena is involved here, including: the
function of movement transformations; modal particles; the use of
pronouns, articles, conjunctions and tenses; and so on. Lists of such
phenomena which are missed by conventional linguistic description
are given by Longacre (1978) and by Labov and Fanshel (1977: 23).
On the other hand, this impressive variety of phenomena is often

seen as lying within the clause. Extra-sentential phenomena are often grudgingly admitted only when they are seen to affect the traditional concerns of core linguistics: when they become intrusive, and cannot be ignored. It is this approach to language which characterizes *pragmatics* as this is defined by several recent collections of articles (e.g. Cole, ed., 1978). Certainly the syntax of the clause is basic in many ways. It appears to be the unit about which the most complex and interesting structural statements are to be made. It is the unit most relevant to the logical analysis of propositional information. It tends to coincide with basic intonational units (e.g. the tone group). And in turn there is evidence that such phonological units are indications of units of neurological planning.

Although it is clear that sentence grammars are often missing important facts, it does not, however, seem possible to identify an autonomous area of discourse phenomena, which are not also matters of syntax and semantics. The general conclusion to be drawn from the kinds of phenomena discussed here may seem rather confused. No elegant account of discourse function is at present available to explain the range of facts discussed here. A narrow logico-semantic account clearly has some explanatory power; but a broader pragmatic account is also required.

Nevertheless, the arguments in this chapter lead to clear conclusions in one area. By definition, sentence grammars ignore the syntagmatic chaining of clauses and sentences in larger exchanges or sequences. My main argument has been that certain phenomena involving particles, adverbs and conjunctions can only be explained with reference to the syntagmatic chaining of linguistic units at the clause or above. At least sometimes this chaining requires that syntactic and semantic units be reclassified as functional units such as speech acts. The facts about syntagmatic chaining argue that discourse is a rank above the clause. The facts about reclassification argue that discourse is a level of linguistic description above syntax. It is this study of syntagmatic organization and of the relationship between forms and functions which distinguishes discourse analysis from other studies of spoken interaction which draw their inspiration from other disciplines.

In order to develop the argument further, I will now have to discuss in more detail the concept of well-formed discourse sequences, and the concept of conversational exchanges. This is the topic of the next three chapters.

5

A Linguistic Approach to Discourse: Structures and Well-Formedness

The moment a conversation is started, whatever is said is a determining condition for what, in any reasonable expectation, may follow. What you say raises the threshold against most of the language of your companion, and leaves only a limited opening for a certain likely range of responses.

(J. R. Firth, 1935)

Many examples in chapters 1 to 4 have illustrated the general point that speakers may say one thing and mean another. Probably all linguists would agree with statements such as: the meaning of an utterance depends on its context of use, including its co-text. Or, phrased rather more carefully: the literal (propositional, logical, conceptual or cognitive) meaning of a sentence is only one factor in determining how an utterance of that sentence will be interpreted on particular occasions of use. In addition, it is widely recognized that most, if not all, sentences have multiple possible meanings in isolation, although hearers can reduce the ambiguity by reference to the context of the utterance, in ways that are not at all well understood.

Linguists disagree, however, over whether such phenomena fall within the scope of linguistics proper, or whether linguistic semantics should be restricted to studying literal meaning, ignoring stylistic and metaphorical meaning, irony, conversational implicature, and so on. They disagree, in other words, over whether such phenomena can have a linguistic-semantic explanation, or only a pragmatic explanation. There is a general debate, in fact, over whether linguistics has given too central a place to the referential and propositional meaning of isolated sentences, and whether it is wrong to relegate other kinds of meaning to a secondary domain of stylistic meaning, social meaning, connotation, and so on. Are the contrasts of meaning involved here really less fundamental?

However, the theoretical consequences of agreeing or disagreeing with such restrictions in the scope of linguistics are extremely difficult to determine (cf. Kempson, 1977: ix), since the decision is inseparable from other decisions about where, if anywhere, to draw the borderline between: competence and performance; sentence and utterance; semantics and pragmatics; presuppositions and entailments; and whether one opts essentially for a truth-conditional semantics or a speech-act semantics. Further, these areas are themselves interrelated and a decision in one area may trigger off unfortunate consequences elsewhere: if only one is clear-thinking enough to work out what these consequences are. For example speech acts are not performed by sentences, and are not entirely determined by the syntactico-semantic form of sentences, but are conveyed by utterances in context (cf. chapter 8). They might therefore seem to be a matter of performance and not of competence, at least as this distinction is often drawn. Sentences do not even always have a truth value in the abstract, but only relative to their use in some context (cf. example 1.4). In fact, a detailed consideration of this area soon draws into question whether the often cited two-way oppositions (such as competence–performance, sentence–utterance) are valid. For example, are the stimulus 'sentences' used to elicit grammaticality judgements actually sentences, or are they *utterances*? Do such judgements tap competence or only a small aspect of performance?

1   *A linguistic approach to discourse*

I will try in this chapter to give a more precise interpretation of statements such as: the meaning of an utterance depends on its place in a discourse sequence (see especially section 8). This requires a more precise definition than I have given so far of several closely related concepts. It requires the concept of *structure*, regarded as constraints on linear sequence. This is closely related to the concept of *well-formedness*: the possibility of distinguishing coherent and incoherent sequences of discourse. It is also closely related to the concept of *predictability*: conversationalists can predict what other speakers are likely to say, because there are constraints on linear sequence. The concept of structure is not definable independently of the concept of *system*: different systems of choice are available at different places in structure. Finally, all of these concepts are applicable to language only under the assumption that the data are considerably *idealized*. This is a very brief list of concepts which I will discuss at some length below.

These concepts have all been worked out in considerable detail in phonology and syntax. This chapter therefore also discusses whether discourse is amenable to study using the same concepts which linguistics has developed to study phonology and syntax: primarily the concepts of system and structure. In other words, how similar is discourse to other levels of linguistic organization? Discussing such questions is therefore a way of studying the boundaries of linguistics as a discipline: are discourse phenomena amenable to linguistic explanations?

It may seem that the concepts of system and structure are rather old-fashioned and simplistic. However, it is worth bearing in mind that discourse analysis is at a very elementary stage, compared with phonology and syntax. As regards connected discourse or text in English, we do not have even basic taxonomic descriptions or statements of basic distributional constraints, either structural (syntagmatic) or systematic (paradigmatic). We have only the rather fragmentary statements of the kind which I illustrated in chapter 4. (see also Labov, 1971, for a defence of the concept of system as the most basic concept in linguistics.)

It is obvious not only that linguists study language, but that they study it in very particular (some would say 'peculiar') ways. It is therefore interesting to see whether discourse can be studied in those same ways. If it cannot, and this has been argued, then this has serious consequences. For it might imply that the concepts that linguists have developed for studying phonology and syntax (and, in general, areas of core linguistics) are mere artefacts of very highly idealized and artificial kinds of study, and have value only in dealing with data which are highly contrived and idealized in two ways: by being restricted to examples which are both smaller than sentences and also studied out of context. Alternatively, it might imply that discourse is not linguistically organized at all. Discourse obviously displays recurrent linguistic patterns, but these might be the result of non-linguistic organization: the result, for example of much more general characteristics of human thinking and puzzle solving.

It may seem that the argument in this chapter is straying rather a long way from sociolinguistic concerns, or even from the analysis of natural language, and is based rather on the kind of contrived and isolated linguistic fragments which I criticize elsewhere. However, as Hymes and Labov have both consistently argued, the distinction between linguistics and sociolinguistics is ultimately to be resisted. On the one hand, sociolinguistics could not exist in its present form without the long history of attempts at rigorous formal description within theoretical linguistics. On the other hand, the weakness of the data base of theoretical linguistics is an open secret, and linguistics must ultimately be based on the analysis of real language used in social contexts. A major question discussed in this chapter is how much idealization is justifiable or inevitable in the description of natural language. The argument therefore concerns the relationship between the logical analysis of idealized languages and the linguistic analysis of natural language. These are more important questions than the precise boundary, if any, between linguistics and socio-linguistics.

2 Predictability and well-formedness

Mandelbrot (1965: 263) succinctly states the apparent paradox which we have to disentangle before we can proceed any further: 'Human discourse is both something highly structured and something highly unpredictable.' It is the old question of whether words and thoughts follow rules; and of whether something which appears intuitively to be so flexible and creative can be described by a formal system.

It is often argued that discourse analysis faces particular analytic problems, because in connected discourse 'anything can follow anything'. I gave a brief and informal answer to this argument in chapter 1, but it now requires a more detailed response. People arguing in this way will generally admit that much conversation and writing is, as a matter of fact, very predictable and repetitive, and extended fantasies have been constructed on this theme. For example, Frayn (1965) in his novel *The Tin Men* satirizes the repetitiveness of many stories in the popular press. One of the characters has the job of computerizing the writing of articles on stock and trivial themes, such as 'Child told dress unsuitable by teacher' or 'A loyal leader on a royal occasion'. The automatic writing procedure consists essentially of a macro-plot-structure plus a finite state grammar for sentences. The narrator of Dahl's (1970) story, *The Great Automatic Grammatizator* has essentially the same idea for short fiction. However, it could be said, this is satire of bad and repetitive practice: in principle, it might be argued, there is no way of predicting what will be said or written next, whether in good or bad practice.

The implication of the claim that 'anything can follow anything' is that discourse is not subject to the same kind of rules and constraints which are found in phonotactic and syntactic sequences. This objection must be answered, since it is often maintained that the whole enterprise of phonology and syntax relies on the possibility of making reasonably clear-cut distinctions between well-formed and ill-formed strings of elements. Before we can discuss systematic and structural organization in discourse, there is therefore a logically prior question which must be decided: does it make sense to talk of well-formed and ill-formed discourse? It is clear enough that the pre-theoretical notion of acceptability applies to sequences of discourse, since speakers may complain of utterances being missing or deviant by saying things such as: *You didn't answer my question*, *He didn't say 'hello'*, or *He never sticks to the point*; and teachers may complain that students' essays are incoherent. My whole discussion in chapters 2, 3 and 4 has largely assumed that discourse sequences can be judged as acceptable or deviant. However, many linguists would question whether speakers' notions of acceptability can be turned into the theoretical concept of *well-formed*.

First of all, it is important to emphasize that the concept of well-formedness in phonology and syntax is more problematic than is often admitted, and operates only under extreme idealization. (Some linguists, for example Halliday, reject the concept of a clear boundary between well- and ill-formed strings. However, the concept is widely held, and must be discussed.)

3   Phonotactics

In phonotactics, it seems easy to distinguish well-formed from ill-formed sequences of phonemes. However, it is possible to specify phonotactic constraints with confidence only if the data are very severely restricted. Usually, English phonotactic constraints are taken to apply only to the citation forms of isolated words. It is very much more difficult, if not impossible, to specify constraints on segments of naturally occurring conversational data. In fact, some phonologists (e.g. G. Brown, 1977: 16) argue that it is quite impossible to make a phonemic transcription of connected informal speech at all.

Certainly, forms which regularly occur in informal speech break what are normally taken to be the phonotactic constraints in English, for example, the initial consonant clusters in the following perfectly normal pronunciations: *giraffe* [dʒræf]; *potato* [ptɛɪtə ɒ]. Such cases can be accounted for by general rules which specify vowel reduction or deletion in informal speech. However, many other different kinds of idealization must also be made. Various styles of speech, in addition to a general informal style, are normally excluded from phonotactic data: for example, stereotyped drunk, lisping and baby talk. Data also have to be restricted, of course, to individual accents. Further, the range of lexical items taken for idealized citation forms has to be restricted to, roughly speaking, fully assimilated native words in common currency. Some studies may be yet further restricted to morphemes rather than words, or even to monosyllabic words. The most consistent position is probably that phonotactic constraints apply to syllables. All this normally excludes the initial clusters in recent loans such as *schmaltz* and *Buenos Aires*, imitative noises such as *vroom*, rare words such as *sphragistics*, and so on. I suspect that many linguists forget the number of different kinds of idealization which they normally accept. (Cf. Lyons, 1977: 586–9.)

Such difficulties in establishing phonotactic constraints are fully discussed by Algeo (1978), who points out the remarkable disagreement in studies of English phonotactics, which is mainly due to different decisions about how idealized the data base should be. On the basis of the extreme idealization involved in specifying phonotactic constraints, Algeo argues also that there is no clear dichotomy between well- and ill-formed phoneme strings, and that the set of consonant clusters in English is not a well-defined set. This does not mean that the distinction is meaningless, only that the boundary is fuzzy.

4   *Grammaticality*

The confidence in the possibility of clear-cut grammaticality judgements, which was evident in early transformational grammar, has clearly waned. It is now well known that grammatical intuitions are not a clear window on competence, but are themselves open to performance errors and to manipulation in experimental conditions (Labov, 1972a: 192–9; 1975a). Intuitions about grammaticality, and also about semantic relations, have turned out to be particularly unreliable areas of crucial importance to transformational theory, for example, with sentences which have quantifiers such as *few*, *some* or *any* in surface structure. Nevertheless, even if there are many dubious instances, there are many sentences which are clearly grammatical and others which clearly are not. In practice, but not always with

a well-argued rationale, linguists often set up a grammar on the basis
of the clear-cut cases, and then 'let the grammar decide' the dubious
cases for itself. (N. Smith and Wilson, 1979: 233–8, do defend this
practice; but Lyons, 1977: 384–5, simply states that he will follow
it.)

Note, however, that the category of strings which are often cited
as grossly ungrammatical is largely an invention of Chomskyan
linguistics. Strings of the type:

5.1   *By by and hockey puddle takes.

would usually be regarded by traditional linguistics, as well as by
linguistically naive informants, not as ungrammatical, but just as
nonsense. Lyons proposes (1977: 379ff) that the main test of ill-
formedness is *corrigibility*, but it is impossible to correct such strings
as 5.1. The same comment applies to strings which Chomsky cites as
grammatical but semantically anomalous, such as:

5.2   Sincerity admires John.
5.3   Colourless green ideas sleep furiously.

Such strings cannot be interpreted, in isolation at least. A test of this
assertion is that they could not be reliably paraphrased. The concept
of ungrammatical might seem to apply better to strings which any
native speaker could correct (in a non-prescriptive sense, of course):

5.4   *The car who is in the garage.
5.5   *Come you here often?
5.6   *He am here.

The problem of grossly deviant strings such as 5.1 sometimes fudges
the issue, but is probably not very important, since any grammar
which can block the corrigible strings will automatically block the
grossly deviant ones as well.

Given these various problems, Lyons (1977: 385) argues that the
pre-theoretical status of grammaticality is one of the fundamental
issues which divides present-day linguists. The issue clearly divides
transformational and systemic linguists, for example. A standard
Chomskyan view would distinguish sharply between grammaticality
(believing that clear-cut judgements are possible here) and acceptability in context (believing this to be subject to too many extraneous
performance factors to be investigable). Halliday, on the other hand,
argues (e.g. 1978: 38, 51–2) that no distinction should be drawn
between what is grammatical and what is acceptable (although not all
systemic linguists take this view).

Less radically, even if one accepts the concept of grammaticality, no one has ever demonstrated that grammaticality has to be a binary distinction. There is in fact every reason to assume that grammaticality judgements lie on a continuum, and that the set of grammatical sentences (like the set of well-formed phoneme strings) is indeterminate. This may be the most important objection to 'letting the grammar decide' dubious cases: it imposes a binary decision on what may be inherently continuous data. Chomsky himself, having taken the concept over from mathematics, simply appears to assume without argument that the class of well-formed sentences in a language is well-defined. The notion has been very fruitful in linguistic theory, but would appear to be wrong. This aspect of Chomskyan theory is attacked in detail by Hockett (1968).

The point of this excursus into phonotactic and grammatical well-formedness has been to show that, although the concept of well-formedness clearly applies, it is not as clear-cut as is often assumed. In discussing well-formedness in discourse, we would therefore not wish to apply criteria which are more rigorous than those applied in well established areas of linguistics.

5   Intuitions about discourse sequences

As regards the use of intuitive data, if intuitions are dubious in syntax, they may seem even more dubious in discourse. However, this may be because our grammatical intuitions have been developed by two thousand years or more of detailed grammatical study. This is itself an objection to the use of intuitive data in syntax, since the data may have been created or at least modified by the process of studying them. It takes some considerable effort, for example, to mould the intuitions of beginning linguistics students until they can make distinctions between grammatical, meaningful, and acceptable in context.

One problem with the criterion of corrigibility is that the ability to correct errors is largely restricted to surface morphological and syntactic features, illustrated by 5.4, 5.5 and 5.6, and to segmental phonology. However, if a foreign learner of English makes a mistake in intonation, or in omitting a discourse marker (for example, utterance-initial well), native speakers are unlikely to be able to give a clear judgement on just what is wrong. In fact, they may not realize that a linguistic mistake has been made at all, but instead judge that the speaker is impolite, brusque or whatever. Similar cases, where the native speaker may recognize that something is wrong, but be unable to specify precisely what it is, are likely to occur with features of textual cohesion and collocation. For example, a student essay which shows inadequate or misleading cohesion may be judged to be stylistically poor, rather than as containing linguistic errors. In any case cohesion is a matter of degree, and the notion of corrigibility applies to cases where there is a sharp boundary between well- and ill-formed.

Nevertheless, errors of some kinds do occur and are corrected in the course of natural conversations. Corrigibility and the fact that errors are corrected by speakers in the course of conversation is itself evidence of a norm. This has been taken as a topic for empirical investigation by Schegloff *et al.* (1977) and Schegloff (1979) who have studied what happens when speakers make different kinds of mistakes in conversation, including slips of the tongue, choosing the 'wrong' word, or referring to someone in such a way that they cannot be identified by hearers. They find, in general, a preference for self-correction. That is, if speakers make a mistake of some kind in speaking, they are most likely to correct it themselves, whether they notice it themselves first, or have it drawn to their attention by another speaker. On the much rarer occasions when A corrects B, the correction is likely to be mitigated by being marked as uncertain or hesitant. The main apparent exceptions to this (pp. 380–1) occur in the type of asymmetrical adult–child interaction which I have discussed in detail in chapter 3.

It is clear from much of my previous discussion in this book, especially in chapter 4, that I believe introspective judgements of discourse well-formedness to be valuable. We certainly require to use them with caution – but precisely the same is true of judgements in phonology and syntax. I will argue in more detail in chapters 7 and 11 that introspective judgements require to be controlled by being combined with other kinds of data, both experimental and naturalistic.

6   *Predictability*

Closely related to the concept of well-formedness is the concept of a syntagmatic chain, in which one item sets up predictions that other items will or will not occur. It is easy enough to demonstrate that discourse sequences set up predictions in terms of propositional content. Many anecdotes would serve here. When I was in Australia recently, I was taken to a national park by the ocean north of

Brisbane. A woman in the party explained to me that there were four beaches in separate little bays along the coast. The convention was that on the first beach, nearest to the car-park, bathers had to wear swimming costumes. On the second beach they could go topless. On the third beach nude bathing was allowed. And we were going to the fourth beach ... Hearers were left trying desperately to use the first three propositions as a discourse frame to predict the fourth, although our predictions turned out to be wrong. (The fourth beach was less crowded.)

Further, whatever two utterances occur next to one another, hearers will attempt to relate them: to use the first as a discourse frame for the second. This is the case even when the utterances were not intended to be related, hence the humour of this introduction to a magazine programme on Scottish radio:

5.7   Today we have a discussion of vasectomy, and the announcement of the winner of the do-it-yourself competition.

In appreciating the humour of this fragment one has to realize both that the two items were not intended to be related, and also that they can easily be related. There is no explicit relation in what is said: the relation has to be inferred from simple juxtaposition. It is difficult therefore just to list items in discourse without also implying some temporal or causal relation between them. (Cf. chapter 4, section 5 on the distinction between logical & and natural language *and*.)

Many other informal demonstrations of the predictive power of utterances could be given. Consider, for example, the way we can often overhear one end of a telephone call and predict much of what the person at the other end of the line is saying. The American comedian, Bob Newhart, bases whole comedy routines on this principle, by giving the audience just one half of a conversation: his well-known driving instructor sketch is based on this principle.

Such examples do not show, however, that such predictions are specifically linguistic. On the contrary, the appreciation of the Australian anecdote is obviously based on a non-linguistic sequence. It would be superficial to conclude that because phonology, syntax and discourse all display 'structure', the structure is similar in each case. (Morgan and Sellner, 1980, make this point very clearly.) For example, our knowledge that English allows the phoneme sequence /nd/ word-finally but not word-initially is specifically linguistic knowledge. So is our knowledge that English word order usually allows adjective–noun, but not the reverse. Such knowledge appears related to no other knowledge about the real physical world, culture, and so on. An appreciation of the Australian anecdote, and also of example 5.7, on the other hand, obviously does depend on non-linguistic knowledge.

This is a particular example of the question of whether discourse is linguistically organized, or organized according to non-linguistic features such as content, defined by references to events or states of affairs outside language. Predictability may be the single most important feature of human communication, precisely since it is central not only to all levels of language, but also central to memory and to thinking in general.

7   Predictability and idealization

Since we are dealing with predictions and expectations, it is evident that the resulting model of discourse will involve considerable abstraction away from particular conversational data. What is involved is a model of norms, rather than merely the analysis of particular texts; although the description will have to be controlled by naturally occurring data. Clearly, also, we are not dealing with patterns in the sense of statistical frequencies: the number of times a particular category or sequence occurs. It is not possible for example to code utterances as isolated units, such as *request*, or *respond*, and then at a later stage to look for recurrent patterns. This is an impossible procedure for two reasons. First, such coding often involves knowledge of how utterances are sequentially placed (see section 8): that is, the outcome, the analysis of sequencing, is presupposed in the initial coding. Second, such a procedure would reveal sequences only in the very weak sense of successive positions of hands on a clock face, to use Schegloff's (1972) metaphor. It would not be able to account for the intuition that certain utterances set up expectations in the hearer that other utterances of a particular kind are yet to come. The argument I am putting forward is therefore also a demonstration that hearers construct the coherence of what they hear, by themselves performing a structural analysis on the discourse in which they participate.

However, it is often argued that the predictions set up by items in a discourse sequence are not as binding as constraints in phonology or syntax. It is argued that anything may follow anything, since irrelevance is always one of the speaker's options (Coulthard and Brazil, 1981: 84). Of course, the ability to recognize irrelevance means itself that deviation from expectations, and therefore expectations, are recognizable. Similarly, the breaking of expectations in jokes, irony, sarcasm and so on, is itself an indication that there are expectations to be broken. We often recognize norms only when they *are* broken. (For detailed examples, see chapter 3, section 8, and chapter 11.)

It is obvious both that utterances set up predictions and that the predictions may be broken. These facts are exploited in children's stories of the following kind (from Hofstadter, 1979: 675):

5.8   A man took a ride in an aeroplane. Unfortunately, he fell out. Fortunately, he had a parachute on. Unfortunately, it didn't open. Fortunately, there was a haystack below him. Unfortunately, there was a pitchfork sticking out of it. Fortunately, he missed the pitchfork. Unfortunately, he missed the haystack.

Another way of analysing such sequences would be to say that each utterance sets up a frame which comes with built-in default expectations; but these default values can be overridden if necessary.

However, it might be that in discourse we are dealing not with clear-cut mandatory rules, but rather with maxims of co-operativeness (Grice, 1975) or guiding principles (G. Wells *et al.*, 1979). One very simple reason why discourse structure is likely to be less deterministic than phonological or syntactic structure is that discourse is the joint construction of at least two speakers. It is difficult to see how A could place absolute constraints on what B says. The fact that there are always at least two participants (speaker and hearer for monologues, if not two speakers) raises also the problem of intentionality and different points of view. Does A intend to convey to B what B understands? Or are we dealing with two only partly compatible interpretative schemas? In principle, the question is unanswerable, but it is probably a pseudo-problem, since it is possible to study how speakers display their understanding of each other's utterances (cf. chapter 2, section 6). G. Wells *et al.* (1979: 5) give these two examples. A child produces two holophrastic utterances with identical falling intonation on both. It is clear from the mother's response that one is taken as a request and the other as an inform, whatever the child intended:

5.9   Child: chocolate
       Mother: no – mummy says you can't have any chocolate
5.10   Child: beamer (sic)
       Mother: that's daddy's beaker yes

So B's utterance may display an interpretation of A's utterance. And B may say anything, but whatever B says will be interpreted in the light of what A has said. It is therefore meaningful to talk of the 'predictive power of the structural frame' (Coulthard and Brazil, 1981: 83). Alternatively, Labov and Fanshel (1977: 75) talk of invariant rules of discourse. Conversation is highly variable, but the interpretative rules are invariant in that they will always be applied to candidate utterances. (Many further examples will be discussed in chapter 6.) A basic concept is therefore continuous classification: each utterance sets up predictions and therefore provisionally classifies the following utterance. As Sinclair and Coulthard (1975: 120) put it, 'the meaning of an utterance is its predictive assessment of what follows'. This is only one kind of meaning conveyed by utterances, but it has to do with the organization of the discourse itself. (It is important here to distinguish between speech acts and conversational moves: it is the latter that Sinclair and Coulthard are discussing. (Cf. chapter 8, section 2.) So, each utterance is pre-classified – before it ever occurs – but can still choose whether to follow this classification or not.

In summary so far then, utterances predict forward; or rather hearers predict forward on the basis of utterances. But interpretations may operate backwards: we look backwards in discourse to discover the relevance of an utterance to its predecessors, especially if a mismatch is evident. It is therefore hearers' interpretations which create the coherence of discourse. Gunter (1974: 81–98) discusses these issues in rather similar terms, but he seems to draw the wrong conclusions. He is clearly wrong, for example, in claiming (p. 96) that 'we do not predict'. We do predict, but we may predict wrongly, and have to interpret what occurs in the light of wrong expectations. Predictability and structure can be seen as opposite sides of the same coin. Predictions (something which language users make) are possible because language is structured. Such intuitive predictions are in turn a crucial part of our data in setting up language structures.

Predictability is sometimes reformulated in terms of redundancy, but this can be misleading. The standard information theory view is that if a piece of language is totally predictable, then it is redundant, has no surprise value and communicates nothing. If we are looking at language in use, this view has to be modified, since even repetition has various discourse functions: for example, to emphasize, check, query, express irony, and so on. (Cf. Ochs Keenan, 1977; and see Coulmas, 1979, on the sociolinguistic relevance of routine formulae.) In other words, repetition is not redundant, as might be thought if only propositional meaning were taken into account. It is in any case not always possible to predict that an utterance will be repeated, for whatever purpose.

8   Structure controls meaning

Brazil (1981) provides a useful discussion of these issues, and a way of solving Mandelbrot's apparent paradox (see section 2). He points out that the concept of structure both separates the possible from the impossible (that is, it separates well- and ill-formed), and that it also provides a way of interpreting what does occur. The structural frame contributes to meaning by classifying items. It is in this way that we are able to interpret such examples as Dylan Thomas's well-known: *a grief ago*. We recognize the structure involved and the identity of structure with *a week ago* or *a year ago*. The structure therefore reclassifies *grief* as a time expression. Here is another example which requires the structure to be understood to understand the joke:

5.11   The noblest of all dogs is the hot-dog: it feeds the hand that
            bites it.

One way of showing that we are dealing with structural (syntagmatic) organization in discourse is to show, therefore, that structure controls meaning. It is easy to find examples where the meaning of an utterance is not retrievable from its syntactic or semantic organization in isolation, but only from its position in a discourse sequence. Consider the following hypothetical sequence:

5.12   Telephone rings. A answers.
            A: Hello
            B: Hello. Is Jim there?

We know intuitively that a response from A such as *Yes. Is that all?* is ill-formed. We know that *Is Jim there?* is not to be taken literally, but as a directive or request (cf. Ervin-Tripp, 1976) meaning approximately "I wish to speak to Jim: if he is there, please fetch him." This meaning could also be conveyed by other sentences, including: *I want to speak to Jim*; *Is that Jim?*; *Could I speak to Jim?*; *Give me Jim, please*; *Jim, please*. Such sentences are all different in surface syntax: declarative, interrogative, imperative, and moodless. And they are all semantically different: they differ in the propositions which are asserted, presupposed and entailed. However, in this position in the discourse sequence, these syntactic and semantic differences are neutralized, to make them equivalent as discourse moves. In such a case, then, the discourse structure controls the meaning which can be conveyed. In this case, only one meaning appears to be possible. If that seems too strong a statement, consider the following data, audio-recorded from a telephone call. I had rung a local College of Education, and the call was taken by a secretary:

5.13   S: hello X college of education
        MS: hello can you tell me what department mister A is in
              I just want ⌜to
        S: ⌞just a moment please
              (long pause)
        S: I'm sorry I can't find him he's not in his study or the staff room
        MS: no I don't want to speak to him I just want to know what his department is so that I can post him some papers

These data show how difficult it is to convey a different meaning at this place in structure: in this case, I tried and failed. I propose the following interpretative rule:

If someone is named in a telephone call immediately after the initial exchange of greetings, this will be interpreted as a request to speak to the person named.

The interpretative rule is most obviously applicable to telephone calls, but also operates elsewhere, as these field-note data show:

5.14   A: Have you seen David Brown?
        B: He's in the refectory.
        A: It's all right, I don't want to see him, I wondered if you'd seen him.

Schegloff (1968) and Godard (1977) discuss the structure of inter-action at the beginning of telephone calls. Godard compares the differences in the sequences used in France and the USA. The very fact that there are such differences shows that we are dealing with a discourse structure which is partly conventional. It might be thought that the structure is not entirely arbitrary, since it depends in part on logical considerations. For example, it is the caller who knows both his own identity and can also make at least good predictions about the identity of the answerer; whereas the answerer usually has less chance of predicting the identity of the caller (cf. R. Brown, 1980). However, if such logical considerations were of primary importance, then we would expect the caller to identify himself first and to speak first. This does happen in some cultures, for example, in Japan (Trudgill, ed., 1978: 7). However, in Britain, France and the USA, the general rule is that the person called speaks first. Godard argues rather that such differences in sequencing are due to differing views of rights and obligations. In France it is almost obligatory to check the number at the beginning of the call, whereas in the USA it is normal to have no check. She argues that in France, a call is assumed to cause a disturbance, and that callers therefore use an obligatory remedial interchange. She relates this further to the generally high cultural value placed on the telephone in the USA which means that telephone calls take precedence over other activities which they may be interrupting.

Ervin-Tripp (1976: 40) and Morgan (1978) explain the meaning in context of items such as *Is Sybil there?* as being due to conventionalized usage which leads to their apparent indirectness of meaning being lost. But the explanation appears to be more interesting than this, and to depend on very general principles. Sentences which are paraphrases at one place in discourse are not synonymous elsewhere. The principle that synonymy is context-dependent is accepted in syntax and lexis (e.g. Lyons, 1968: 448) and holds also in discourse.

Such analyses demonstrate the way in which the meaning of an utterance depends on its place in a discourse structure. The structure involved is bigger than a clause or sentence, and sentence grammar cannot therefore explain the data. In addition, the discourse structure involved is conventional and varies from culture to culture. On the other hand, it is still not entirely clear that we are dealing with specifically linguistic knowledge. For example, it is possible to reformulate the interpretative rule above as a Gricean conversational maxim (cf. Grice, 1975), such as: do not ask questions without some reason. For example, do not ask after X's whereabouts, if you do not wish to speak to him, hide from him, or whatever. Such a formulation clearly draws again on non-linguistic inferences.

9   *Canonical discourse and idealization*

To talk of interpretations is to see things from the hearer's or reader's point of view. From the speaker's point of view, he has to make the initial decision whether to break out of this classification, that is, whether to support or to reject the preceding discourse. After any utterance there is therefore a systemic choice, which can be initially represented as:

$$\left[\begin{array}{l} \text{support} \\ \text{reject} \end{array}\right.$$

Reject here means ignoring a previous utterance, being irrelevant, and so on. Since it implies breaking discourse expectations, it means producing discourse which is by definition ill-formed. Since anything *is* possible under *reject*, the possibilities here are not in principle stateable. It is, however, often possible to set up systems of choices for which *support* is the entry condition, and discourse analysis therefore has to operate under this simplifying assumption. What we are centrally concerned with, therefore, is the set of canonical responses which do conform to very precise expectations and for which *support* is an entry condition. *Support* will be defined in more detail elsewhere (chapter 9, section 6), but for the present *canonical support* can be taken to include utterances which do not question the presuppositions or felicity conditions of preceding utterances. It is also possible to define a set of predictable types of *queries*: thus it is possible to query presuppositions, pre-conditions for speech acts, particular lexical items, and so on, but often in highly restricted and principled ways. It is therefore possible to modify the system as follows:

$$\left[\begin{array}{l} \text{support} \left[\begin{array}{l} \text{canonical} \\ \text{query} \end{array}\right. \\ \text{reject} \end{array}\right.$$

Reject is the bucket category which every descriptive system requires: it implies that the discourse has broken down, and only if too many utterances end up in the bucket of category need we be worried. (For further discussion of supporting utterances see Burton, 1980, chapter 7; and Berry, 1981b.) These points make explicit another layer of idealization required before we can make statements about discourse well-formedness.

10   Analogies

I should also develop a few further points about constructing arguments in discourse analysis by analogy with arguments in phonology and syntax. Why should one argue by analogy? One reason is that the concepts of phonology and syntax can be a valuable source of ideas; and that one would expect at least some of the same kinds of patterning in discourse as elsewhere in language. As Sinclair and Coulthard (1975: 119) say, one might be 'suspicious of structural proposals that (have) no parallel elsewhere in linguistics'. However, analogies are always dangerous and misleading if pushed too far: the important point here is to see how far the analogies hold between discourse, syntax and phonology, and where they break down. As I have pointed out, we cannot simply transfer the concept of structure unthinkingly to discourse.

A point where an analogy does hold with phonology and syntax is that phonotactic and syntactic rules differ in detail according to the style of language used, formal, casual, written, spoken, and so on. Berry (1981a) has proposed that it may be necessary to distinguish social discourse from discourse which has practical ends. There are folk terms which underlie this distinction. Terms for social discourse include 'small talk', 'just chatting' and 'passing the time of day': these correspond to the linguists' term 'phatic communion'. Since the purpose of social discourse is its own smooth going-on, to use a Goffmanesque expression, one would expect different rules than in transactional discourse. The Gricean 'be relevant' and 'be brief' maxims will be relaxed (Grice, 1975); on the other hand, requirements for supportive feedback and back-channel behaviour (Duncan, 1972) will be more stringent. (Cf. chapter 7, section 11.) Rules for initiation will be different, since everyone will be expected to chip in, and this will clearly affect discourse sequencing.

On the other hand, a difference between discourse and phonology or syntax is that discourse rules may be used strategically. Developing the traditional chess metaphor, a chess player can play within the rules, but also use the rules to create openings, attacks and defences (cf. Widdowson, 1979a). In an often quoted statement, Labov (1972a: 252) writes that: 'The fundamental problem of discourse analysis is to show how one utterance follows another in a rational, rule-governed manner.' But rule-governed and rational do not mean the same thing (Mohan, 1974). One may play chess irrationally, without breaking the rules. There is no analogy with phonological or grammatical rules here. Conversational responses may be irrational but rule-governed, or may exploit the rules for humour. The concept of a conversational gambit makes sense, but there is no grammatical equivalent. Speakers can refuse to answer questions, but they cannot refuse to speak grammatically for any conventionally recognizable communicative ends. Speakers may, of course, use syntactic choices strategically, but only in a context defined by a larger discourse sequence. For example, formal syntax may be used to create a formal or frozen atmosphere, or a switch to non-standard dialect syntax may be used to convey social or ethnic identity.[1]

In addition, the notion of incoherent conversation makes perfect sense, and might be applied to speakers who are drunk, half asleep, senile, mad or whatever. However, such people would be judged socially incompetent, not merely linguistically or communicatively incompetent. Similarly, talking to oneself breaks the normal assumption that conversation is interactive. Probably everybody does it, but to be caught doing it is to risk social condemnation. Some manifestations are on the margins of social acceptability, for example, humming or singing to oneself, or talking to a pet. (Goffman, 1981, provides a detailed analysis.) There are no analogies in syntax to such deviance.

11   Conclusions

Conversations are infinitely varied and utterances can be indirect, obtuse, devious, strategic, ironic, witty, rude, irrelevant and silly. Nevertheless, the concept of well-formedness does apply, and it makes sense to talk of discourse as having structure. This provides the basis for investigating the organization of discourse with traditional linguistic concepts. There are unfortunately no terms analogous to *grammatical* and *ungrammatical*. It seems preferable to use the terms *well-* and *ill-formed* discourse, rather than the collocation *(un)grammatical discourse* or neologisms such as *(un)discoursical*. This may serve as a reminder that I am using the terms *well-* and *ill-formed* under the idealizations that I have defined above, and that they are theoretical terms and different from a pre-theoretical concept of acceptable discourse.

We must also be particularly cautious in making a superficial analogy with phonological and syntactic structure. To say that discourse has structure does not necessarily mean that this structure

---

[1]   I am grateful to Lesley Milroy for these examples.

is specifically linguistic (Morgan and Sellner, 1980). The structure may be the surface manifestation of much more general organization, including the causal relation between events in the world and our inferences about such events. The next chapter will discuss further whether the relationship between utterances in sequence are syntactic, semantic or pragmatic.

6

Initiations and Responses

In previous chapters, I have tried to show that the concept of structure applies to discourse (with the reservation that the structure need not be specifically linguistic); and that it therefore makes sense to study the relationship between units above the clause, possibly reclassifying these units as functional acts or moves.

This chapter will continue to discuss such syntagmatic chaining of discourse units by discussing certain kinds of conversational exchange. For the present I will define an exchange as the minimal interactive unit, comprising at least an initiation (I) from one speaker and a response (R) from another. The simplest structure for an exchange is therefore IR. The most obvious example of such an exchange is probably a question–answer pair, with the structure QA.

This definition of exchange is based on Sinclair and Coulthard's (1975) work, and will be further developed in chapter 7.

1   Questions

I will start with some discussion of question–answer (QA) pairs. They may seem artificially simple, in that interrogative syntax places unusually powerful constraints on what can follow. One has to start somewhere, however, and they turn out not to be all that simple.

It is usual to distinguish between two broad types of questions, which I will refer to as yes–no questions and x-questions. An example of each type, respectively, is: *Is Harry in the pub?* and *Where is Harry?* Several other more or less equivalent pairs of terms are used: yes–no versus wh-questions (e.g. Quirk *et al.*, 1972); closed versus open questions, and confirmation–denial versus information-seeking questions (e.g. Robinson and Rackstraw, 1972). The term polar question is also used for yes–no questions. Jespersen's (1933: 305) terms and definitions are particularly relevant to my concerns here.

He uses the term nexus questions for what I am calling yes–no questions, in which 'we call into question the combination (nexus) of a subject and predicate'. And he uses the term x-questions for items in which 'we have an unknown quantity x'. Note that the various terms used to categorize questions refer both to features of the surface syntax (e.g. the presence of a wh-word such as *where*), and also to features of the expected answer (e.g. *yes* versus *no*). I have chosen the terms yes–no and x-question to focus attention on the discourse sequence. Such a discourse-sensitive concept of questions is also evident in Fries' (1952: 165) comment that: '... the question itself is part of the frame in which the answer as an utterance operates.'

Such a concept calls into question Bloomfield's (1933: 170) famous definition of a sentence as 'an independent linguistic form, not included by virtue of any grammatical construction in any larger linguistic form'. Some utterances are not independent, since they are interpretable only in the light of a preceding utterance, and this may be due to elliptical syntax.

A full taxonomy would also have to distinguish other question types, including tag questions, so-called rhetorical questions, and conducive or biased questions (see Bublitz, 1980). The literature on questions is enormous. For bibliographies, see Egli and Schleichert (1976) and Ficht (1978); and for a succinct summary of some of the main issues see Lyons (1977: 753–68). Here I am concerned only to discuss the problem insofar as it throws a little light on whether the relation between question and answer is syntactic, semantic or pragmatic.

2   Yes–no questions

Given a yes–no question such as *Is Harry at home?* it is true, in a sense, that anything may follow it, but clear constraints are placed on the interpretation of the utterance which does follow (cf. chapter 5, section 8). Hearers will try and interpret whatever follows as meaning either "yes" or "no". This is not to say that only the forms *yes* and *no* can occur; but that whatever does occur is already pre-classified as meaning either "yes" or "no", or, if this is impossible, then as querying or refusing assumptions made by the questioner. The meanings "yes" and "no" may be selected simultaneously with other choices from other systems, including ± certainty, which I will represent here as a binary choice, although it is a continuum. So, we have the following system in the response slot after a yes–no question:

$$
\left\{
\begin{array}{l}
-\!\!\left[\begin{array}{l} \text{yes} \\ \text{no} \end{array}\right. \\[1em]
-\!\!\left[\begin{array}{l} +\,\text{certainty} \\ -\,\text{certainty} \end{array}\right.
\end{array}
\right.
$$

For example, an answer such as *I don't think so* has co-selected "no" and − certainty.

The constraint between question and answer is clearly not purely syntactic, since any surface syntactic form could realize the terms in the systems: say,

6.1   Chance would be a fine thing.
6.2   Don't make me laugh!

as a realization of "no". The relationship is semantic and is expressible in terms of propositions. The question sets up a propositional frame: a proposition with one value (polarity) unspecified. The polarity is supplied by the answer which is the propositional completion. In the case of 6.1 and 6.2, however, the proposition is not supplied by the surface form of the utterance in isolation: it has to be inferred. (I have adapted the terms propositional frame and propositional completion from Berry, 1981a.)

Note that these points immediately suggest a way of classifying responses. They may fit both syntactically and semantically, or only semantically. A semantic fit may rely on inferring a proposition which is not asserted. Making a response fit at only one level is a way of exploiting features of an utterance to produce manipulative discourse, as in:

6.3   A: Have you left the door open again?
        B: Yes.

where B's response fits syntactically and semantically with A's, but thereby treats A's utterance as a question, rather than as a complaint or request (to shut the door).

Also, I have implied that "yes" and "no" are in simple contrastive distribution. This is not always, if ever, the case, and the constraints on "yes" versus "no" are more powerful still. Before discussing this, however, I will make some comparable points about x-questions.

3   X-questions

X-questions have interrogative syntax and begin with one of a closed class of words: *where*, *when*, *who*, *whose*, *which*, *what*, *how*. Alternatively, the wh-word may introduce an embedded clause, as in: *Do you know where he is?* which could be answered as either a yes–no or an x-question.

X-questions might appear initially to be a case where there are syntactic constraints between adjacent utterances. Thus a where-interrogative must normally be followed by a place adverbial, and a when-interrogative by a time adverbial.

6.4   A: Where's Harry?   B: In the pub./*At six o'clock.
6.5   A: When will he be home?   B: At six o'clock./*In the pub.

However, it is easy to find counter-examples to such a claim, and to find items which are syntactically place adverbials answering when-questions:

6.6   A: When did this happen?   B: In the pub.

The point is that the when-interrogative predicts a time adverbial, and therefore hearers will attempt to interpret an answer in this way, as, for example, "When he was/we were/etc. in the pub." Again the constraint is therefore seen to be semantic. The question sets up a propositional frame which has one variable. This pre-classifies any following utterance, which is searched to provide a value for the variable. This is essentially the kind of analysis proposed by Jespersen (1933: 305), who writes that such questions 'have an unknown quantity x exactly as in an algebraic formula'. Alternatively, this can be expressed in terms of the presuppositions of the question. The presupposition of the question in 6.4, has one variable which requires a value.

Note also that such cohesion between place and time adverbials is possible elsewhere:

6.7   A: Are you going to the pub?
       B: Yes.
       A: See you *then*.

Although place adverbials can substitute for time adverbials, the reverse is not possible:

6.8   A: Where did this happen?   B: *At six o'clock.

Examples such as the following complicate matters, but do not alter these basic points. Suppose we have:

6.9   A: Where's Harry?   B: He's not well today.

The answer is still searched for a possible place adverbial such as "At home", although the answer *At home* might be conversationally inappropriate on its own, since some reason might be required. Further, examples such as:

6.10   A: Where's Harry?
        B: (What do you mean?) He isn't anywhere.

may appear philosophically peculiar, but they are conversationally normal, and indicate that questions are not asked against a neutral background, but against a background of assumptions of normality. Such assumptions allow such utterances to be interpreted as, for example, "He is where you would expect him to be – so why are you asking?" (Cf. my comments below on Lyons', 1977, analysis of neutral questions.)

The conclusion would seem to be that questions may make syntactic predictions about answers, but such predictions are seldom, if ever, absolute. Major constraints are propositional. Questions are not asked without expectations of the propositional content of answers, but against a background of what is taken for granted as normal. Major constraints are semantic, but pragmatic factors (for example, beliefs about normality in the world) are involved.

The pragmatic assumptions underlying an x-question may be complex. In one of the Father Brown stories (Chesterton, 1929), an admiral is drowned. His death is announced to the assembled company:

6.11   'Admiral Craven was drowned before reaching home.' ...
        'When did this happen?' asked the priest.
        'Where was he found?' asked the lawyer.
        'He was found,' said the Inspector, 'in that pool by the coast, not far from the Green Man ...'

The lawyer's question reveals him as the murderer. Father Brown argues as follows:

> 'Now when you are told simply of a seaman, returning from the sea, that he has drowned, it is natural to assume that he has been drowned at sea. ... there would be no reason to expect his body to be found at all ...'

The pragmatic assumptions underlying Father Brown's reasoning can be set out as a series of propositions which are suggested by the scenario of a seaman returning from the sea. We have a noun phrase *Admiral Craven*, with a unique referent and an existential presupposition; a second noun phrase *a seaman*, with no unique referent; and a general interpretative frame, *returning from the sea.* The indefinite noun phrase and the frame bring into being constants which need not be explicitly mentioned, but which it is natural to assume (as Father Brown says). A more obvious example of such a discourse frame might be a school. If a school is mentioned in conversation, we automatically assume it to be populated with teachers and pupils, without need for them to be explicitly introduced into the discourse. So if I say:

6.12   I used to teach in a school. *The pupils* were horrible.

I do not expect the definite noun phrase to be questioned with *What pupils?* (Cf. Karttunen, 1976, for a discussion of discourse referents.)

4   *An Initial Definition of Exchange*

Such examples of QA pairs suggest a very general concept of exchange. I will indicate briefly the definition here, and develop it at length in chapter 7. An exchange comprises an initiation, where the possibilities are open-ended, followed by utterances which are pre-classified and therefore increasingly restricted. If the possibilities are opened up again, this marks either a new exchange, or at least a bound exchange. Alternatively, the exchange may be regarded as an information unit, the propositional frame being defined by the initiation. Any utterances which function to complete the proposition, by, for example, giving a value to a variable, form part of the same exchange. The exchange can therefore be defined in terms of decreasing options: that is, increasing predictability. That is, the exchange can be defined in semantic terms. Predictability and semantic completion have their formal realization in increasingly elliptic syntax as the exchange progresses. It may be, in fact, that it is the exchange and not the sentence which is the upper limit of semantic units (such as proposition) and of syntax (for example, sequences of clauses defined as ellipticity classes). This is proposed by Berry (1981b).

I gave examples above of a proposition being distributed across two turns. It is possible, in fact, for a complex proposition to be distributed across more than two turns, as in:

6.13   A: I'm going to London.
      B: When?
      A: Tomorrow.
      B: By train?
      A: Yes.

The question of how propositional information may be concentrated into single turns or, as it were, diluted, by being distributed across several different turns, is a general one, which will have to be further developed elsewhere. The problems have to do with the amount of redundancy which an audience may be thought to need. This pragmatic concern with the effect on the audience, means that such questions have been one of the traditional concerns of rhetoric, although they have seldom been explicitly treated. The issue has also to do with the function of the utterance: for example, whether the information is concentrated into a summary or abstract. (See Linde and Labov, 1975, for discussion of why propositions in spoken language may be concentrated into one sentence or spread across more than one.)

It is possible also to find a speech act which is similarly jointly constructed by more than one speaker. Speech act theory generally starts from the speaker as an isolate, and operates from this point of view under much the same idealizations as sentence grammar. But it is easy to find examples of co-operative illocutionary acts such as:

6.14   A: Will you go tomorrow?   (1)
      B: Yes.   (2)
      A: Promise?   (3)
      B: Yes.   (4)

In 6.14 the explicit conveying of the illocutionary force of promise is separated from the propositional content. Since (3) and (4) have no propositional content of their own, this would be grounds for regarding (1) to (4) as one exchange. Other examples of co-operative illocutionary acts include any kind of verbal contract, in addition to promises, or statements of agreement. Hancher (1979) discusses a range of such co-operative acts. (Cf. chapter 9 for further discussion.)

5   Yes and no

I may have seemed to imply above that "yes" and "no" are in contrastive distribution after yes–no questions. However, they are rarely, if ever, equally predicted. And more generally, positive and negative propositions and syntactic forms do not have equal distribution either in syntax or in discourse.

To regard "yes" and "no" as being in straightforward contrastive distribution might mean that they are being confused with logical negation. But negation provides a clear case where the logical operator (∼) approximates only very roughly to natural language *not* and related forms. In propositional logic, the following basic relationship holds: $p = \sim \sim p$. But the following sentences are not synonymous, . despite superficial similarity of form:

6.15   (a)   He is interested.   (b)   He is not uninterested.

The latter may also be contrasted on occasions with:

6.16   He is not disinterested.

(This point, incidentally, disposes of prescriptive statements that so-called 'double negatives' cancel each other out and are therefore incorrect.) Assuming that both are in standard English, the following two sentences are not synonymous:

6.17   (a)   He did some work.   (b)   He didn't do no work.

The second would typically be used in different circumstances – for example, to deny a prior accusation. Compare:

6.18   He didn't exactly do no work, but I admit he didn't do much.

Positive and negative sentences are used to perform different speech acts. (See Givón, 1978, for detailed arguments in favour of this view. However, see also Kempson, 1977: 153, who questions this distinction between denials and other uses of negation.)

Another indication that logical negation is not equivalent to natural language negation is that *not* is not always synonymous with the prefix *un-*. For example, the following two sentences are not synonymous:

6.19   (a)   Susan is not happy.   (b)   Susan is unhappy.

The second is synonymous with *Susan is sad*. But (a) allows a wider interpretation: Susan's feelings lie somewhere between actually sad and just not overtly happy.

Yes and *no* are oddities on syntactic grounds. They are often regarded as clause or sentence substitutes. However, as Halliday and Hasan (1976: 137–8) point out, they are better regarded as elliptic forms, since they express just the polarity of the clause. This distinguishes *yes* and *no* from superficially similar items in other languages such as French, where they express agreement or disagreement with what has gone before (although, for a modification of this, see below).

6.20   A: Are you coming?   B: Yes./No.
6.21   A: Are you not coming?   B: Yes./No.
6.22   A: Tu viens?   B: Oui./Non./*Si.
6.23   A: Tu ne viens pas?   B: *Oui./Non./Si.

Yes and *no* can also co-occur with other elliptic forms of the clause.

6.24   A: Are you coming?   B: Yes, I am.

Second, because *yes* and *no* are highly elliptic, they must be non-initial in discourse. They cannot be initiations, but have to be a response to a preceding utterance. This, in itself, makes them essentially an interactive or discourse phenomenon. They will therefore not normally occur at all in written language, unless rarely after 'rhetorical' questions.

Yes and *no*, and more generally the contrast between positive and negative, might normally be considered to be a matter of syntax or even lexis. In isolation, *yes* and *no* or positive and negative, appear to be in straightforward contrastive distribution. And they are clearly contrastive in at least some discourse sequences:

6.25   A: Do you like whisky?   B: Yes (I do)./No (I don't).

However, unless positives and negatives are considered in their contexts of occurrence, then facts are likely to be missed about them. This provides a motivation for going beyond lexico-syntax, or the kind of systemic contrast which I suggested above is available after yes–no questions.

Even within syntax, positive and negative do not have identical privileges of occurrence. For example, only positive clauses may be exclamative:

6.26   What a long way it is!/*isn't!

So, the polarity of a clause is an entry condition for a syntactic choice (cf. Martin, 1981):

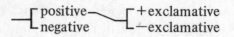

Givón (1978) provides other such examples to show that negatives are marked by having a more restricted distribution than corresponding positives.

There are other cases where the contrast between positive and negative is cancelled within sentences. In sentences such as:

6.27   Will/won't you join the dance?

the contrast is not one of polarity. The negative form might be considered as more polite. Or in such examples as:

6.28   You might consider whether you can/can't do it.

several politeness markers co-occur, and the choice of *can* versus *can't* does not alter the logico-semantic meaning. In such cases, politeness is marked by the modal verb, the past tense form of the modal, the embedded request and possibly by the negative. Negative forms are often used to mark politeness in discourse, as in this field-note data:

6.29   A shop-assistant is offered a £5 note.
        Shop-assistant: You wouldn't have anything smaller I don't
                          suppose?
        Customer: No, sorry.

Such a request form strongly predicts the answer "no", facilitates a rejection of the request, and therefore does not put the customer on the spot. English has a range of such syntactic means for conveying that either "yes" or "no" is expected. (Cf. Bublitz, 1980, on conducive questions.) It follows that "yes" and "no" will rarely, if ever, convey equal amounts of information. One will usually be more strongly expected than the other and therefore will have less information or surprise value when it does occur.

Note in 6.29 that *no* is followed by an apology, whereas *yes* would not have been. After routine questions or small requests, *no* will characteristically be followed by an apology or an account or both, as in:

6.30   Q: Have you got a light?
        A: No, sorry, I don't smoke.

This is further evidence that "yes" and "no" are not in simple contrastive distribution and not equivalent as discourse moves.

The usual rule for agreeing with a preceding utterance is to choose *yes* after a preceding positive and *no* after a negative. That is, the form is determined by what precedes, and *yes* and *no* are in complementary distribution. Compare:

6.31   A: And I am not quite sure what time they're coming
             exactly.
       B: No./*Yes.

A clear case where the linguistic form is determined by the preceding utterance is illustrated by the confusion often caused by asking an adult stranger for permission to occupy an empty seat on a train, in a restaurant or other public place.[1] Thus, assuming that the request is granted, the form *Is this seat taken?* or *Is anyone sitting here?* predicts *No*. Whereas *May I sit here?* predicts *Yes*. Since both forms seem to occur with about equal frequency, and since the actual form is often lost due to noise, confusion over the answer is frequent. If the form is often obscure, one might wonder how the question is understood at all. The answer is that the question is largely predictable from non-verbal behaviour and from context, since there are very few requests which adult strangers can normally make of one another in public places.

However, both *yes* and *no* can be used to express agreement with a negative sentence, and in this context they may be interchangeable without any necessary change in meaning, and the contrast between them is therefore neutralized. In this case, however, *yes* can be ambiguous: it can be used to disagree with the preceding negative sentence, in which case it will be followed by an expansion. Compare:

6.32   A: So he's not coming then?   B: No./Yes.

where both *yes* and *no* can express agreement. Versus:

6.33   A: So he's not coming then?   B: Yes – he is.

Further, the contrast between *yes* and *no* is particularly likely to be neutralized after an utterance with different polarity in the matrix and embedded clauses, as in this example:

6.34   A: And I think I'm probably right in assuming that there
             are no further objections.
       B: Yes./No. (Low pitch, falling intonation.)

Yes would agree with the polarity of the matrix sentence and mean "yes, you're right"; whereas *no* would mean "no, there aren't." The fact that *yes* and *no* are in free variation here is often seen in meet-

---

[1]   I am grateful to Margaret Deuchar for this example.

ings. After such utterances, participants can often be seen both nodding and shaking their heads, whilst all agreeing with what has been said. Here is such an example from field-note data, with the same speaker saying *no* and nodding:

6.35   Two neighbours are talking about a spell of good weather.
        A: But the weathermen say it won't last, will it?
        B: No. (Nodding head.)

The ambiguity of *yes* on its own after a negative sentence is illustrated by the following field-note data of an exchange noted in a supermarket. The customer had taken a bag of tomatoes off a shelf.

6.36   Assistant: They're not priced yet.   (1)
        Customer: Yes. (High fall rise.)   (2)
        Assistant: No, they're not.   (3)
        Customer: Yes, I know.   (4)
        Assistant: You'll have to take them over there to get them
                      weighed.   (5)

The customer presumably intended (2) as "Yes, I agree with you." The high fall rise intonation conveys also: "the information is known to me and is obvious." A motivation for this interpretation is the customer's expanded version in (4). But the assistant takes (2) as contradicting (1) and meaning "Yes, they are." The lack of communication may have been caused by the use of the high fall rise intonation, which may be a characteristic of Received Pronunciation, but not of all accents of English (G. Brown *et al.*, 1980).
    Some sentences, such as:

6.37   Is the door open?

do not appear to expect either "yes" or "no" more strongly. Lyons (1977: 765) claims that such questions can be 'neutral with respect to any indication of the speaker's beliefs as to the truth-value of p ... unweighted with respect to the speaker's expectation of acceptance or rejection of the proposition'. However, it is important to distinguish between sentences and utterances. Sentences such as 6.37 may convey entirely unbiased questions, but it is doubtful if they are ever used as utterances to ask entirely unbiased questions. Speakers do not go around asking questions at random. They ask questions which they have reasons for asking, and have hopes and expectations about answers. A question such as *Is dinner ready yet?* may be prepared for the answer "no", but is probably hoping for "yes"! There is likely to be a preferred response.

Data on the answers expected by yes–no questions is provided by cases where the expectation is challenged. Consider the following field-note data. A lecturer was giving a typist an appendix to an already lengthy article she had to type for him.

6.38   Lecturer: Can I add that to the back?
      Secretary: What would you do if I said *No*?
      Lecturer: I'd take it away and come back when you're in a better mood.
      Secretary: You'd have years to wait then, wouldn't you.

Givón (1978) has argued in detail that syntactically corresponding positive and negative sentences perform different speech acts, in that they differ in their assumptions about what the addressee is likely to believe. Negative sentences are typically used to correct or deny false beliefs, and positive sentences therefore make fewer assumptions. This means that corresponding pairs of sentences have different discourse consequences. He discusses examples such as:

6.39   A: We saw a movie last night.
      B: Oh! That's nice!
6.40   A: We didn't see a movie last night.
      B: Oh! ... Were you supposed to?

Givón is certainly correct to argue that positive and negative sentences are characteristically used in different ways. It is clear that the initiation in 6.39 could be the first mention of the topic, whereas the initiation in 6.40 assumes a previous mention. However, positive sentences are not used against an entirely neutral background. They can also be used to contradict or deny assumptions which the addressee may be thought to hold. This may be tested very simply by going up to a colleague and saying something such as:

6.41   Your car is still safely in the car park.
6.42   Your wife was faithful to you last week.

Even utterances about innocuous subjects, say:

6.43   The milk was delivered this morning.

would only be used to convey the end of a milkman's strike, to deny a belief about a lazy milkman, or in some way to contribute to some universe of beliefs. Adults do not go around stating the obvious.

Further, "yes" and "no" may be in contrastive distribution as regards answering a request for information, but may in addition contrast in the discourse possibilities they open up. Consider this piece of field-note data. I had rung up a married couple of my acquaintance:

6.44   MS: Hello, this is Mike Stubbs, is that Alastair?   (1)
        A: Yes.   (2)
        MS: Is Beryl there?   (3)
        A: Yes, but she won't be on Thursday.   (4)

The question is: why does A say (4)? (It turns out that Beryl is leaving for South America later that week.) A takes (3) as a pre-sequence: quite correctly, since I was ringing to invite them to dinner! An answer of *Yes* alone at (4) would open up such possibilities.

In summary, if we look at "yes" and "no" or positives and negatives in discourse sequences, it turns out that they may be in contrastive distribution, although rarely if ever equally expected, in potential free variation (i.e. synonymous) or in complementary distribution. As I argued in chapter 5, section 8, such cases where the discourse sequence can be shown to control meaning, are themselves indications that the concept of well-formed discourse is a valuable one.

6   Observational studies of yes and no

Wooton (in press) provides an empirical study of the different distribution of *yes* and *no* in mother–child discourse. He studied over a hundred request sequences in a corpus of audio-recorded data between mothers and four-year-old children. Here *yes* and *no* and related positives and negatives are used to grant or refuse the request. He found that granting and refusing were done in quite different ways. In granting a request, the mother would often simply say *yes* or its semantic equivalent, typically after a pause of less than half a second. But refusals were not performed by saying *no*. In fact negative forms were routinely omitted. Refusals were often performed in positive syntax, with added mitigation and accounts, and often after considerable time delays. Refusal sequences could be long interchanges in which the mother moved progressively towards negative forms. In a comparable study, Pomerantz (1975) studies positives and negatives as agreements and disagreements after previous utterances. She again finds a preference for agreements, and therefore that the forms are not in straightforward contrastive distribution. In other words, *yes* can be a simple granting of a request or an agreement. But *no* is not a simple refusal or disagreement: it would in addition convey some other meaning, for example abruptness, annoyance or rudeness. Similarly, it is impossible simply to refuse a formal invitation to a dinner or whatever, without also conveying rudeness. Such an invitation would have to be declined, with an apology, or a reason for absence. Some sequences of speech acts are, in fact, impossible.

Bald (1980) reaches very similar conclusions about the asymmetry of *yes* and *no* in a study done from a rather different theoretical perspective. He studied 372 responses of *yes* and *no* to utterances in audio-recorded interview data. First, *yes* was much commoner than *no* (309 versus 63 occurrences). This is partly due to the situation: an interview prompts the interviewee to express agreement rather than disagreement. However, in addition, most *yes* responses are in a tone unit of their own, whereas about half of the *no* responses are part of a tone unit. This is due to the convention that disagreement has to be explained. Bald found comparable, although not such sharp differences, in the distribution of *yes* and *no* in conversation between intimates.

We have established so far, then, that there are distributional restrictions on the forms *yes* and *no*, and on the propositions completed by "yes" and "no", which cannot be accounted for within sentence grammar. The restrictions can be stated only by studying the syntagmatic chaining of units above the clause.

7   *A-, B- and AB-events*

Having established that "yes" and "no" are not equally distributed after other utterances, we can use these facts to provide tests for what Labov and Fanshel (1977: 62–3) call A-, B- and AB-events (cf. chapter 4, section 4).

A-events are events to which the speaker has privileged access, and about which he cannot reasonably be contradicted, since they typically concern A's own emotions, experience, personal biography, and so on. Examples include *I'm cold* and *I don't know*. Notice how, in school classrooms, a statement such as *I don't know* may be the only one to which a pupil is not open to correction. B-events are, similarly, events about which the hearer has privileged knowledge. A cannot therefore normally make unmitigated statements about B-events, such as *You're cold*, unless A is in authority over B, for example, as mother to child. Statements about B-events would normally be modalized or modified: *You must be cold* or *You look cold.* In either case, Labov proposes a rule of confirmation (Labov and Fanshel, 1977: 100):

> If A makes a statement about a B-event, it is heard as a request for confirmation.

This rule shows that knowledge is assumed by speakers to be differently distributed amongst other speakers, and that although it may be A who makes a statement, it is B who, as it were, has to give the stamp of authority to the proposition involved. Thus there is a separation between A, who asserts a proposition, and B, who confirms or denies it:

6.45   A: You look cold.   B: Yes, I am.

(Berry, 1981a distinguishes between primary and secondary knowers in this connection.)

Labov also uses three other related terms. AB-events are defined as knowledge which is shared by A and B, and known by both to be shared. O-events are known to everyone present, and known to be known. D-events are known to be disputable. There is therefore a classification of utterances according to the amount of shared knowledge involved. These definitions of AB- and O-events are comparable to the way in which the term *pragmatic presuppositions* is often defined, as propositions which are established by the preceding discourse, or which can be assumed to be generally agreed.

Labov and Fanshel are interested in the interactional consequences of statements about different kinds of event, and propose, in effect (1977: 101), that statements about different kinds of fact may be classified according to what follows them in the discourse.

Initiation		*Response*
	A-event	minimal acknowledgement
	B-event	confirmation
A makes a statement about	AB-event ⎱	
	O-event ⎰	minimal response
	D-event	evaluation

No formal definitions are given which might distinguish minimal acknowledgements or responses from confirmations. Only evaluation is clearly distinct. However, after statements about A-, B- and AB-events, the possibility of occurrence of *yes* and *no* is quite different and provides a test for the distinctions.

After statements about B-events, *yes* and *no* are in contrastive distribution:

6.46   A: You're a Catholic.   B: Yes./No.

In statements about A-events, A already has privileged access to the information involved. Therefore both *yes* and *no* will be equally inappropriate:

6.47   A: I'm a Catholic.   B: *Yes./*No.

Since statements about AB-events or O-events are about topics already assumed to be shared knowledge, *yes* and *no* will be in complementary distribution:

6.48   A: The Pope's a Catholic.   B: Yes./*No.
6.49   A: The Pope's not a Protestant.   B: *Yes./No.

In conversation, such statements might be used to establish what is taken for granted, and the polarity is likely to be more explicitly marked:

6.50   The Pope's a Catholic, right?
6.51   The Pope's not a Protestant, right?

So the distribution of *yes* and *no* is as follows:

A makes a
statement about
$\left\{\begin{array}{l} \text{A-event} \\ \text{B-event} \\ \text{AB-event} \\ \text{O-event} \end{array}\right.$
  both inappropriate
  in contrastive distribution
  in complementary distribution

The general principle here is that items can be classified according to their discourse predictions.

8   *Truth and certainty*

Expressed more generally, we are dealing here with how the certainty of propositions is expressed. Speaker A cannot normally be contradicted about A-events, for example. Both the grammar and discourse sequences provide possibilities of marking propositions as being inherently decidable or not. Tense selection is an obvious area where a grammatical feature depends on the status of the proposition being claimed. For example, simple present tense is used for eternal truths

(*Oil floats on water*); past tense forms are used for marking tentative-ness either in hypothetical worlds, for example, in counterfactual statements (*If he was here, we could go*), or in order to mark polite-ness (*I was wondering, if I might* ...). Simple present tense may be used to refer to future events if they are predictable and certain, but not if they are by their very nature unpredictable:

6.52   Celtic play Rangers tomorrow.
6.53   *Celtic beat Rangers tomorrow.

In a well-known article, G. Lakoff (1971) discusses such examples as 6.52 and 6.53. His general argument in the article is that grammati-cality makes no sense in isolation, but depends on assumptions about the nature of the world. He appears to take the view, however, that such assumptions are more or less constant, including general cultural beliefs and values. However, we can make 6.53 grammatical by con-structing a local discourse context which makes the certainty of the event plausible:

6.54   I've rigged everything, bribed the referee and the linesmen: *Celtic beat Rangers tomorrow* – and then lose their next game.

In any event, the grammaticality depends whether the event referred to is certain or not: developing Labov's terminology, we might call these C-events.

Note also the general methodological point which such examples raise. If you agreed initially that 6.53 was ungrammatical, and were then persuaded, when I put it in a discourse context in 6.54, that it was after all grammatical, then your grammaticality judgement was manipulated in a very simple way. If we accept the competence-performance dichotomy, then we might say that grammaticality judgements are open to performance errors: initially you had not noticed a possible interpretation. On the other hand, if your judge-ment was so easily manipulated by such an argument, then perhaps the judgement itself is merely an artefact of such experimental manipulation: and different judgements, and therefore different data, could be produced by different techniques. The relationship between such artificial judgements and real language in use becomes very problematic. Or, alternatively, perhaps such grammaticality judgements are never really made in isolation anyway, it is just that informants imagine their own contexts, and some contexts are more obvious than others. In other words, such examples throw very con-siderable doubt on the whole enterprise of eliciting grammaticality judgements on isolated sentences, since they question whether such judgements are ever truly decontextualized.

This discussion bears on the very general issue of the relation between formal logic and the analysis of natural language. Logic has traditionally been based on the view that there are only two truth-values: a proposition is either true or false. (Some versions of logic, which admit the concept of semantic presupposition, therefore also admit a third truth value or truth value gap, cf. chapter 10.) However, if we are considering real language in use, and in particular the relation between yes–no questions and answers, then we have to consider the possibilities: (a) that there are many possible intermediate values between true and false; and (b) that the concept of truth value is not precisely the required concept at all. (See McCawley, 1981: ch. 12, which discusses such questions.)

The problem arises for two reasons. First, we have to distinguish between the truth or falsity of propositions (the topic of logic) and speakers' certainty about the truth or falsity of propositions. Second, we have to admit that propositions about real world events and states of affairs are often complex and may be partly true and partly false. In general, the problem arises due to the distinction between the highly idealized data for which formal logic tries to account, and the much more complex situations in which natural language is used.

For example, given a question such as:

6.55   Is Harry a Catholic?

there are various answers apart from "yes" and "no". Possible answers might indicate the state of knowledge or degree of certainty of the answerer, for example: *I don't know*; *I'm not sure*; *I think so*. Although, as I discussed above, there are ways of interpreting some of these answers as "yes" or "no" plus a certainty component. Other answers can indicate to what degree the proposition is true, for example: *Very much so*; *Well, sort of*; *Strictly speaking, yes*; *Yes, but not a good one*; *He is and he isn't*; *In some respects*; *In name only*; and so on. Such answers indicate that there is a range of values intermediate between true and false; or, more exactly, that some propositions depend on a range of truth values in different dimensions. There are, in fact, words which can pick out and distinguish such dimensions (cf. McCawley, 1981: 385):

6.56   A: Is Harry a Catholic?
         B: Well, *technically* or *nominally* he is, but he isn't *really*.

Rather than a two-valued system of truth values, Belnap (1977) has proposed a four-valued system which would seem to be required for a question-answering device:

O: I have not been informed whether p or not.
T: I have been informed that p.
F: I have been informed that not p.
B: I have been informed that p and not p.

In response to the question *Is Harry a Catholic?*, possible values might be conveyed by forms such as:

O: I don't know.
T: Yes.
F: No.
B: John said he was but George said he wasn't.

The value B is required, in other words, to deal with contradictory information. The value T could be subdivided to deal with how reliable or certain the information is, or whether the speaker has privileged access to it, in ways I have discussed above.

It would seem then that the traditional logical approach to truth values has only limited application to discourse sequencing. First, a many valued logic is necessary. And second, it is often not the concept of truth as such which is relevant, but a related concept of state of information or information value.

I have given examples above, where judgements about grammaticality or acceptability appear to depend on knowledge about what is normal in the real world. Compare the Father Brown example 6.11 or the football example 6.52. However, it is important to distinguish between cases where such real world knowledge is really crucial, and cases where it only appears to be.

9   Knowledge and beliefs

It is important, in other words, not to rush to the opposite extreme and to conclude that linguistic knowledge is indistinguishable from knowledge about the world. On the contrary, we should try to delimit the kinds of knowledge that are required in understanding the coherence of discourse sequencing. One reason that has certainly kept many linguists away from studying real discourse is the fear that once the door is opened, there is no way of preventing the whole world from rushing in.

Labov (1972e: 434) cites an argument by Bever and Ross. They argue that understanding the relation between sentences involves understanding of the world. This may sometimes be true, but it is not the case with the two sentences they cite:

6.57   Everyone should read the Bible. Deuteronomy is one of the great books of the world.

They argue that discourse analysis cannot be part of linguistics, since an account of the coherence of this sequence depends on the knowledge of a particular fact: that Deuteronomy is a book of the Bible. However, this argument is false, as can easily be shown by making up nonsense sequences, which are still interpreted as coherent, although the knowledge could not previously have been known by anyone:

6.58   You ought to read *Wombats Galore*. Bruce McQuarrie is a great author.

Arguments in this area are often confused by a failure to distinguish what can be interpreted from the language itself, and what has to be imported from the real world. For example, a sentence such as *My children are sick* has as one of its presuppositions "I have children." But as M. Atkinson and Griffiths (1973) point out, if this presupposition is not shared by a hearer as part of his real world knowledge, the communication does not break down simply because a felicity condition for such a sentence has been broken. The hearer infers the presupposition and is more likely to say *Oh dear!* than *What children?*

10   Actives and passives

There are other cases where the syntax of a question may partly determine the syntax of the answer. A grammar of English clearly has to account for the fact that active and passive versions of most sentences are synonymous. (Well-known counter-examples to this generalization are sentences which have quantifiers such as *some*, *few* or *any* in surface structure. It would probably be generally admitted that such sentences are often ambiguous, but have different preferred interpretations in their active and passive versions.) Thus the follow-

Glasgow University Library
Checkout/Renewal Receipt

Customer name: YAZGIN, NAGME

Title: Working with texts : a core introduction to
language analysis / Ronald Carter ... [et al.].
ID: 30114011578013
Due: 06-12-06

Title: English words : a linguistic introduction /
Heidi Harley.
ID: 30114013515542
Due: 03-01-07

Title: Semantics : a new outline / F. R. Palmer.
ID: 30114002513474
Due: 06-12-06

Total items: 3
29/11/2006 14:47

4hr & 24hr loan items cannot be renewed.
Please return short loan items on the self-return
machine.

ing two sentences are synonymous, insofar as they have the same truth conditions:

6.59.   Harry hit John.
6.60   John was hit by Harry.

These two sentences have the same entailments, and in fact entail each other. It is assumed here that entailments are propositions which can be inferred from sentences in isolation.

However, the fact that they are synonymous in this idealized sense, does not mean that they have the same privileges of occurrence in discourse. For example:

6.61   A: What did Harry do?
         B: Harry (He) hit John./*John was hit by Harry (by him).

There are also other sentences which are perfectly grammatical and synonymous with 6.59 and 6.60 but which would be inappropriate answers. These include:

6.62   *It was John that Harry hit.
6.63   *What happened to John was that Harry hit him.
6.64   *HARRY hit John. (Where upper case represents contrastive
         stress.)

Note that such answers would be corrigible (cf. chapter 5, section 4). (Cf. Widdowson, 1979b: 220ff who discusses such data.)

We therefore require a distinction between synonymy, which is a relation holding between sentences in isolation, and some concept such as discourse equivalence. Many descriptions would simply note the formal relation between active and passive, and note their synonymy. Their different uses in discourse sequence would, by implication, be a matter of mere performance. However, more recently some scholars (e.g. Creider, 1979; Langacker, 1974; Radford, 1979) have begun to discuss transformational relationships within a functional perspective. As Langacker (1974: 630) argues, the question of why languages have various properties is a more interesting question than just describing the properties.

We can explain the lack of discourse equivalence between 6.59 and 6.60 with reference to their thematic structure. There is considerable variation in terminology in this area, and terms used include: topic–comment, subject–predicate, theme–rheme and given–new, although some linguists distinguish between these sets of terms (cf. Lyons, 1977: 500–11). As a general rule, given or known information comes first in a sentence, since it is logical to use something known as a point of departure. In:

6.65   What did Harry do?

it is presupposed that Harry did something, and we would therefore expect the answer to start from this point of known or presupposed information. 6.59 does this, whereas 6.60 assumes that we know something about John. Since passivization in English reverses the order of subject and object noun phrases and allows the logical subject to be deleted, one of its functions is to provide a way of distributing information differently within sentences, and of preserving the themacity appropriate to the presuppositions of the question. In other words, the relation between syntax and discourse equivalence is not arbitrary in such examples.

So a word-order (or more accurately group-order) phenomenon is here being explained with reference to assumed states of knowledge of speakers. What is otherwise an optional transformation is shown to have discourse consequences. A better formulation might be to say that the function of the forms relates to the current topic of the discourse. This is the kind of idea which is often discussed, albeit inexplicitly, by writers on good style (e.g. Strunk and White, 1979: 18).

Again, the data are explicable in terms of a propositional base set up by the question. *What did Harry do?* (6.65) presupposes "Harry did something", and therefore leaves a variable "something" to be given a value. We would expect this value to be placed in the characteristic slot for new information, and the syntax functions to do this via movement rules.

We still seem to be dealing here with fairly well-defined syntactic matters, although we are discussing how syntax is organized to fulfil communicative needs, as defined by states of knowledge of speakers. The way in which propositions are encoded according to the communicative context and the states of knowledge of speakers has, of course, been discussed in detail by the Prague School linguists (e.g. Danes, 1968) and by Halliday (e.g. 1970) and others (e.g. Chafe, 1974; Kuno, 1978). Prague School Linguistics has, for example, developed the concept of 'communicative dynamism' within the theory of functional sentence perspective, to explain how less dynamic parts of a sentence, carrying old information, tend to occur first. Alternatively, the phenomena seem to have to do firmly with cohesion rather than coherence, as these terms are defined by Widdowson (1979b: 96–9). Cohesion has to do with relations between surface linguistic forms and between propositions, whereas coherence refers to relations between communicative acts. The phenomena discussed in this section have to do with the appropriate order of presentation of propositions, but makes no reference to the illocutionary force of the utterances.

It is possible to generalize the points I have made also to cover other transformations whose function is to topicalize certain items of information. For example, Prince (1978) discusses the function of wh-clefts and it-clefts in discourse; and R. Longacre (1978: 262-3) discusses the function of nominalization as one way of taking the emphasis off an event when it is repeated in a narrative. He gives examples such as:

6.66   He went to the shop. *Having arrived*, he shot the manager.

In addition, there are lexical means of sequencing information in ways which take into account the knowledge already held by listeners. For example, the following two sentences entail each other:

6.67   George sold the car to Harold.
6.68   Harold bought the car from George.

Other lexical pairs which can similarly reverse the surface sequence of syntactic units include: *father, son; give, take*, and so on. In other words, this kind of functional explanation can relate what is otherwise a disparate set of unrelated surface phenomena, syntactic and lexical. Further, one function of marked topic is to perform the speech act of correcting a misunderstanding. Consider an exchange such as:

6.69   A: When did John call?   B: It was Harry that called.

11   *Conclusions*

Although many of the phenomena discussed in this chapter have their realization in different syntactic forms, we are dealing not only with the internal syntactic structure of sentences. We are dealing also (a) with the distribution of whole clauses of sentences relative to each other, (b) with the ways in which propositions may be distributed across more than one conversational turn, and therefore across more than one syntactic unit, and (c) with the way in which speakers' states of knowledge influence such distributions.

7

Analysing Exchange Structure

In chapter 5 I discussed how far the concept of prospective or predictive structure is applicable to discourse. In chapter 6 I discussed
the concept of a conversational exchange with a minimum structure
of IR. Even in a superficially simple case of a QA exchange, it turned
out that the relation between I and R is complex. In this chapter
I will pick out one topic which relates chapters 5 and 6, and pursue it
in more detail: the concept that conversational exchanges are pros-
pectively structured.

There are several concepts central to discourse analysis, which
seem intuitively appealing and in fact rather obvious once they are
pointed out, but which, on closer inspection, turn out to be difficult
to define. One such concept is the conversational exchange, which
I provisionally defined in chapter 6 as the minimal interactive unit.
I also proposed that exchanges have to be defined syntactically (in
terms of sequences of ellipticity classes) and semantically (as a
propositional frame and its completion). Other intuitively
plausible candidates for such interactive exchanges include:
inform–acknowledge; greeting–greeting; complaint–excuse; request–
compliance–thanks; and so on.

1   *Theory, methodology and data*

Such interactive units seem well established by a large body of
research (see sections 4 and 5 below). In addition a concentrated
amount of work on discourse analysis since about 1970 has demonstrated that spoken discourse is highly organized and amenable to
analysis using traditional linguistic concepts such as sequential and
hierarchic organization, system and structure, and so on. However,
the demonstration has so far been largely informal: insights have
been gained, features of conversational organization have been
noticed, but few attempts have been made to develop such insights
in a rigorous fashion. Two main problems are as follows.

Many structural analyses of spoken discourse have now been published, but little attempt has been made to motivate different rival analyses of the same data, and to decide which analysis is the best. This is a powerful procedure and is standard in phonology and syntax, where much of the literature consists of analyses followed by counter-examples and rival analyses. A prerequisite of such a procedure is, of course, the statement of analyses in a form which allows counter-examples to be searched for and found: that is, a degree of formalization.

Second, there is the problem that intuitions about discourse sequences may be useful but are notoriously untrustworthy (cf. chapter 5). Some control over the analyst's intuitions is therefore required, as well as the development of techniques for collecting other types of data. Methodology therefore requires more attention than it has often had so far (cf. chapter 11).

In this chapter I will therefore discuss the use of different methods (e.g. observational and experimental) and different kinds of data (e.g. naturally occurring and introspective) in order to motivate analyses of conversational exchanges. In a relatively new area of study such as discourse analysis, the only reasonable course would seem to be to combine different methods of study. Linguists are often accused of ignoring the study of actual utterances located in specific inter-actions. Conversely, linguists often accuse others of refusing to idealize and generalize, and therefore of working with unclear statements and undeveloped theory. What is needed is a balance in which emergent theory is controlled by data. Further, the control should be exercised by different kinds of data, both naturally occurring discourse and also deliberately elicited data. A corpus of naturally occurring data is necessary, but it has exactly the same limitations in discourse analysis as in syntax. The study is restricted to forms which happen to occur, and it is therefore impossible to study rare forms and the full range of complete paradigms. A corpus therefore requires to be supplemented by introspective data, and, since these are not always reliable, by data elicited from other informants by controlled experimental techniques.

2   Well-formedness in discourse

As I discussed at length in chapter 5, linguistics has traditionally been concerned with characterizing well-formed versus deviant strings, that is, with stating the constraints on the distribution of units such

as phonemes and morphemes. The basic aim is to predict the correct
surface distribution of forms, and the basic assumption is that any
given string is recognizably well- or ill-formed, with only a few
doubtful cases if any. This assumption is certainly fruitful in phonotactics and in syntax, although many problematic cases arise (cf.
chapter 5, sections 3, 4). And, as I have argued, under appropriate
idealization, the concept of well-formedness also applies to discourse.
Thus in the following genuine interchange between a husband A and
wife B, utterances (3) and (5) indicate that (1–2) has been heard as
an ill-formed sequence by one of the participants:

7.1   A: I'm going to do some weeding   (1)
        B: yes please   (2)
        A: what   (3)
        B: yes please   (4)
        A: you don't listen to anything I say   (5)
        B: I thought you said you were going to pour some
             drinks   (6)
        A: no I said I'm going to do some weeding   (7)

   In the normal course of events, deviant phoneme strings or grossly
ungrammatical sentences simply do not occur, unless they are produced by non-native speakers. Yet it is quite common to find conversational interchanges, such as 7.1, which are ill-formed but do
occur, and to find that speakers then have routine ways of recogniz-
ing and repairing the ill-formed discourse. Note also, therefore, that
although judgements of well-formedness are usually applied in syntax
to contrived data, such judgements can equally well be applied to
naturally occurring discourse.

   Second, although utterance (2) above does appear to be inappropriate, and due to a performance error, there is no real difficulty in
thinking of a way to interpret (2) so that it makes a perfectly
coherent response to (1). It could be interpreted, for example, as
"yes, please, that's a good idea, it's about time you did tidy up the
garden a bit." Given any two utterances in discourse, it is usually
possible to relate them, even if they were not intended to be related.
(Cf. example 5.7.)

3   *Notational conventions*

The rest of this chapter will develop some of these ideas with reference to the concept of *exchange*, which is the unit of discourse

which seems most amenable to linguistic-structural analysis. I will use the following notational conventions:

[ ]   Square brackets indicate exchange boundaries.
( )   Round brackets indicate optional items.
n   Indicates recursion, e.g. F^n: any number of Fs.
→   Predicts a following utterance, and is therefore non-terminal in an exchange.
←   Is predicted by a preceding item, and is therefore non-initial in an exchange.
←→   Is predicted and predicts, and is therefore medial in an exchange.
I   Initiation.
R   Response.
R/I   Response/initiation.
F   Feedback.
Ir   Re-initiation.
Inf   Inform.

An exchange is a minimal interactive unit, in which an initiation I by A is followed obligatorily by a response R from B, and optionally by further utterances. The minimal structure is therefore

$$[\overrightarrow{I}\ \overleftarrow{R}].$$

4   Research on exchange structure

Several researchers have proposed concepts which are broadly comparable to *exchange*. For example, Sacks (1967–72) uses the concept *adjacency pair*, which includes two-place structures such as question–answer and greeting–greeting. If the second-pair-part is missing, it is 'noticeably absent', giving, in the terminology I am using here, an ill-formed string *[I]. Such a string *could* occur, for reasons discussed above; but if it does, it will be recognized as deviant and interpreted accordingly. Goffman (1971) uses the term *interchange* to refer to various structures, of up to four places. And Sinclair and Coulthard (1975) propose the term *exchange* for structures of up-to-three-place structures which they label [IRF], for initiation–response–feedback, and which are particularly applicable to teacher–pupil interaction of the type:

7.2   T: can you tell me why you eat all that food – yes   I

P: to keep you strong   R
T: to keep you strong yes – to keep you strong   F

I will discuss in more detail below how the structure of such three-part exchanges might best be represented.

Concepts such as *exchange* and *adjacency pair* are useful and intuitively appealing. It does give insight into the organization of some conversations to regard them as comprising question–answer or statement–acknowledgement pairs, or initiation–response–feedback triplets, which in turn form larger units. But there are many unsolved problems, such as the following: Is it possible to give formal recognition criteria for exchanges? Are exchanges always well-defined units, with clear-cut openings and closings? Or do they have well-defined openings, but ill-defined ends? As Labov and Fanshel (1977: 62) suggest: 'ending is a more complex act than beginning.' Or are some utterances simply Janus-faced, closing one exchange and opening the next? Is all conversational data analysable into exchanges, or is the concept applicable only to a narrow range of discourse (e.g. teacher–pupil dialogue) whilst other discourse (e.g. casual conversation) drifts along in a less structured way? Can one exchange be embedded within another, giving discontinuous exchanges? And so on. Any work which makes structural claims about the organization of spoken discourse must provide answers to such questions.

This chapter will not answer all these questions, but it will at least propose three ways of beginning to tackle them: first, the use of a restricted set of intuitive judgements by the researcher about well-formed discourse; second, the use of informants' judgements elicited by manipulating naturally occurring conversational data; and third, the use of further naturally occurring data to provide corroboration or refutation of structural claims.

5   Sinclair's work on discourse

My own use of the term *exchange* in this chapter is based on work done mainly at the University of Birmingham, England, and derives in its major characteristics from work by John McH. Sinclair. An early informal presentation is by Sinclair (1966). The main outlines were circulated in Sinclair *et al.* (1972) which was revised for formal publication by Sinclair and Coulthard (1975). The main developments of work on exchange structure are contained in Sinclair (1980), Coulthard and Brazil (1981), and Berry (1980a, b; 1981a, b). Related work on intonation in discourse is published in Brazil *et al.*

(1980) and other informally published work by Brazil (e.g. 1975). And there are several unpublished theses, deriving more or less closely from this approach, including Burton (1978), Carter (1979), S. Harris (1980), Montgomery (1977), Richardson (1978) and Willes (1980). I do not have room here to review all of this work. However, introductions and reviews are available elsewhere: in Burton (1981a; and 1980: ch. 6 – two slightly different versions of the same article), Coulthard (1977), and Stubbs and Robinson (1979).

Sinclair and Coulthard (1975) are concerned with the particularly distinctive exchanges with an [IRF] structure, illustrated above in 7.2, which characterize much formal teaching. However, they have claimed (e.g. Sinclair, 1980: 122), that if the exchange is defined as the minimal unit of interaction, then [IRF] is a primary structure for interactive discourse in general. In any case, it is proposed by Sinclair and Coulthard (1975) that the most characteristic exchange in traditional teaching has a structure comprising these three moves. An I predicts a following R, and R occurs in response to a preceding I: I and R are therefore symmetrically related. F functions to close an exchange. (Very similar proposals have been made independently by Mehan, 1979, also in work on teacher–pupil discourse.)

There are however variations on the basic structure. A teacher-elicit exchange, where the teacher elicits a verbal response from the pupil, has the full [IRF] structure, with all three elements of structure obligatory. A teacher-direct exchange, in which the teacher directs a pupil to do something, has the structure [IR(F)], where R is a non-verbal response. A teacher-inform exchange has the structure [I(R)]. That is, a teacher conveys propositional information, as in lecturing, and pupils may or may not respond. Note that it is not given the structure *[IF] since this would imply an evaluation of the teacher's I. A checking exchange has the structure [IR(F)]. Here the teacher does not know the answer to his initiating question: it might be a procedural question, such as *Can you see the board?* or *Have you finished your work yet?* What Sinclair and Coulthard are emphasizing, in the different sequential ordering in these exchanges, is that different kinds of I make different predictions about what will follow. For example, a test question or pseudo-question, to which the teacher already knows the answer, leads to a different exchange structure from a genuine question in which, for example, the teacher is checking on a piece of information which only the pupil has. (Berry, 1981a, develops in much more detail some of the consequences of the ways in which information may be differently distributed between speakers.)

The overall framework presented by Sinclair and Coulthard (1975) is much more complex than this. They distinguish free from bound exchanges, and teaching exchanges, illustrated above, from boundary exchanges, which mark the boundary of major sections of a lesson. They also situate the whole discussion of exchange structure within a scale and category model of discourse in general. However, what I am concerned with here is the concept of exchange.

There are various limitations on this approach to discourse structure. These have to do mainly with the degree of idealization involved in the description. Teacher–pupil interaction is already much simpler than casual conversation in many rather obvious ways. Further, Sinclair and Coulthard deliberately concentrate only on traditional lessons in which there are clear status and power relations. The situation is also peculiar in that knowledge is very unequally distributed between teacher and pupils: teachers often ask questions to which they already know the answers. Further, the model appears to be a consensus model, in which there is agreement about the norms and conventions. It is quite possible that teacher and pupils may have different views about how the discourse could and should develop. It is difficult to know how to handle deviance within such a model: deviance tends to imply meaninglessness, since actions only have meaning within a framework. Sinclair and Coulthard's description therefore has the effect of playing down the way in which meanings are negotiated in the course of interaction. Finally, they tend to imply that utterances have a single function, for example, of initiating or responding, whereas all utterances are multi-functional, and the same utterance may be an initiation as well as a request and complaint: *Haven't you finished yet?*

I make these points since they also apply to the model of exchange structure which I propose below. I should therefore also present a brief defence of this approach. There is nothing wrong with idealization in itself: indeed, it is inevitable in any description. The important point is whether the idealization advances knowledge, or whether it ignores crucial features of the language being modelled, and throws the baby out with the bathwater. No matter how delicate an analysis is, there is always dispersal of meaning at different levels of language. And there is always a residue of meaning due to the particular context of situation of a text. Conversations are not well-defined, unitary events, and no exhaustive account of their organization is possible. Categorization is always problematic, and it is never possible to say in so many words exactly what is meant. Some aspects of language are inherently indeterminate, and therefore all conversations are less determinate than formal methods of analysis can admit. None of this means, however, that formal methods of analysis are worthless: only that studies of discourse must combine different methods of study with different limitations. What I want to do in this chapter is to pursue the kinds of formalism which Sinclair and Coulthard propose a little distance in one direction.

Sinclair (1980) develops several of these points at a more general level. He still maintains (p. 122) that:

> there is little doubt that the exchange is a defensible linguistic unit, the minimum unit of interaction, relatable to a primary structure of initiation, response and feedback. ... the rules of exchange structure provide the essential organization of utterances.

He argues further (p. 116) that the exchange is 'an accumulation of shared meaning (hence the tendency to elliptical structures in non-initial position)'. This point is developed below. Utterances within an exchange display compliance: anything else signals a new exchange. The basic notion is, then, that an exchange comprises an initiation and any contributions which tend to close that mini topic: by completing a proposition (cf. chapter 6); by acknowledging it (cf. chapter 9), and so on. We are dealing with the predictive power of the unfinished linear structure (p. 112).

Coulthard and Brazil (1981) further develop several of these ideas. They define the exchange as 'the unit concerned with negotiating information', and attempt on this basis to propose a general exchange structure, based on the concepts of: predictive structure; increasing ellipticity as the exchange progresses; and a structure comprising initiation plus any moves tending to complete or close the information introduced in the initiation. I will now develop at some length the approach to exchange structure proposed by Coulthard and Brazil.

6   Basic discourse categories

First, I will discuss a way of defining basic discourse categories, and then see what implications follow about exchange structure. We have seen in chapter 5 that a starting point for discourse analysis is to use the concept of continuous classification (Sinclair and Coulthard, 1975: 120): each utterance is classified or interpreted in the light of the structural predictions, if any, set up by the preceding utterance. That is, given any utterance we ask whether it predicts a following item, whether it is itself a response to preceding items, whether it marks an initial boundary of a relatively large unit of discourse and thus predicts such a unit, and so on (cf. Sinclair and Coulthard, 1975: 14). Such an approach proposes a small number of minimal interactional categories, at primary delicacy, which might include moves such as initiate, I; respond, R; respond-initiate, R/I; and feedback, F.

Coulthard and Brazil (1981: 97) define elements of exchange structure in terms of two features, ±predicting and ±predicted. This gives four logically possible combinations of features:

	Predicting	*Predicted*
I	+	−
R	−	+
F	−	−
R/I	+	+

Let us follow through what such definitions imply for exchange structure.

First, these features entail other features. The feature +predicting entails −terminal: if an utterance predicts a following utterance, it cannot be terminal. Similarly, the feature +predicted entails −initial: another utterance must have preceded it. But the features −predicting and −predicted do not entail anything about the position of utterances within an exchange. We can therefore immediately expand the matrix as follows:

	Predicting	*Terminal*	*Predicted*	*Initial*
I	+	−	−	
R	−		+	−
F	−		−	
R/I	+	−	+	−

The intention of Coulthard and Brazil's definitions is clearly that I is +initial, and F is −initial, but these features do not necessarily follow from their definitions. So, for example, exchanges such as [F] and [I R I R] are not explicitly ruled out. Several structures are ruled out, however, including *[I F] and *[I R/I].

A further possible anomaly is that both R and R/I are defined as +predicted. If R/I occurs then it is in response to a preceding I. But it need not occur, since the choice is between R on its own or both R/I and R. Possible exchanges include:

$$[\vec{I}\ \overleftarrow{R}\ (F)]$$

$$[\vec{I}\ \overleftrightarrow{R/I}\ \overleftarrow{R}\ (F)]$$

As it is defined, F is optional, and the round brackets are redundant, but I will continue to use them for clarity.

As I noted above, Sinclair and Coulthard (1975) analyse three-part teacher–pupil exchanges as [I R F]. But F is now defined as —predicted and therefore optional. A better analysis for such exchanges, with an obligatory third move, would be [I R/I R]. Coulthard and Brazil (1981: 97–8) propose such an analysis for exchanges such as 7.3. The teacher shows a road sign to the class:

7.3   T: can anyone tell me what this means   I
       P: does it mean "danger men at work"   R/I
       T: yes   R

It is tempting to analyse the pupil's utterance in this particular case as R/I, merely because it both answers the question and explicitly requests a response. But a third move is predicted from the beginning of the exchange, irrespective of the syntactic form of P's utterance. The correct analysis would seem to be to regard the pupil's syntactic choices as being largely neutralized in such exchanges, so that interrogative, declarative and moodless items are all equivalent as R/I moves. Forms such as:

7.4   does it mean "danger men at work"
7.5   it means "danger men at work"
7.6   "danger men at work"

differ in the certainty versus tentativeness they convey (cf. chapter 6, section 2), but they all expect a following R.

Such exchanges can therefore be distinguished from the following which begins with a genuine request for information (from chapter 2, data appendix, 86–8):

7.7   MS: what time does this period end is it ten   I
       G: quarter past   R
       MS: quarter past oh that's all right   F

These two exchanges are intuitively different: the first begins with a test question to which the teacher already knows the answer; the second begins with a genuine question. This difference is captured in two distinct structures. Note also that it is at R in each case that the piece of information conveyed is given, as it were, its stamp of authority. (Cf. Berry, 1981a, for a detailed discussion of this issue.)

Another problem arises since the definitions of moves rule out four-part exchanges with the structure:

$$*[\overrightarrow{I}\ \overleftarrow{R}\ \overleftrightarrow{R/I}\ \overleftarrow{R}]$$

since R/I is defined as predicted, but the prediction of I is already fulfilled by R which makes no further predictions. It is easy, however, to find data which seem to require some such four-part structure, as in this audio-recorded interchange:

7.8	A:	can you tell me where the Savoy Cinema is	I
	B:	ooh yeah it's only round the corner here	R
	A:	is it?	?
	B:	it's not far like	R
	A:	cheers thanks very much ta	

An alternative would be to analyse this as two exchanges [I R] [I R]. But this would fail to account for the coherence of the interchange. Also, A's *is it?* is intuitively non-initial.

A solution to some of these problems would be to specify ±initial separately from ±predicting and ±predicted. (Tests for ±initial are given below in section 8.)

		Predicting	Terminal	Predicted	Initial
1	I	+	(−)	−	+
2	R	−		+	(−)
3	F	−		−	−
4	R/I	+	(−)	+	(−)

The features in brackets are redundant, being entailed by other features, but are left in for clarity. I is now explicitly defined as +initial, and F as −initial.

If we add ±initial to the feature specifications, this gives in turn four further possibilities for combining features:

		Predicting	Terminal	Predicted	Initial
5	*	+	(−)	+	+
6	*	−		+	+
7	Inf	−		−	+
8	Ir	+	(−)	−	−

Possibilities 5 and 6 are logically contradictory: an utterance cannot be both initial and predicted. Possibility 7 could define an Inform, as in lecturing, where no R is expected: this would allow one-part, non-interactive exchanges. Possibility 8 could define a non-initial initiation: Ir for re-initiation.

Let us see more systematically what other exchange structures the revised matrix generates. It may be that they are mere artefacts of the model, but they may turn out to have descriptive value.

The model allows one one-part exchange:

[Inf]

This was ruled out by the initial informal definition of exchange above, which regarded [I R] as the minimal exchange. But it would seem intuitively acceptable for, say, moves in a lecture where no response is required or expected. The model allows the two-part exchange:

[Inf F]

Feedback *may* be provided by a lecture audience, therefore [Inf F] seems intuitively acceptable. Inf is at least potentially interactive. But as we have noted, F is optional; therefore:

[Inf (F)]

Even in casual conversation, it is arguable that one finds sequences of Inf's, with only some acknowledged. In this data fragment (from chapter 2, data appendix, 1–4), a twelve-year-old boy is talking about the area of Edinburgh where he lives:

7.9   G: there's quite a lot of they old fishermen's houses –   Inf
             I used to go along there when I was much younger
             but they've demolished most of the Haveners   Inf
       M: aye   F

Inevitably there will be problems in distinguishing Inf and I: that is, in distinguishing utterances which do or do not expect a follow-up utterance. But it is possible to distinguish F and R on formal grounds (cf. chapter 9). F can be restricted to a closed class of items including: low pitch *yes* or *no* (depending on the polarity of the preceding utterance), *uhuh*, and so on. That is, I and Inf differ both in terms of whether they predict following items and in the form of the items.

Taking again the example of moves in a lecture: there seems to be no constraint on two feedback moves after an Inform. The model will, in fact, allow Inf followed by any number of Fs, therefore:

[Inf (F^n)]

similarly, it will allow [I R] or [I R/I R] followed by any number of Fs:

[$\overrightarrow{I}$ $\overleftarrow{R}$ (F^n)]

[$\overrightarrow{I}$ $\overleftrightarrow{R/I}$ $\overleftarrow{R}$ (F^n)]

The move R/I is itself recursive, therefore:

[$\overrightarrow{I}$ $\overleftrightarrow{R/I}{}^n$ $\overleftarrow{R}$ (F^n)]

Re-initiations, Ir, which are non-initial and predicting, but not predicted, can occur after [Inf ...], [I R ...] or [I R/I R ...], for example:

[Inf $\overrightarrow{Ir}$ $\overleftarrow{R}$]

[$\overrightarrow{I}$ $\overleftarrow{R}$ $\overrightarrow{Ir}$ $\overleftarrow{R}$]

[$\overrightarrow{I}$ $\overleftrightarrow{R/I}$ $\overleftarrow{R}$ $\overrightarrow{Ir}$ $\overleftarrow{R}$]

Finally, [... Ir R ...] is recursive.

The basic exchange structures generated are therefore:

[Inf], [I R] and [I R/I R].

Each of these may be followed by any number of Ir R pairs and/or any number of Fs.

The method I have proposed in this section is to follow the formalism as far as it leads. We may decide that it leads, in some cases, to unacceptable conclusions: this is the only way of testing the initial concepts which were the starting point.

So far I have looked only at some structures which appear to follow automatically from the initial definitions of basic discourse categories. These structures do not seem to be merely artefacts of the model, as I have shown from a few illustrative examples. However, in order to motivate the proposed exchange structures, we would have to show that they can account for naturally occurring data. We could also attempt to elicit informants' intuitions about discourse sequences and see whether they correspond with the model. The rest of this chapter will indicate briefly how we might go about this.

7   Analysis of complete interchange

First, let us see what complications arise if we try to account for the coherence of a short but complete interchange. The data cited below comprise the whole of a short speech event between two neighbours, A and B, calling to each other between their allotments. B could not see A, but recognized the voice. The data were not audio-recorded, but were noted down verbatim immediately after the event. It can be assumed that the interchange was recorded word-perfectly. It was impossible to recall the intonation contours used, but utterances printed on separate lines and numbered will be assumed to have been spoken as one separate tone group each.

The interchange is, on the face of it, rather banal. But it is highly structured in some fairly obvious ways, and although it is simple enough to allow different analyses to be proposed and compared, it is rather more complex than may be apparent at first sight.

7.10	A:	John	(1)
		have you got your watch on you	(2)
	B:	yes	(3)
	A:	what time is it	(4)
	B:	five fifteen	(5)
	A:	is it	(6)
	B:	yes	(7)
	A:	thanks	(8)
	B:	OK	(9)

My intuitions would allow various combinations of utterances to be deleted and still leave a well-formed interchange. For example (4-5-8) and (4-5-6-7) seem well-formed, but *(2-6) does not. My intuitions would allow over forty well-formed combinations. However, the superficial banality of the data also allows the possibility of comparison with other very similar interchanges.

The main aim of an analysis of such an interchange must be to account for its perceived coherence: it occurred as a complete speech event, and an analysis should make explicit that it is a well-formed, complete unit. Also, any structural claims should be as powerful as possible and make interesting predictions about other data. And, of course, the analysis, which may well turn out to be wrong in detail, should at least be specific enough to allow counter-examples to be found.

8   *Tests for ±initial*

The definitions of I, R, R/I and so on above are based entirely on logical distinctions. We require also some tests for the defining criteria. A test for ±initial is as follows. An utterance is −initial if its lexis or surface syntax requires to be expanded from preceding utterances, and could not otherwise be understood in isolation. Thus, in the data, (3) can be expanded into (3a) but not (3b):

(3a)   yes I have got my watch on me
(3b)   *yes I'd like a drink

Similarly (5) can be expanded into (5a) but not (5b):

(5a)   it is five fifteen
(5b)   *the train arrives at five fifteen

Similarly (8) can be expanded into (8a) but not (8b):

(8a)   thanks for telling me the time
(8b)   *thanks for the lift

On the other hand, (1), (2) and (4) cannot be expanded in this way, and are therefore +initial. Utterance (9) has no obvious expansion, and it may be best to treat it as a boundary marker for this reason. In this case a closing boundary, although *OK* can also be an opening. Such boundary markers cannot be expanded since they have no lexical content which can be regarded as having been deleted: they are not 'about' anything, but function purely to mark units in the discourse. (Cf. chapter 4.)

I am making the assumption that the expansion of such elliptical utterances is uncontroversial. Of course, such expansion is open-ended. For example, (4) might be expanded as:

(4a)   I ask you what time it is
(4b)   do you know what time it is

and so on. But then any utterance may be expanded with explicit performative verbs in this way. (Cf. Labov and Fanshel, 1977, and McTear, 1979, for a discussion of problems in the open-ended expansion of utterances.)

Although the expansion of elliptical sentences in their discourse context is in principle open-ended, informants will nevertheless usually agree on appropriate expansions. In other words, the correct expansions are themselves amenable to experimental investigation and test. This distinguishes this kind of ellipsis from the ellipsis found on signs and headlines, which do not occur in a discourse sequence; and to which informants do not give replicable expansions. Gunter (1974) distinguishes between these two types of ellipsis, respectively, as contextual and telegraphic. Thus a note to the milkman reading *Two pints today* could be expanded in many ways as, for example:

7.11 $\left\{ \begin{array}{l} \text{(Please) could/would/will you leave} \\ \text{We need/want} \end{array} \right\}$ two pints of milk today

This definition of ±initial suggests a way of defining the exchange as an information unit, in which major information is introduced and then supported by elliptical syntax in the rest of the exchange. There is no room to discuss this further here. (See Berry, 1981a.)

9 Some candidate analyses

Let us now consider various analyses of the data and their advantages and disadvantages.

1   (1) could be regarded as an I which is realized by a Summons, and which gets no R. This would leave us with an ill-formed exchange *[I], but no deviance appears to be recognized by the participants. It also leaves us with two exchanges over the first three utterances, and no account of the relation between them: [I] [I R].

2   Alternatively, (3) could be regarded as both the Answer to the Summons and the response to (2). We now have one item as an element of structure in two different exchanges, one of which is discontinuous.

3   Alternatively, (1) could be regarded as a Summons which gets pushed down to an O(pening) by (2), giving a single exchange: [O I R]. This introduces a new move: O. It also introduces a new concept of a push-down mechanism, where a move is interpreted, then re-interpreted in the light of what follows. Such a concept could, however, be motivated from other data. For example, teachers often ask strings of questions, but pupils only answer the last one: the first questions could be regarded as pushed down to Openings. (Sinclair and Coulthard, 1975: 35.)

4   Various analyses of (4-9) suggest themselves. The simplest might appear to be [I R] [I R] [I R]. But (6) and (8) are non-initial. And this analysis would leave us with three unrelated exchanges, whose coherence would have to be accounted for in some other way, for example, by grammatical cohesion.

5   Alternatively, since (6-7) appear to be deletable as a unit, leaving (4-5-8-9) as well-formed discourse, we might propose [I R [I R] F F]. This would give one exchange embedded within another. Again (6) is coded as I, but is non-initial.

6   Alternatively, we might propose [I R Ir R F F], which accounts for the coherence of (4-9) by analysing them as a single exchange. As I suggested above (9) might more appropriately be regarded as a C(lose).

A candidate analysis is therefore:

[O I R] [I R Ir R F C]

This is compatible with the exchange structures proposed above. But, as we would expect, an attempt at an analysis of a whole speech event, even such a short one, has introduced further complications.

We would further have to account for the relation between the two exchanges. Note here simply that a question such as *Have you got your watch on you?* is predictably heard as a preparatory to a following question.

10   *Eliciting informants' intuitions on discourse*

As I have noted above, intuitions about discourse sequences are unreliable. However, it is possible to place some control on informants' intuitions, by starting from a real piece of data and manipulating it in various ways. (Cf. Gazdar, 1974; Clarke, 1975, for discussions of similar experiments.) One experiment which was tried with the data above was to print the numbered utterances on separate pieces of card, without information about who was speaking, shuffle the pieces and give them to about thirty informants with the following instructions:

1   Try to reconstruct the conversation from the pieces of the jigsaw. (A piece of card does not necessarily represent the whole of a contribution to the conversation. There are no long pauses in the middle of the conversation.) Copy out your conversation and label it "FIRST VERSION".

2   Can you put the conversation together in any *other* way? Copy it out and label it "SECOND VERSION".

3   Which bits of the conversation would you regard as essential? Copy them out and label them "ESSENTIAL ELEMENTS OF CONVERSATION".

4   Is there any order of the bits of the conversation which you
    would regard as impossible? Copy it out and label it "IMPOSSIBLE
    VERSION". Can you say why?

First, none of the informants appeared to have any difficulty in
following the instructions, and produced both plausible and impossible versions. In other words, they appeared to have strong intuitions
about the data. Versions proposed as impossible, for example,
included:

7.12   A: What time is it?
       B: *Yes./*Is it?/*Thanks.
7.13   A: John.
       B: *Is it?

Second, all the informants, in attempting to reconstruct the
original order, produced versions identical or very close to the
original. Versions with minor differences were due to: (1) and (2)
being reversed, which makes no difference to the turn-taking; (8) and
(9) being attributed to one speaker as *ok, thanks*, and the order being
given as (1), (3), (2), i.e.

7.14   A: John.
       B: Yes.

which involves a change at the end. This gives some weight to an
analysis which treats (1) *John* as an I which could be followed by R,
but is not, and is therefore pushed down to O.
    Consider the following subproblem in exchanges such as:

7.15   A: What time is it?
       B: Five fifteen.
       A: Thanks.

Is the *thanks* obligatory? That is, should this be analysed as an
obligatorily three-part exchange [I R/I R], or as an optionally two-
or three-part exchange [I R (F)]? The questionnaire data were
ambiguous. In answering question 3, most informants allowed two-
part exchanges, but a few gave three- or four-part exchanges including
an obligatory *thanks*. Observational data were therefore collected.
Students and colleagues collected naturally occurring instances of
people asking the time: examples of speakers asking them, or
examples overheard. And they noted down a brief description of
who the speakers were and the situation. The findings were quite
clear-cut: two-part exchanges occurred only between family or

friends. But three-part exchanges occurred between both friends and strangers. (Only strangers were offered a *thanks*, but friends were offered other acknowledgements.) With strangers the structure is [I R/I R]; with family or friends it is [I R (F)].

In this way, emerging theory can be made to control data collection. That is, once our emerging concepts have given us precise questions to answer, we can use *theoretical sampling* to collect the data to answer them (Glaser and Strauss, 1967). A next obvious step is to collect data in broadly comparable situations: for example, adult strangers asking each other for well-defined pieces of information in the street and other public places.

11   Concluding comments

I will end with a brief note on a problem which is often raised in connection with the kind of model of exchange structure proposed above: how widely applicable is such a model? It is often argued that not all discourse is as highly structured as this chapter may seem to have proposed and that the concept of exchange is primarily applicable to relatively formal social situations in which a central aim is to formulate and transmit pieces of information. Such situations would include teacher–pupil interaction, doctor–patient consultations, asking strangers for directions and service encounters in shops. The concept is not so obviously applicable to casual conversation between social equals, where the general function of much of the discourse may be phatic and social, rather than to transmit information.

One way in which this objection may be answered is to regard the exchange structures proposed above as a relatively restricted set of possibilities which are generated by a more general exchange structure which has fewer constraints (e.g. as proposed by Burton, 1981b). Often statements about conversational structure are formulated too loosely to allow different descriptions to be compared with any precision. A central aim of discourse analysis should be the development of a formalism which will allow such comparisons.

8

Beneath the Surface of Discourse: Indirection in Speech Acts

If speakers always said what they meant, then there would be few problems for speech act theory or for discourse analysis. But, of course, they do not, and in principle could not, say in so many words exactly what they mean on any occasion of utterance. A central problem for analysis is therefore the depth of indirection involved in much discourse: the distance between what is said and what is meant, and the multiple layers of meaning between the literal propositional meaning of an utterance and the act which it performs in context.

In order to account for the coherence of discourse we need accounts not only of surface lexical and syntactic cohesion, and of logical propositional development. We need also an account of speech acts, indirect speech acts (in which the illocutionary force of an utterance is overlaid by markers of mitigation or politeness), the context-dependence of illocutionary force, and the sequential consequences (predictive power) of certain speech acts. In other words, we have to have multiple theories of discourse coherence.

1 Austin: utterances as actions

It has long been clear that language conveys many different kinds of meaning: propositional, stylistic, social, affective, and so on. However, it was the British philosopher, J. L. Austin (1962) who made very explicit for the first time that there are many different things which speakers can do with words. His most basic insight was that some utterances are not statements or questions about some piece of information, but are actions. Austin pointed out, for example, that if a speaker produces utterances, in appropriate circumstances, such as:

8.1   I bet you a pound that Harry falls off the ladder.

8.2   I promise to play Scrabble with you tomorrow.
8.3   I bequeath you all my back copies of *Playboy*.

then the speaker has not made statements about betting, promising
and bequeathing. Such utterances are a bet, a promise and a bequest.
No sooner said than done. Or, in fact, the saying and the doing are
inseparable in two senses. The acts could not be done without using
language, and the saying counts as the doing.

It would not be possible here to attempt a comprehensive review
of the enormous literature on speech act theory. What I will do is
discuss some aspects of the concept that utterances are actions which
are particularly closely related to the analysis of connected discourse,
and which have tended to be neglected by speech act theory. These
concern mainly: the question of whether such utterances can be
brought fully within linguistic modes of explanation; and the
problems which arise when the concept of speech act is applied to
natural conversation. For it is something of a paradox that speech
act theory emphasizes the uses of language, and in fact applies to
utterances not sentences, but has depended largely on introspective
judgements of isolated sentences. It has largely ignored both
naturally occurring data, and also connected sequences of speech
acts. Problems which arise with naturally occurring connected discourse include: co-operative speech acts performed jointly by more
than one speaker; the use of explicit performatives for reasons of
formality or style; and the great depth of indirection in many speech
acts.

The two classic books on speech act theory are Austin's (1962)
original discussion of 'how to do things with words', and Searle's
(1969) discussion of speech acts. Searle (ed., 1971) contains important papers by Austin, Searle and Strawson. Sadock (1974) is an
important book. Searle (1976) is an important updating of the
theory. Cole and Morgan (eds., 1975) contains several important
papers, especially on indirect speech acts. Cohen (1974) provides a
comprehensive review of work up until that date. And Butler
(1982) provides a review which relates speech act theory to discourse
analysis and is therefore particularly relevant to my concerns here.

2   *Discourse acts and speech acts*

One source of difficulty in discourse analysis is that utterances perform acts at very different levels of abstraction, which can probably
be hierarchically ordered. There is a large literature which emphasizes

that language serves different functions, but such discussions differ greatly in the level of abstraction which they propose. For example, Halliday (e.g. 1970) proposes three broad functions of language: ideational, interpersonal and textual. Jakobson (1960) and Hymes (1962) propose about half a dozen: directive, referential, contextual, and so on (cf. chapter 3, section 6). Whereas Austin (1962) postulates hundreds or even thousands of speech acts, which Searle (1976) then regroups into half a dozen basic categories. It is clear that rather different notions of speech act or language functions are being discussed.

Interpreted in a narrow way, discourse analysis appears to have to do with discourse acts, which are defined entirely according to their internal function within the discourse itself. What I have referred to in chapter 7 as basic discourse categories are basic only in the sense that they organize the discourse itself, by initiating, continuing and terminating exchanges, and so on. Such acts therefore have to do with local organization of sequences of utterances: initiations which require responses, and the like. On the other hand, speech acts, as they have generally been discussed by the speech act philosophers, are rather different. They are defined according to psychological and social functions outside the on-going discourse. They include, for example, the expression of psychological states (e.g. thanking, apologizing), and social acts such as influencing other people's behaviour (e.g. warning, ordering) or making contracts (e.g. promising, naming). Such acts typically have long-term consequences. If you make me a promise, give me a warning or appoint me to a job today, the speech act may still be in force in ten years' time.

Several scholars have pointed to this distinction. Franck (1979) distinguishes conversational moves from speech acts; and Widdowson (1979b: 138) distinguishes interactive acts from illocutionary acts. And Labov and Fanshel (1977: 60) talk of metaactions which regulate the discourse itself by initiating, responding, interrupting or redirecting. The distinction is not always as clear as it might seem however. Much of the speech act literature attempts to define illocutionary acts independently of context. However, in interpreting the illocutionary force of an utterance, hearers often draw on their knowledge of the preceding discourse.

In addition to metaactions and what would normally be called speech acts (e.g. requests), Labov and Fanshel (1977) also identify actions at a deeper socio-psychological level, such as challenges, defences and retreats. In fact, they more or less dismiss the study of discourse acts (metaactions) as a rather superficial and obvious feature of discourse which follows automatically from their analysis of more abstract acts (p. 60, note). This seems rather an unfair dismissal of work such as Sinclair and Coulthard's (1975) which deals precisely with this level of discourse acts. First a very significant percentage of certain kinds of discourse consists precisely of overt signals of discourse organization (cf. chs. 3, 9). Second, these explicit markers of structure are one feature which distinguishes discourse from syntactic structure. And third, in concentrating on a deeper level of socio-psychological interaction, Labov and Fanshel may be giving undue weight to the therapeutic interview which constitutes their data. In fact they admit that even in analysing the challenges and retreats in such psychotherapy, they may be exaggerating the agressive character of the interaction and presenting a level of conflict which it did not have for the participants at the time (p. 345). This is always a danger in microanalysis: that it focuses enormous analytic attention on details of interaction which had no significance at the time. The details may only be observable at all when the discourse is audio-recorded and transcribed and listened to repeatedly. This is not how conversationalists experience interaction in real time. The analysis may, for example, explicitly separate propositions from the modes of mitigation or politeness which co-occur with them. Labov and Fanshel nevertheless claim (p. 360) that all conversation apart from casual encounters between, say, strangers in the street or in shops, are carried out at this great depth of inter-action which is not explained by either discourse acts or illocutionary acts.

3   Austin's theory of speech acts

Austin's original insight was that stating or describing is only one function of language. In fact, he argued, statements (constatives, in Austin's term) do not even have any privileged position. They are often thought of as somehow basic. However, adults do not go around simply making unsolicited statements or describing the world. The important distinction between constatives and performatives is that only constatives can be true or false. Performatives are used to perform actions, and it does not make sense to enquire about their truth conditions. For example, if A says:

8.4   I promise to come.

then it makes no sense for B to say *That's not true.* In saying 8.4, A
has performed the act of promising. B might say *I don't believe you.*
However, this would be to question A's good intentions. Performative utterances may be inadequate in various ways, but they cannot
be untrue. This test would distinguish the constative *I'm sorry* from
the performative *I apologize.* One can say *I'm sorry* without being
sorry at all. However, to say *I apologize* is itself to apologize. One
can of course also *use* the sentence *I'm sorry* in order to perform the
act of apologizing.

A way to reformulate Austin's main point is to show that propositions are distinct from acts. Suppose that a lecturer says:

8.5   Students are a lazy bunch these days.

A student might respond in various ways. He might say:

8.6   That's untrue.

In this case, *that* would refer anaphorically to the propositional
content of the sentence. Truth and falsity are a relevant consideration only when referring to propositions. Speech acts can go wrong
in various ways, but the concept of truth conditions does not apply
to them. An alternative response to 8.5 might be:

8.7   You're always complaining about something.

In this case the word *complaining* refers to the speech act performed,
with no reference to the propositional content.

Lyons (1977: 667ff) has set out a general framework for the
different kinds of entities in the universe of discourse to which
speakers may refer. These include surface linguistic forms,
propositions and speech acts. It is also possible to refer to parts of
utterances or propositions. For example, one could query the scope
of the subject of 8.5:

8.8   Well, *some* students may be.
8.9   That's rather a generalization.

Or one can query the predicate:

8.10   *Lazy* is hardly the word I would use.

Phrased in this way, it should be clear that work on speech acts
can be related to work on textual cohesion, by studying the way in
which speech acts (and other units) are referred to in the course of
conversation. This would avoid the usual focus on the illocutionary

force of contrived and isolated sentences. It would also investigate how conversationalists themselves orient to and formulate speech-act categories in the course of conversation.

Having reformulated Austin's point in this way, by separating the proposition and the speech act conveyed by an utterance, it is also clear that Austin's original distinction between constative and performative is faulty, as Austin himself realized. For the same proposition may be stated, questioned or denied; I may remind you of it, use it as a complaint, and so on. In other words, stating is a speech act like any other. Thus if A says, with or without the explicit performative verb *state*:

8.11   (I state that) students are a lazy bunch these days.

then the truth of the proposition may be queried. However, it cannot be false that A has stated.

From this observation, Austin developed his more general theory of speech acts. Utterances can perform three kinds of act. The locutionary act is the act of saying something: producing a series of sounds which mean something. This is the aspect of language which has been the traditional concern of linguistics. The perlocutionary act produces some effect on hearers. Persuasion is a perlocutionary act: one cannot persuade someone of something just by saying *I persuade you.* Comparable examples are convincing, annoying, frightening and amusing. This has been the traditional concern of rhetoric: the effect of language on the audience. The illocutionary act is performed in saying something, and includes acts such as betting, promising, denying and ordering. Some of the verbs used to label illocutionary acts can themselves be used performatively. Thus, to say *I deny that X* is to deny that X. The distinction between perlocutionary and illocutionary force is not always entirely clear. For example, a request has a part of its essential force the intent to produce an effect on the addressee by getting him to do something. This difficulty in definition again arises from the sequencing of actions which speech act theory has largely ignored. It also arises from the basis of the definitions in speakers' intentions, which are unobservable psychological states.

Speech act philosophy sees language as a set of activities in concrete situations. (Cf. Turner, 1970, for an ethnomethodological development of this point.) Language cannot be reduced to some logical structure which has priority. The propositional and predicate calculus set out valid patterns of formal inference and obviously explain some features of natural language. However, natural language cannot be reduced to the notation of formal logic. Activities cannot be reduced to the formal devices of an ideal language. On the contrary, Austin stressed the great variety of uses which words have, and argued that the hundreds of different uses of language cannot be reduced to just one or two logical, propositional or conceptual uses. This emphasis on the multi-functional nature of language has its own dangers, and Gellner (1959: 191) has criticized what he calls 'the cult of the idiosyncracy of various kinds of use of language' in ordinary language philosophy.

One of the weakest aspects of Austin's theory is that there is apparently no end to the number of speech acts which language may perform. Basically, there are two ways to control the proliferation of linguistic categories. One is distributional. Two potential speech-act categories would be admitted as distinct if they have different discourse consequences. For example, are *hint* and *suggestion* separate speech acts? If it could be shown that they elicit different responses, either verbal or non-verbal, then the answer is clearly 'yes'. However, I can envisage no such differences, and would therefore argue that they are different labels for the same speech act, although they may differ on some related dimension, such as directness or transparency. This way of defining speech acts has been largely ignored by speech act theory, since, as I have already pointed out, it largely ignores the use of speech acts in discourse sequences. (Cf. chapter 4, section 4.)

The second way is to define recognition criteria for the linguistic forms which realize speech-act categories. Functions are controlled by forms. I will discuss some problems with this kind of definition in the next section.

4   Identifying speech acts

If speakers always said what they meant, in the sense of overtly indicating the illocutionary force of their utterances, then again there would be few problems for speech-act theory. However, speakers can perform speech acts without overtly indicating what they are doing: not all utterances have illocutionary force indicating devices (IFIDs, see Searle, 1969: ch. 3). And, conversely, the simple insertion of an explicit performative verb in an utterance need not uniquely determine the illocutionary force of that utterance.

Austin's original examples of speech acts often involve particular set forms of words (sometimes including performative verbs) uttered with well defined meanings in ritual or ceremonial settings. Such examples will inevitably be the clearest cases. They include items such as:

8.12   I name this ship ...
8.13   I pronounce you 'Guilty'. (As said by a judge.)
8.14   I will. (As uttered in a marriage ceremony.)

Alternatively, they involve the use of explicit performative verbs in non-ceremonial settings:

8.15   I promise; I apologize; I warn you; etc.

In general, highly conventionalized settings often provide the easiest cases for identifying the illocutionary force of utterances, whether or not an explicit performative verb occurs. Games provide such clear-cut cases, as when an umpire declares *Out!* or a card-player calls *Snap!* Note, in such cases at least, the close relationship between the speech act and the non-linguistic situation. In fact, to define the meaning of the speech act in such cases would require defining the role of the utterance in the game as a whole, rather than in a discourse sequence. One objection which has been raised against speech-act theory is that it seems inevitably to lead away from language. It does after all point to the relation between acts of language and social acts in general. This makes it questionable whether speech-act theory can be integrated into linguistics. A good place to study such ritualistic utterances is in the situations in which children use formulaic utterances to contract bargains, bets, gain possession of objects and so on. Thus an item such as *Bagsy!* is a prescribed form of words which gives the speaker rights if uttered in appropriate circumstances. Whereas *Bagsy no backs!* asserts the status of a preceding utterance or action by affirming a contract already made. Opie and Opie (1959) give much information on the historical and geographical distribution of such forms in Britain. However, I do not know of any study of their use in connected discourse.

Before emphasizing the indirectness and non-literalness which is often involved in identifying which speech act is being performed, it is worth mentioning that some speech acts can be identified through fixed or partly fixed forms of words or syntactic constructions, even outside highly conventionalized settings. Chomskyan linguistics has often over-emphasized the creativity of everyday language. In practice, a significant percentage of conversational language is highly routinized into pre-fabricated utterances. Thus utterances such as the following are lexicalized in two senses: they are set expressions; and they express commonly occurring meanings. They are neither syntactically nor semantically creative. On the other hand, they are not idioms: their meanings are retrievable from their lexical and syntactic forms; and they are not absolutely fixed in form.

8.16   (In a bar.) Have this one on me.
8.17   I don't believe a word of it.
8.18   Who does he think he is?
8.19   I thought you'd never ask.
8.20   It's very nice to meet you.

A very long list of such common examples could be given. Ervin-Tripp (1976) also argues that non-literal directives with the surface form:

8.21   modal verb + *you* + feasible action

are routinized, and do not have to be interpreted by inference on every occasion of utterance. Therefore, forms such as:

8.22   Can/could/would you do X?

are the unmarked form for requests between adults.

Sociological and anthropological theory recognizes the importance of ritualization in human behaviour. However, recent linguistics has tended only to emphasize the creativity, and to ignore the stereotyping and standardization in much language use. As Halliday (1978: 4) says, 'In real life, most sentences that are uttered are not uttered for the first time. A great deal of discourse is more or less routinized.' We might quibble over the word *most*: however, the balance of routine and creativity is an empirical question which has been neglected.

Austin proposed various tests to identify performative verbs. The simplest is that *hereby* can be inserted before the verb. Thus one can say:

8.23   I hereby promise ... ; I hereby warn you ... ; etc.

but not:

8.24   *I hereby sing.

The use of *hereby* would of course mark the language as stylistically formal, probably written and possibly legal. Speech act theory has generally disregarded the stylistic implications of IFIDs.

Another way to test for performative verbs is to ask whether the saying of an utterance is the only way to perform the act. For example, one cannot apologize, thank or promise without saying something to someone. Whereas one can be sorry, be grateful or intend to do something, without saying anything. This test, incidentally, excludes *threaten* as a performative verb, although Austin regarded it as one. One can threaten someone either verbally or non-verbally, by shaking a fist, for example. (For a detailed discussion of threats, see S. Harris, 1980: ch. 4.) Also, *I threaten you* is only marginally acceptable at best.

A more accurate formulation is that someone must say something in using a performative verb. So one might have:

8.25   A: Do you promise?
        B: (Nods head.)

which commits B to the promise although B has said nothing. In fact, the proposition, the identification of the speech act and the commitment to the speech act may all be separated and distributed across different utterances by different speakers (cf. chapter 6, section 4).

8.26   A: Are you coming?
        B: Yes.
        A: Promise?
        B: Yes.

Since speech-act theory has been based primarily on contrived, isolated sentences, it has largely ignored the ways in which illocutionary acts may be co-operatively constructed across different speakers' utterances. Hancher (1979) discusses several aspects of such co-operative illocutionary acts, which involve more than one agent, and bilateral contracts between speakers.

If a performative verb occurs in first person, simple present tense and in a lone main clause, then it will have performative force. However, other forms may also have performative force, and this complicates their recognition. Examples, from both spoken and written language, include:

8.27   I *can promise* you I'll be there.
8.28   I *will* (now) *ask* Harry to take the chair.
8.29   I *am warning* you not to do that.
8.30   *Warning!* Deep water.
8.31   Passengers *are* (hereby) *warned* not to cross the line.

Some of these forms are also clearly determined partly by the formality of the style involved, a factor which speech act theory has not usually considered.

The easiest speech acts to recognize would appear to be those which contain explicit performative verbs, such as:

8.32   I promise I will come tomorrow.
8.33   I tell you, he's an idiot.
8.34   I insist that he is an American.

However, utterances need not contain explicit performative verbs; and, in addition, omitting the explicit performative verb may actually change the speech act being performed. For example, corresponding forms without a performative verb are:

8.35   I will come tomorrow.
8.36   He's an idiot.
8.37   He is an American.

Arguably, these items 8.32–4 have a different illocutionary force from 8.35–7. At the very least they differ in style and emphasis. In other words, the actual use of explicit performative verbs depends on the formality of the context, on the emphasis expressed or on the function of an utterance in denying a preceding utterance.

Such cases appear to have been ignored by Searle (1969: 68) when he states the principle of expressibility. Searle admits that it is possible to perform an act without using an explicit IFID. However, he then argues that if the illocutionary force of an utterance is not explicit, it can always be made explicit. Whatever can be meant or implied can be said. Austin (1962: 103, 120–1) also held the view that illocutionary forces are conventional in that they can be made explicit by a performative formula. However, it would be quite wrong to think that just adding an IFID to an utterance makes the illocutionary force explicit without otherwise changing its meaning. For example, the following two sentences are not normally used to mean the same thing. They are certainly not interchangeable in the same social or discourse contexts, and would have different responses:

8.38   I'll come tomorrow.
8.39   I hereby promise that I'll come tomorrow.

The differences may be explained via Grice's (1975) maxim 'Be brief'. Speakers do not use extra words without reason: there are no true paraphrases without stylistic changes.

The conclusion here appears to be as follows. To almost every kind of speech act there corresponds a performative verb. Such verbs can be used to refer to the illocutionary force of utterances. For example, if I say:

8.40   I'll come on Tuesday without fail.

but do not come, then you can later accuse me by saying *You promised to come.* Or if I say:

8.41   I'll punch you on the nose.

you can say *Don't threaten me.* Many such verbs can also be used in the performative utterances themselves (although *threat* is a dubious case, as I pointed out above). However, it is important not to confuse the actual verbs with the illocutionary force of the utterance. The two things are closely related, but not always the same thing. Austin himself appears to fall into this confusion when he proposes his classification of performative verbs in English (1962: 150–63). He appears to be classifying surface, lexical verbs in English, not illocutionary forces. Searle's (1976) classification, on the other hand, is of illocutionary forces.

A major problem, then, is the extent to which the illocutionary force of an utterance inheres in an explicit IFID, and to what extent it depends on the conventions of interpretation. It has been pointed out by R. Hudson (1975), Palmer (1976) and Sinclair (1980) that utterances lie on a dimension of lesser or greater ambiguity in conveying illocutionary force. Least ambiguous are the rather rare instances, overemphasized in the literature, in which an explicit first person performative verb is used in a ritual context.

The most serious obstacle to a coherent speech act analysis, on the other hand, is probably such a sentence as Austin's example:

8.42   There's a bull in the field.

In such cases, there is no overt IFID: declarative syntax is typically much more ambiguous than interrogative or imperative. Nor is the sentence part of any well-defined, conventionalized social situation. It is easy enough therefore to imagine different occasions of use on which it could have different illocutionary forces including: casual remark, warning, complaint, order and so on. Such cases also make it clear that illocutionary force is a property of utterances, not sentences, since the same sentence may have different illocutionary forces on different occasions of utterance. It is this ultimate dependence of illocutionary force on non-linguistic context which provides the most serious problem for attempts to integrate speech act theory into linguistics. More generally, such examples raise the question of whether speech act theory can ever be entirely principled, since contexts appear to vary without limit. There therefore appear to be as many speech acts as there are imaginable contexts of utterance.

On the other hand, it is obvious that not all forms can perform all speech acts. Constraints between forms and functions therefore provide an important linguistic study. Consider the oddity of some of the following combinations:

8.43   'Fancy meeting you here!' she exclaimed/?complained/ *asked/*ordered.
8.44   'Have this drink on me,' he offered/?ordered/?complained/ *bet.

Such co-occurrence restrictions can be studied by informant techniques, although experimental methods have not generally been used in speech act theory. However, Butler (1982) has used elicitation techniques to test informants' perceived politeness of utterances and therefore to test for their perception of speech act categories such as order, request and suggestion.

5   Speech acts and social roles

The following complication in speech act theory has been pointed out (e.g. by Cohen, 1974). The felicitous performance of certain speech acts, such as christening, excommunicating people, naming ships and pronouncing people guilty in court, requires that their speakers have social roles bestowed on them by the framework of some social institution. It has been argued that such acts cannot be explained within linguistic theory, since they require special powers to be conferred upon speakers. They do not therefore fall within an individual's normal communicative competence. This argument does not appear to have much force as it stands. Even if I do not have the authority required to marry two people at sea, I may or may not know the forms of words required of each party, and I may still be able to interpret such words correctly if I hear them as a witness or best man.

However, the objection does point out that there is more connection between social roles and speech acts than is often made clear in the literature, and that the correct interpretation of some speech acts requires an understanding of this connection. The study of speech acts is therefore more of a *socio*linguistic enterprise than is often made clear. (Cf. Turner's, 1970, sociological interpretation of

Austin.) For example, speech acts may be classified into acts in which the speaker is speaking on his own behalf, and acts in which he is speaking in a role on behalf of some group. As Hancher (1979) points out, collective speech acts may allow pronominal forms other than first person singular to be used for committing speakers to promises and so on:

8.45   We agree to the proposal.
8.46   We promise to abide by this decision.
8.47   We wish to question your interpretation.

Such cases naturally arise, for example, in a negotiation, where individuals are speaking on behalf of others who have elected them and authorized them to speak on their behalf. In such cases, in fact, first person singular forms may be unusable. See below in 8.64(16) where I cite a piece of data from a trade union spokesman in a negotiation who makes overt references to the fact that he is speaking *from a union point of view*, and therefore to the collective speech act which he is performing. And see also chapter 9 where I discuss some of the surface realizations of prefaces to collective versus personal speech acts. As Goffman (1981: 145) points out, such cases of speaking as the incumbent of a social role show the concept of speaker as an unanalysed folk notion.

In some discourse, the situation is more complex still, for the same speaker may sometimes produce utterances which are to be interpreted as +official since he is speaking as the incumbent of some social role; whereas other utterances may be interpretable as his individual point of view. For example, in a committee meeting, the chairman may sometimes speak as chairman, when opening and closing items in the agenda, and so on. No one else present could felicitously perform such speech acts. Other acts, such as summarizing the mood of the meeting or asking for a participant's point of view, might usually be done by the chairman, but need not be. In other utterances, the chairman might simply make a point in the discussion as an individual committee member.

Here are some examples from a committee meeting recorded in an industrial setting. The meeting was discussing job specifications and wage rates. All the utterances are by the chairman. The clearest chairman-talk consists of explicit control over large scale features of the discourse, such as whole topics on the agenda:

8.48   Ch: well before let me just try and see if: er – – if we need
              to continue at length here – er – – the grading is

> recommended at nine – does anybody – – wish to continue discussion feel that there is a case for other than nine

In 8.49 the chairman again refers to the whole topic under discussion, and marks a major boundary paralinguistically and by *well*:

8.49   Ch: (click) well what's the general feeling then.

In other cases, the chairman summarizes an individual's contribution for the benefit of the meeting, although this example is highly mitigated by an explicit apology as well as by the pseudo-hesitation:

8.50   Ch: well the the answer you *seem* to be giving I'm sorry to be seeming – trying to cross-question you but I think (laughter) people are interested in this one – is really that...

In other utterances, however, the chairman contributes to the discussion as any other committee member might:

8.51   Ch: there is the problem of course that if you bring new people in it takes some time before they've caught up with what's going on...

It would be possible to test the recognition of such utterances by informant techniques. For example, a transcript could be prepared with speakers' names deleted, and informants asked to identify which utterances were spoken by the chairman.

The general point is that there is a relationship between the speech act performed and the social role of the speaker, which has largely been ignored by the speech-act literature. The correct interpretation of the illocutionary force therefore depends both on the linguistic form of the utterance, and also on an understanding of the social network, for example the authority status of speakers. In addition, for a correct interpretation of, say, 8.51, hearers have to be able to recognize whether Ch. is speaking as an individual (in which case the illocutionary force is probably making a point in a discussion), or whether Ch. is speaking in his role as a chairman (in which case the illocutionary force could be summarizing the discussion).

6   Problems for hearers and readers

Given the depth of indirection involved in many utterances, it is not surprising that conversationalists themselves often have difficulties in inferring just what speech act is being performed. This is illustrated in this exchange, noted during a conversation among some postgraduate students. They were discussing participation in seminars. A addresses B:

8.52   A: But, I mean, you've got no compunction about sticking your oar in.
          B: (Says nothing.)
          C: That's a compliment, Dave, work on it.

In isolation, A's remark could have many intended illocutionary forces, including a rebuke.

In seminars with my students, I often find it difficult to convey suggestions which are not interpreted as requests or orders. Students often interpret utterances such as:

8.53   You might be interested in having a look at X's article on this.

as instructions and respond with questions such as:

8.54   Do you want us to read that for the next essay?

They interpret my utterances in accordance with my social role, and given my authority status in that situation, they are very sensitive to interpreting anything possible as an indirect command. Since almost any utterance can be interpreted as a hint to do something, I am often left with little room for manoeuvre.

Addressees also have difficulties in knowing how literally to interpret the propositional content of utterances. It is common for hearers not to be sure how literally something is to be taken. The most elaborate cases of this kind appear in literature, where there is often uncertainty over the 'logical status of fictional discourse' (Searle, 1975b). The most common case is where an author assures readers that his novel is not a true story. Here is an elaborate instance from Priestley (1946):

8.55   Because this novel is written in the first person and its action swings from the West Riding I once knew to the contemporary film world, a special word of caution is probably necessary. This work is pure fiction, containing no autobiographical material, no portraits of actual persons living or dead, no reporting of scenes ever visible to my outward eye. I beg the reader to accept this not as a mere formality but as a solemn assurance.

Note the explicit references to speech acts (e.g. *reporting*) in this quote, and also that it ends with an explicit commitment to the sincerity of the statement itself – in case readers do not know how to interpret the statement! The converse case is rarer, but also occurs. This example is from Hoyle (1966), from the beginning of a science 'fiction' story:

8.56   The 'science' in this book is mostly scaffolding for the story, story-telling in the traditional sense. However, the discussions of the significance of time and of the meaning of conscious-ness are intended to be quite serious, as also are the contents of chapter fourteen.

I make these points to emphasize that the kinds of indirection and interpretative procedures discussed here are not merely an abstruse problem for speech-act philosophy, but can have important conse-quences in the real world. Questions of comprehension and interpretation obviously have important practical consequences in all kinds of teaching, in legal contexts, in cross-cultural communication, and so on. Various sociolinguistic studies have been done on communication problems caused by indirect speech acts: in school classrooms (Willes, 1980), and in courtrooms (S. Harris, 1980). As Harris points out, there has been too much emphasis in the literature on trivial requests to do with passing the salt or taking out the garbage. As a result, the range and complexity of directives in real situations have been underestimated.

Fascinating data on the depth of indirection which may be involved in giving directives has been provided by Lerman (1980) in her analysis of Nixon's language in the Watergate transcripts. She discusses what she regards as the puzzling hesitation, softness, casualness, frivolity and constant mitigation used when the most powerful politician in the Western world gives commands to his aides: what she describes as a maximally distant style.

A social setting in which speakers are likely to be particularly sensitive to possible misinterpretations is a trade union negotiation between management and trade union in industry. Consider this example from an audio-recorded negotiation: at one point the chairman, who is on the management side says:

8.57   what exactly are y: y y you er – asking or or or suggesting here

He explicitly queries both the propositional content of what has been said, and also the illocutionary force, question (or request) or suggestion.

The extract continues as follows: M1 and M2 are management spokesmen, T1 and T2 are trade unionists, and *Ron* is T1's pseudonym.

8.58 M1: what exactly are y: y y you er – asking or or or
            suggesting here Ron   (1)
      T2: well what I'm suggesting is that er – when these
            people are em – offered a job – it's pointed out
            to them what the appropriate union is   (2)
      M2: are we talking the er – the last column   (3)
            (utterances omitted)
      T1: we're not even talking about areas where there's a
            bit of disagreement that's been going on for
            about two years   (4)
            (laughter)
      M1: yes – er   (5)
      M2: I shall need a com ⌈ parison if you (   )   (6)
      M1:   ⌊ I'm not quite sure what
            you – you're asking yet 'cause I mean   (7)
            (utterances omitted)
      M1: but I don't think Ron's asking this point out
            that you ca – can't sort of – do arm twisting
            but I think all you're saying is point out are
            you – ⌈ 'cause   (8)
      T1:   ⌊ we never said twist anybody's arm   (9)
      M1: no I mean Bill was hhh (laugh) worried   (10)

Note simply the considerable hesitation which mitigates M1's request for clarification in (1); that in (2) T1 uses an explicit performative *suggesting*; that in (3) M1 is still questioning the propositional content of the talk, and that T1 explicitly comments on the topic in (4); that in (7) M1 is still querying what is being asked, using a different performative verb from T1. It is obviously not the case that propositional content and illocutionary force are unambiguously retrievable from utterances and clear to all speakers.

7   Finding the answer

I will conclude this chapter by discussing two pieces of data which illustrate some of the problems of identifying the act performed by utterances in naturally occurring discourse. In both cases, the problem arises through the indirection involved: an indirect answer to a question, and an implicit challenge to a proposal.

I discussed in chapter 6 the relation in question–answer (QA) pairs, and suggested that after yes–no questions, following utterances may be interpreted as "yes" or "no", whatever their surface form. It is obvious enough that questions may receive indirect answers. In a QA exchange such as:

8.59   A: Are you coming to the pub tonight?
        B: I've got to work.

the answer will normally be interpreted as "no", and as an elliptical form of some proposition such as "No, because I've got to work". Thus a reason may be substituted for a direct answer, and the hearer left to infer the answer from the reason. In this case, the inference would depend on our knowledge that going to pubs is usually regarded as relaxation, and that this is incompatible with work. It is easy enough to interpret the answer as "yes" if the questioner knows that B is a barman.

There may be further difficulties in interpretation if there is no guarantee that the answer occurs in the utterance following the question. The hearer may have the additional problem of first finding the utterance which conveys the answer. Consider the more complicated piece of data in 8.60 which, I will argue, has the structure Q(X)A, where the inserted sequence X consists of fifteen utterances and several exchanges. They are an extract from a committee meeting audio-recorded in an industrial organization. The meeting was discussing the job-grading and wage-rate of different categories of employee. Ch. is the chairman. Bill has been out of the room to take a telephone call and has therefore missed some preceding discussion.

8.60   Ch: question we put to you is do you agree with
                the unanimous view of the rest of us   (1)
        Bill: hmhmhm (laughs)   (2)
        Ch: he sees the joke   (3)
        Roger: he daren't turn round   (4)
        Bill: what are the what are the s senior
                specification ⌈ clerks   (5)
        Ch: ⌊ I'm sorry I – don't mean to – I
                don't really –   (6)

Dave:	well – ( )	(7)
Ch:	I don't mean to pressurize you	(8)
Dave:	you can say they're coming through as (plant name) six	(9)
Ch:	we have discussed this that's what I'm saying	(10)
Bill:	they're grade six	(11)
Dave:	well – they're b. l. n. grading you see Bill	(12)
Bill:	yeah	(13)
Dave:	which is about	(14)
Bill:	which is equiv – they equate to grade six weekly do they	(15)
Dave:	yeah	(16)
Bill:	well there isn't any ruddy option then is there	(17)
	(laughter)	(18)
Ch:	you're hap – seriously you're ⌈happy with with six ⌊yeah all right	(19)
Bill:	( ) OK	(20)
Ch:	OK the panel ratify this	(21)

One way of understanding the fragment in commonsense terms is to say that at (1) Ch. asks a question, addressed specifically to Bill as the previous context makes clear, and that Bill finally answers it at (17). In the intervening exchanges, Bill shows that he sees the joke (2–4), checks on some items of information in preparation to answering the question (5, 9; 11–13; 15–16), and Ch. apologizes for putting pressure on Bill (6, 8, 10). Participants appear to take (17) as some kind of conclusion to the sequence, since (17) is followed by Ch. checking if Bill is happy with the decision. I want to concentrate on the pair of utterances (1) and (17) and discuss some points involved in the claim that they form a coherent QA pair. In other words, suppose (17) is heard as an answer to (1), then what analysis and operations would this involve?

Something of the complexity of the fragment can be seen by setting it out as follows. The labels are for identification only. I do not wish to attach particular importance to them, except of course to *question* and *answer*. It can be seen that hearers have to deal with overlapping items, interrupted items, and, if my analysis is correct, with discontinuous items.

Ch.	(1)	question
Bill	(2)	laugh
Ch.	(3)	comment
Roger	(4)	comment
Bill	(5)	request for information
Ch.	(6)	apology
Dave	(7)	answer//
Ch.	(8)	apology
Dave	(9)	answer
Ch.	(10)	apology
Bill	(11)	request for confirmation
Dave	(12)	answer
Bill	(13)	accept
Dave	(14)	X//
Bill	(15)	request for confirmation
Dave	(16)	answer
Bill	(17)	answer
	(18)	laughter
Ch.	(19)	request for confirmation
Bill	(20)	answer
Ch.	(21)	{closes item

Where // denotes interrupted item, and where braces denote exchange boundaries. The diagram ignores overlaps.

A possible objection to a structure such as Q(X)A is that the inserted sequence has in some way changed the discourse situation, so that the answer cannot simply pick up where the question left off. Thus a possible adjacent QA pair is:

8.61   Q: Do you agree?
A: Yes.

However, one cannot have just *yes* as item (17) in the present data. In general, short form answers, such as *yes, no, maybe*, do not occur if the answer is separated from its question. In other words there are distributional constraints on the occurrence of elliptical clauses. In items such as *yes* and *no*, everything is elided except the polarity of the clause (cf. chapter 6). This means that in the present data, we do not interpret Bill's *yeah* at (13) as an answer to (1). Routinely, the speaker takes account of the talk between question and answer by marking the answer in some way, but what we can call disjunction marking (DM). So we can propose an obligatory transformational rule of the form:

$$Q(X)A = Q(X)A + DM$$

For the present data, my intuition allows as an adjacent QA pair:

8.62   Q: do you agree with the unanimous view of the rest of us
        A: (well) there in't any ruddy option (is there)

That is, A can include either both or neither *well* or the tag question. But not:

8.63   Q: do you agree with the unanimous view of the rest of us
        A: *(well) there in't any ruddy option *then* (is there)

Then appears to act as a disjunction marker. An alternative realization might be *in that case*. Although *well* and a tag question may typically co-occur with disjunction markers, they are not restricted to occurrence in disjoined items. Another form of disjunction marking is a non-elliptical answer. (Owen, 1981: 112 proposes a similar analysis of disjunction marking.)

The issue of whether (17) is an answer to (1) is, however, still more complex. First, the surface form of (17) is itself a tag question, although I proposed above that the tag is optional. Second, (17) is not literally an answer at all. A literal answer would be some equivalent of *yes I agree*. But (17) is a reason why Bill would answer "yes": the "yes" has to be inferred, and Ch. asks for confirmation of it in (19). As I suggested via the hypothetical example 8.61, reasons are frequently substituted for answers.

Usually, then, it is easy to find answers: they occur immediately after questions. The claim that an answer may occur fifteen utterances after a question involves the claim that position of occurrence is not the only criterion by which answers are recognized. Nor is there any certainty in the form of (17), although it might be regarded as having a partly routinized form for utterances which express unwilling agreement. In order to identify the answer to the question, it would seem that hearers must do a great deal of interpretative work. They must pay attention to the surface form of utterances, although there is no IFID which can identify an answer. Nothing can identify an answer as an isolated utterance, therefore its interpretation involves reference to its position of occurrence. As in this data, the sequence may be complex, and identifying (17) assumes that hearers can do some kind of structural analysis into exchanges of all the intervening utterances. There are many other factors involved in correctly interpreting (17). However, I have already taken the argument far enough to show that it involves reference to discourse sequences of a type which speech act theory has entirely ignored.

8 Motivating underlying acts

I will argue in chapter 9 that a great deal of conversational structure is overtly marked on the surface of discourse. However, if the coherence of a discourse sequence cannot be explained by reference to surface cohesion, then the analysis must rest on underlying acts which are performed by the utterances. It is important to motivate every step away from the surface, from observable cohesive ties to abstract acts. In the data discussed in this section, I will use the evidence of a break in the surface cohesion of a fragment of discourse to try and motivate underlying acts. Labov and Fanshel (1977: 357) recommend this as a general research strategy:

> We have given great attention to breaks in the coherence of surface structure, which provides objective evidence that some relationship more abstract than the surface relations must be found to account for the continued flow of conversation.

I will also argue that it is possible to account for the coherence of the discourse only by supposing that utterances are interpreted simultaneously as acts of different kinds at different levels of abstraction.

The data 8.64 comprise a fragment from a trade union negotiation. The fragment is from near the beginning of the negotiation. The chairman has been talking for several minutes, summarizing the position reached in a previous meeting, and what management are now prepared to offer. The fragment is therefore taken from an intuitively important moment in the discussion: the point where the trade union spokesman breaks in for the first time and takes the floor with a long monologue of his own, after (17). M1 is the chairman, on the management side. T1 is the leader of the negotiation on the trade union side. T2 is his colleague. There were two other management representatives present who do not speak in this extract. Bob is T1's pseudonym.

8.64   M1:   er what I'm asking is   (1)
          in the light of what – has been said – or offered
          today resulting from the last meeting –   (2)

you'll – ll er will drop – any – your objections   (3)
to the contract trainee draughtsman scheme   (4)
so er – er you know this ⌈ is   (5)
T1:   ⌊ you mean *that* –   (6)
(holds up contract paper)
M1:   pardon (1)   (7)
T1:   you mean *that* (1)   (8)
T2:   you're not having that are you –   (9)
M1:   well – again er – ⌈ we've no strong –   (10)
T2:   ⌊ whatever   (11)
M1:   if you want ⌈ us to drop the contract there – Bob   (12)
T1:   ⌊ look – look – let me – let me – let   (13)
M1: ⌈ then er   (14)
T1: ⌊ me – make it – patently clear   (15)
as a – from a union point of view –   (16)
we're not playing with that as a union   (17)

Note, first of all, the lack of connectedness which this fragment shows at surface level. Why does M1 suppose at (12) that T1 wants the contract to be dropped? T1 has not said so in so many words. Certainly T2's utterance (9) is not explicit. So how did M1 interpret him as having meant this? Why does M1 not answer T1's question (6)? Why does T1 interrupt M1 at (13) when M1 appears to be about to make an offer? I will not answer all of these questions fully, but pose them to point out that such questions could not be answered without supposing an underlying structure at least as complex as the one I propose. One could suppose that M1 knew that T1 really meant that he wanted the contract dropped because of previous discussions and because of what he knew of the trade union position. However, this would not solve the problem of how M1 took these particular utterances as expressing this position. How were general principles of interpretation brought to bear on the details of this particular interchange? Expressed in its simplest way, the problem appears to be: why does M1 say (12)?

Let us start with (6) which, intuitively, is the utterance which causes trouble for M1. It is T1's first utterance in the negotiation:

(6)   T1:   you mean *that*

This is intonationally marked as an interrogative so at one level it is a discourse act: a metaquestion or request for clarification. Such questions are privileged in so far as they are much freer in their possibilities of distribution than most questions, and can logically follow any preceding utterance. A negotation is, moreover, a speech event in which the speakers are explicitly oriented to getting things clear (cf. section 6). Thus earlier in this data, M1 has said:

8.65   think it would be useful first of all just to recap on the points you made as I see it – so that eh we can make sure we're all talking about the same thing

This concern would therefore allow T1 to interrupt M1 although he has not finished talking. These observations are sufficient to account for why (6) might occur at this point. I propose below, however, that (6) is not merely a request for clarification: T1 uses (6) and the possibility of placing it here, in order to perform another speech act.

M1 responds with:

(7)   M1:   pardon

M1 does not answer T1's metaquestion, but asks his own meta-question, although it seems unlikely that he has not heard (6) which is very clear on the audio-recording. At (8) T1 does respond to (7):

(8)   T1:   you mean *that*

This seems to be an unproblematic answer to (7), since it is a repetition of (6) with the same intonation. However, exact repetitions do not generally occur in conversation. Labov and Fanshel (1977: 214) observe that 'if a request is repeated in exactly the same words, the action is normally heard as a sharp criticism.' They are discussing requests for action, but the same point holds for other requests for verbal clarification or information. Generally, repetitions are mitigated by changing their surface form. (Cf. also Ochs Keenan, 1977, on the variation of form in repetitions.)

The next utterance is marked by a tag question as an interrogative:

(9)   T2:   you're not having that are you

It is not a straightforward reformulation of (6) or (8), however, but a gloss on what T2 interprets T1 as meaning. A straightforward expansion of (8) might be *do you mean this contract*. But T2 reformulates an underlying meaning. Nevertheless, this expansion is still by no means explicit, and *having that* could mean many things: even the referent of *you* is ambiguous. Note also that we hear (9) as reformulating (8) because of its position in a side sequence. At one level of analysis, a possible structure for (6) to (9) is:

(6)   T1 request for clarification

(7) M1 request for clarification
(8) T1 repetition
(9) T2 reformulation

The sequence continues:

(10) M1: well – again er – we've no strong

The item *well* is ambiguous. When it is utterance-initial, it is always a discourse marker: it refers backwards to some topic that is shared knowledge, marking the utterance as relevant to what has preceded, but admitting a shift in topic. Utterance (10) is also marked by *again* which indicates that (10) is at least the third item in some sequence: it is a modification of some previous statement by M1 following some intervening talk. *Again* can therefore allow the hearer, who has understood M1's previous utterance, to infer the gist of (10) before it is completed: at least it warns the hearer what to expect.

However, our analysis is now in difficulties, since, on the one hand, to propose that *well* marks a shift in topic does not explain the coherence of the fragment. We still have not found a response to (6). If (6) is merely a request for clarification, then we would expect to find M1 saying *yes that's what I mean.* But M1 makes no such remark, and no one appears to miss it. On the other hand, if *well* marks an answer, what is it an answer to? Can we find any way of interpreting (10) as an acceptable answer to (6)? To do this we have to re-analyse (6) to (10) at a deeper level of underlying acts. The simplest way is to return to (6) and to propose an interpretative rule which allows us to hear it as something other than a request for clarification.

Attendance at academic conferences and seminars has convinced me that there is an interpretative rule of discourse that:

> Questions from the floor following the presentation of a paper, will be interpreted as challenges to the position the speaker has presented; and the speaker's response will be interpreted as attempts to defend the presentation.

This might be regarded as a specific example of Labov and Fanshel's (1977: 97) rule for challenging propositions:

> If A asserts a proposition that is supported by A's status, and B questions the proposition, then B is heard as challenging the competence of A in that status.

Speech situations such as academic conferences and trade union negotiations are ones in which speakers are speaking as incumbents of statuses and clearly defines roles: expert, lecturer, chairman, spokesman, and so on. In fact, Labov and Fanshel (p. 124) define challenge as 'any (speech) action that makes problematical the status of the listener'. (For further discussion of the interpretation of utterances as metastatements, and the interpretation of metastatements as evaluative, for example as complaints, criticisms, and so on, see chapter 3, section 9, where I propose a related interpretative rule.) The discourse rules quoted here are clearly *socio*linguistic, since they involve not only speech acts, but refer to the status of speaker and hearer, and therefore to the social structure of power and authority relationships.

Can we find any local justification in the data for interpreting (6) as a challenge? The literal meaning of (9), as a reformulation of an underlying meaning of (6), is at least compatible with interpreting (6) as a challenge: It is direct evidence that T2 takes (6) to be not merely a request for clarification. M1's *pardon* was previously analysed as a metaquestion. But *pardon* is often used when the speaker could, if pressed, repeat what was said: it is often used as a conversational time-gainer. The best local evidence probably occurs in (12) where M1 formulates what T1 might want. T1 has not said what he wants, yet M1 provides us with a translation of what he takes T1 to mean. M1 has apparently heard (6), (8) and (9) as a request to *drop the contract*, which in the context is a challenge: this is logically incompatible with (3–4) in which M1 proposes that the trade union *drop any objections to the contract*. Another way of analysing (6) would therefore be as a pre-challenge, leading to some utterance such as *because if that's what you mean, then we're not having it.*

We therefore have several local cues that my analyst's interpretation is compatible with the participants' interpretation in the situation. These local cues give no indication, however, of how the participants formed their interpretations: to explain this, we must assume an interpretative rule of the type I have proposed. Note also how later utterances have been used to confirm my interpretation of earlier utterances. If we code utterances into acts and exchanges, as I do below, then earlier codings are retrospectively confirmed or denied by later codings. Such a coding reifies precisely this feature of spoken discourse as a process. I prefer to look at such a coding as representing knowledge of structural features of discourse which speakers themselves draw on in making sense of discourse. Some of the points I have made could be summarized in this proposed structure. // indicates interrupted acts. Lines across the page divide exchanges.

		Surface acts	Underlying acts
M1:	so eh – you know this ┌ is	offer//	
T1:	└ you mean that	request clarification	challenge
M1:	pardon	loop	time-gainer
T1:	you mean that	repetition	challenge
T2:	you're not having that are you	reformulation	challenge
M1:	well	starter	
	again er – we've no strong – if you want ┌ us to drop...	offer//	
T1:	└ look – look –	frame	
	let me – let me – let me – make	interruption	
	it patently clear	preface	

It might appear that the kinds of indirectness and ambiguity that I have discussed here are defects of language. If you wish to challenge someone, why not just say so, in so many words? Phrased directly in this way, the answer becomes fairly clear. Language has various ways of allowing speakers to perform speech acts which are then deniable. Labov and Fanshel (1977: 46) point out that intonation provides one such deniable channel of communication, and argue that 'speakers are permitted to deny the communications that they have just made even though they and the hearers may be perfectly well aware of what has just been done.' They argue further that since such paralinguistic channels of communication are inherently ambiguous, they are also inherently gradient, and that this is why there is little agreement on a transcription scheme for paralinguistic behaviour. The more indirectly speech acts are expressed, the more deniable they are by the speaker, and the more options they give to the hearer. Without such imprecision, life in the social world would be impossible. We see here another way in which discourse analysis leads to a study of an essential aspect of social behaviour.

9   Conclusions

Having come this far, it must be admitted that the relations between linguistic forms and actions such as challenges and retreats is unlikely to be entirely definable. The interpretation of such acts will often depend on idiosyncratic or social knowledge, and cannot therefore be formalized, although it is possible to formulate invariant interpretative rules. I have tried to show that the coherence of discourse sometimes depends on acts at such a level of abstraction. The conclusion is not that discourse analysis is not amenable to systematic study. The correct conclusion is that no single level of analysis will ever be able to say all there is to say about a conversation, unless it is of the most routine kind, say, a routine transaction between strangers in a shop, and such interaction, in which nothing of personal or social significance is at stake, has been overemphasized in the literature. We can never learn everything about anything, but it is possible to study with some precision the ambiguity and indirectness which are central to social interaction of any significance.

9

On the Surface of Discourse: Prefaces and Alignments

In the last chapter I discussed the great depth of indirection which is often involved in the expression of speech acts, and the fact that it is often not possible to infer the illocutionary force of an utterance from its surface form in isolation. However, it is important not to go overboard with this idea, and to realize that many aspects of discourse function and sequencing are often overtly signalled in the surface lexis and syntax of discourse.[1]

1   *The indirection argument*

Several researchers have usefully emphasized that the relation between conversational surface forms and underlying meanings, functions and structures, is at best tenuous and at worst downright misleading. This general argument emphasizes that there is no one-to-one correspondence between what is said and what is meant or what is done, and that no analysis of linguistic forms alone will permit an analysis of underlying acts and moves. For example, the social context of the talk must be taken into account in the analysis of discourse structure. I have already discussed in detail some of the reasons for paying attention to indirection in language use. Obviously, such examples provide problems for analysis, but it is important not to conclude immediately that great indirection is characteristic of all discourse.

Consider three statements of what might be called the indirection argument. Goffman (1955), in a famous article, argues that the cues by which an interactant displays his 'line' in a social encounter are displayed not only in talk, but are 'diffusely located in the flow of

---

[1] I take the main title of this chapter and the term *signalling* from Hoey, 1979 and in prep. The rest of my argument is, however, rather different from Hoey's work.

events in the encounter'. Pride (1971: 112) similarly emphasizes the subtlety of this process:

> The language user himself is probably engaged in the more or less continuous exercise ... of handling status relationships of one sort or another, the linguistic markers of which may be *quite minimal* ... (Such markers) matter of great deal, for all their *fleeting appearance* in the stream of speech. (Emphasis added.)

Again, Labov (1972f) asserts that in spoken discourse: 'sequencing rules do not operate between utterances, but between the notions performed with those utterances. In fact, there is *usually no connection between successive utterances* at all' (emphasis added).

Now, such arguments are a necessary corrective to oversimplified attempts at some form of surface text-analysis, which neglect to study the paralinguistic, kinesic and proxemic cues which structure conversation, as well as the social knowledge which contributes to its coherence. On the other hand, a view that minimal and fleeting cues are diffusely located in the flow of events makes no precise analytic claims. In addition, it is methodologically unhelpful: an analyst wants to know what the cues are, and where they are located. (Note, incidentally, that there are no conversational data cited in the articles quoted by Goffman and Pride.) And whilst we have to admit Labov's general argument that discourse analysis must analyse underlying acts, the quote above is overstated, and on a literal reading simply false. In more recent work (Labov and Fanshel, 1977: 350), Labov has in fact modified his position:

> sequencing rules operate between abstract speech actions, and ... they often are arranged in a complex hierarchy. There are no necessary connections between utterances at surface level, though sequencing patterns may take such surface structure into account.

This quote represents the view I take here. Without reverting to a sterile text analysis position (cf. Z. Harris, 1952), I want to emphasize just how many cues of conversational structure are located in what is said. Any discourse analysis must integrate an account of what is said, into an account of what is done: first, because otherwise we have no realization rules or recognition criteria for underlying categories; second, because speakers themselves are condemned to stand by what they say, not by what they mean or intend.

In this book I have neglected almost entirely the kinesic and para-linguistic aspects of conversation. They involve enormous problems of recording, transcription and analysis, which I am not competent to tackle. However, a justification for ignoring them is the great redundancy of most interaction. The same messages are signalled over and over again in different channels: kinesic, intonational and linguistic. It is therefore an empirical question to discover how much is signalled in surface linguistic form.

The correct generalization appears to be as follows. There may be no surface markers relating utterances, and in addition these super-ficial indices (if any) can be deceptive. However, at least in some discourse types, including social casual conversation, a large pro-portion of the talk comprises precisely such superficial indices of underlying organization. I illustrate below what I mean by a large proportion. Much talk has less to do with expressing propositional content than with structuring, repeating, emphasizing, mitigating and generally 'padding'. This sounds like a definition of phatic com-munion (Malinowski, 1923; Laver, 1974), but it is by no means confined to making conversation for its own sake. It is precisely such items which are of interest to the discourse analyst, since they are the items which indicate the underlying structure of the discourse or the underlying functions of individual utterances. The amount and use of such signals of discourse function and structure are also, however, of great sociological interest. Mitigation, in particular, is a basic interactive dimension, as Labov and Fanshel (1977: 84) argue. This is one reason for the great concern with indirection in the literature on speech acts, given that one of the most obvious means of mitigation is to leave things unsaid (Labov and Fanshel, 1977: 336). However, such mitigation is also expressed on the surface. As a speech action which makes the social world tolerable, mitigation is a central aspect of much social behaviour, and discourse analysis can contribute significantly to its study.

2   Limitations on idealized data

One reason why much work on speech act theory and pragmatics has failed to look for overt surface signals of conversational organization is that it is usually based on invented data. (This criticism does not,

of course, apply to Goffman and Labov, although Goffman often
fails to cite data in a form which allows his analyses to be replicated.)

For example, N. Smith and Wilson (1979: 174) invite us to consider how B might be interpreted as a coherent response to A:

9.1   A: Where's my box of chocolates?
        B: Where are the snows of yesteryear?

It is an important issue that part of our discourse competence
involves an ability to discover discourse coherence where it is not
evident in the surface lexical or propositional cohesion. On the other
hand, it is evident that such invented data have been artificially
purified of all possible surface connections in order to make precisely
such a point. And in practice, hearers usually do have a lot of help
from surface markers in interpreting the conversational point of
utterances. (Such examples as 9.1 are also highly idealized by being
presented as isolated exchanges: hearers usually also have help from
surrounding discourse or social context, although I will not discuss
this here.) Here are two other examples of well-known invented
exchanges from the literature on indirect speech acts and implicatures, similarly stripped of almost all signals of surface cohesion
(from Searle, 1975a: 61; and Grice, 1975: 51):

9.2   A: Let's go to the movies tonight.
        B: I have to study for an exam.
9.3   A: Smith doesn't seem to have a girlfriend these days.
        B: He has been paying a lot of visits to New York lately.

Such contrived examples might give the impression that people
characteristically talk in juxtaposed sentences expressing propositions, but stripped of almost all signals of speech act category
(such as a recognizable IFID) or discourse sequence (such as ellipsis
or a discourse marker such as *well*). However, in general, people do
not talk as enigmatically as speech-act theory often implies, and life
would be intolerable if they did! Much of the work on conversational
maxims by Grice and others, and on indirect speech acts by Searle
and others, centres precisely on maxims and procedures which may
relate utterances which, on the face of it, violate semantic and
pragmatic requirements of relevance. Their general position therefore
requires deliberately contriving sentences which have no overt links
between them.

(Crystal, 1980, similarly points out that when contrived intuitive
data are cited in sentence grammar, adverbials are usually omitted
from clause structure unless they are being specifically discussed,

although they are very common in conversational English. Sentence adverbials often signal discourse organization: cf. chapter 4.)

Another danger, discussed by Labov and Fanshel (1977: 352–3) is that if interaction is, as it were, stripped to its logical and semantic content, it may appear much more aggressive than the original. The reason is the number of markers of mitigation which characterize most conversation between adult social equals. Thus 9.1 above is easily interpretable as ironic, and 9.2 as abrupt or short-tempered. (Wooton, in press, and Pomerantz, 1975, provide data on the ways in which disagreements or refusals are mitigated in conversations between adult and child or between adults.)

Rather more characteristic of much real discourse are exchanges such as the following, recorded in a committeee meeting:

9.4   A: there was another person somebody you were going to
              phone – or was that the ⌈ that was the same one wasn't it
        B: ⌊ well I
        A: yes the unit supervisor
        B: yeah that's right well he – er again er – I've got hold of
              Peter now because ...

A 'cleaned up' version of this QA exchange, giving only propositional content might look like this:

9.5   A: "Were you going to ring the unit supervisor?"
        B: "Yes."

However, a major topic for discourse analysis is to study how such propositional content is actually expressed in interaction. In this case, there is considerable redundancy: for example, both *yes* and *that's right* convey the same propositional information. *Well*, repeated twice, marks the answer as relevant to what has gone before, but admits a slight change in topic (cf. chapter 4, section 1). And *again* indicates that the point of the answer is comparable to a previous utterance, so giving hearers some help in predicting what will be said.

3   *Formulating turns at talk*

It is interesting, then, to study how the point of an utterance may be formulated in its own surface structure, or in the surface form of an adjacent utterance. Sacks (1967–72) has discussed in detail the ways in which conversationalists display in their utterances how they have

understood something. We clearly cannot directly observe conversationalists' interpretations. However, Sacks argues that we can
observe the products of such interpretations, and how such analyses
are made available and displayed to others. Garfinkel and Sacks
(1970) also discuss how turns at talk may be 'formulated'.

One way of looking at any utterance is to study how it displays an
analysis of a preceding or following utterance. For example, the form
of a response may display how a preceding initiation has been
interpreted by the answerer.

9.6	Are you doing anything tonight?	I
	John's coming round.	R1
	What have you got in mind?	R2
	Mind your own business.	R3

These three possible answers display different interpretations. R1
treats I as a question seeking information. R2 treats it as a pre-
invitation, predicting that some other question, request, invitation or
whatever will follow. R3 treats it as prying, and rejects the pre-
conditions for asking the question. R1 might also assume a following
invitation, but this is not displayed in its form.

Further a speaker's utterance may convey more or less explicitly
the illocutionary force intended in the utterance being produced.
An obvious, but not typical case, would be the use of an explicit
performative verb. For example, consider this particularly explicit
example from a trade union negotation:

9.7   no but what you said Mr Jones of course doesn't quite tie
        up with the objection I raised

The speaker signals this utterance as at least the fourth in a sequence:
some initial utterance, followed by an utterance characterized with
the illocutionary force of raising an objection, followed by what
Mr Jones said which is characterized as an inadequate response to the
objection, followed by the present utterance which rejects this
response:

X:	utterance
Speaker:	objection
Mr Jones:	inadequate answer
Speaker:	rejection of answer

One might also predict that the speaker will continue to restate or
reformulate his objection: the utterance beginning therefore also

gives hearers clues as to both the illocutionary force and propositional content of the coming utterance.

This is a comparable example, from the same meeting. T1 is a trade union spokesman; M1 and M2 are management spokesmen:

9.8   T1:   (long monologue closes)
we're not gonna take up an inflexible attitude but we are going to be pretty difficult over that one
M1:   yes well
M2:   Mr Mr Bolton can I - please explain our acute problem in engineering er - you're not correct to say that there's now a surplus...

Here M2 both prefaces his own utterance as an explanation, and questions the propositional content of T1's utterance and provides a summary of it.

Such observations seem in many ways a more hopeful approach to a naturalistic study of illocutionary force than the speech act approach of trying to specify speakers' intentions and the sincerity conditions for acts. Such psychological phenomena are unobservable. However, a study of how speakers indicate what point they have grasped or intend can do two things. First, it can provide a way of studying how participants display their own interpretations of discourse, in the sense of how they formulate the point of utterances they produce and hear, without forcing the analyst's interpretations on the discourse. (Cf. especially Schegloff and Sacks, 1973.) Second, it can provide an analysis of one pervasive way in which utterances are chained, in at least certain discourse types.

Such signals cannot, of course, always be taken at their face value. It is a frequent commonsense observation that speakers often get into the stream of conversation by prefacing their utterance in a way which claims a relation to preceding utterances, but then go on to say something which turns out to have no such obvious link. This is a well known tactic in meetings. Thus a speaker might begin an utterance by saying:

9.9   yes in theory this should be the case and I believe for instance...

(example from a radio discussion), or:

9.10   I think we come back to the point you originally made and...

(example from a committee meeting), and then use this superficial linking device as a springboard to turn the conversation to the speaker's own topic. If we look at utterances in this way, we are looking at speakers' own orientations to discourse sequencing, but such prefaces can be used strategically. This again (cf. chapter 5, section 10) illustrates a difference between discourse and syntax: discourse rules may be used strategically. The same is true of the following examples, all from a radio discussion:

9.11   that's only true if you assume that ...
9.12   what is certainly true is that ...
9.13   but are we therefore saying that ...
9.14   but that isn't to say that ...
9.15   but in that case ...
9.16   but what I do believe is that ...
9.17   also perhaps it's ...

Summarizing some of these points, I am proposing that moves in an exchange can be internally structured as follows:

$$\text{move} = (\overrightarrow{\text{preface}}) \text{ continuation}$$

That is, prefaces are optional but very frequent in some speech events. The preface refers back to the previous talk, if only to disassociate the speaker from it, and predicts a continuation of the utterance. The continuations need not be sequentially related to each other, although they may be, for example through lexical cohesion. Preface and continuation could therefore be regarded as acts which are constituents of moves. Prefaces are bound acts. (Edmondson, 1981: 84 makes a similar suggestion.)

4   Prefaces

We need now a more explicit definition of such utterance-initial prefaces. It is intuitively obvious that there is a large class of such items, including: joke prefaces (e.g. *did you hear the one about ...?*), story prefaces (e.g. *I meant to tell you ...*) and topic markers (e.g. *you know we were talking about ...*). (Cf. Sacks, 1967–72). Schegloff and Sacks (1973) identify an important class of conversational items which they call *misplacement markers.* They give as an example *by the way ...* and point out that such items are used to mark utterances which occur out of sequence. More precisely, speakers use such items to indicate to hearers that they should not attempt to use placement in sequence, in order to analyse the point or illocutionary force of the following utterance. They mark a break in the surface utterance-by-utterance cohesion. Sinclair and Coulthard (1975) identify *frames* in classroom discourse (e.g. *now then* ..., *right* ...). These could be regarded as a type of misplacement marker. Since they are boundary markers, by definition they tell hearers that what is coming is not simply linked sequentially to the previous utterance. The use of any misplacement marker also implies that the speaker is assuming control over conversational structure at a high level: not simply taking advantage of an opening set up by the previous utterance. Similarly, Labov and Fanshel (1977: 156) use the term *discourse marker* for items such as *well* and *now*, when they are used to indicate a shift in topic.

Studying such structural markers therefore provides a direct way of studying an aspect of how people listen to each other: the kinds of abstract discourse structures they listen for. By definition, such markers, and misplacement prefaces which I define below, are items whose position, and perceived relevance, cannot be accounted for by an analysis which chains utterances only utterance-by-utterance in a purely linear way. Such items are markers of a hierarchic discourse structure, since at least some of them mark the boundaries of units larger than moves or exchanges.

In data I have studied from committee meetings, if speakers are going to produce an utterance which is out of place in this sense, they typically preface it by an elaborate item such as:

9.18   just one other comment – Mike – er – you asked just now what ...

9.19   can I – I must just say that – I think that ...

9.20   John – you know this other information ...

Such items claim their lack of connectedness to the immediately preceding talk as recognized and therefore accountable. The form of these examples is probably intuitively obvious, but it is possible to define more clearly the form of misplacement prefaces. For these data from meetings, and probably more generally for speech events such as academic seminar or serious discussion, the full form of a misplacement preface is:

1   term of address
2   mitigation
3   account
4   placement marker
5   self-referential metastatement
6   metareference to other speaker's talk

This realization statement is to be read as follows: Such prefaces only occur in formal speech events. All items are optional, but several typically co-occur. The order of the items is not fixed, and markers of mitigation in particular may be distributed across the whole utterance. (In fact, some markers of mitigation, such as intonation and voice quality are non-segmental in any case.) The labels are numbered for reference to the examples below. The labels should be self-explanatory in conjunction with the examples, and all items, except 2, have clear lexical realizations.

A hypothetical full form of such a preface might be:

9.21   1   John –   2   er I think perhaps   3   it would be useful
        4   before we go any further   5   if I sum up   6   some of
        the things Harry was saying . . . .

Here are some real examples from the data:

9.22   2   think   3   it would be useful   4   first of all   2   just
        5   to recap . . .
9.23   4   at this point   2   I think   3   it's worthwhile   2   er –
        5   stressing . . .
9.24   2   I think   6   this has been said to you   3   before . . .
9.25   2   I think   3   bef – time is probably appropriate   4   at
        this point –   5   if I could have a chart put up and   5   go
        through   6   your proposal . . . .
9.26   2   well do you think I could   5   clarify the situation   2
        as we see it   2   just . . .
9.27   5   one comment   1   Mike   2   – er –   6   you asked me
        4   just now what . . .
9.28   3   and the thing is that – as you pro –   2   to just   5   give
        you   3   a little bit of history   2   as you know . . .

As I discussed in chapter 3, some speech events are characterized by much overt signalling of discourse organization. S. Harris (1980) argues that overt references to the discourse and to the speech acts performed are common in courts of law. Thus a magistrate might say to a defendant:

9.29   I'm putting it to you again . . .

However, defendants do not preface utterances with forms such as *I want to make it clear*, although in terms of propositional content alone, there is every reason for using such a preface.

A subcategory of such prefaces is interruption prefaces. Interruptions are an important turn-taking mechanism in certain speech situations, but are an almost entirely unstudied aspect of conversation. (However, see Jefferson, 1973, and Lycan, 1977, for some discussion.) Interruptions turn out to be a very complex speech act. They are clearly not simply defined by the mere overlap of two speakers in time. The interpretation of an utterance as an interruption depends on a complex of facts, including the status of the speakers, and the perceived relevance of the utterance, which relates interruptions to the kind of preface discussed here. Interruptions could be studied from many points of view: their synchronization in time; the points, for example defined syntactically, at which speakers tend to interrupt; whether speakers of higher status interrupt differently from speakers of lower status; and recognizable prefaces (e.g. *could I just come in there? ...*).

There are various surface markers which typically preface utterances designed to break into the flow of discourse. Examples are:

9.30   can I add to that er ...
9.31   can I ask organization-wise why ...
9.32   we've got two people in sales if I can just come in here ...
9.33   if I could ask a question again ...
9.34   look – look – let me – let me – make it patently clear ...

There is probably no way of specifying all the surface forms that an interruption preface will take. On the other hand a large number have a form which makes them a subcategory of the type of preface defined above:

1   term of address
2   can I/could I/I must/let me (i.e. forms of mitigation)
5   self-referential metastatement

In addition the first few syllables are often repeated.

5   *Alignments*

Another type of preface could be called personal point of view prefaces. In speaking, speakers may indicate that their utterances are personal statements, and not to be aligned with the statements of others, as when a speaker says: *personally I think ...* Such personal point of view prefaces are closely related to the prefaces discussed above, since again they indicate a break in the perceived topical coherence of the discourse. Goffman (1981: 285) has discussed such disclaimers, and gives examples such as: *if I may express an opinion* ... Keller (1979) also discusses what he calls conversational gambits and semantic introducers such as: *the way I look at it ...*

Other such examples from meetings are:

9.35   I'm rather unhappy about this because er I would like ...
9.36   personally I think we really ...
9.37   I don't think it really ...
9.38   my real opinion is ...

Alternatively, speakers may indicate that they are not speaking as individuals, but that their utterances are official, in the sense that they are speech acts performed on behalf of a group. Thus a trade union spokesman may preface an utterance by saying:

9.39   let me make it perfectly clear from a union point of view

(Cf. example 8.64.)

Alternatively again, speakers may indicate that they wish to align their utterances with those of other speakers present, by saying, for example, after another speaker's utterance:

9.40   that's the point I was going to make

The previous section discussed ways of signalling breaks in discourse coherence. This section discusses such endorsements, where the central or only function of an utterance is to endorse a previous one.

There are many ways of supporting another speaker's talk. Moerman (1973) gives one kind of example as follows. He repeats Sacks' point that stories told in conversation tend to occur in 'clumps', and that a story will be designed to fit previous stories by being similar to them in recognizable ways:

> To tell a noticeably second story is not only to acknowledge that there has been a first, ... for it is to endorse in the strongest way possible, by doing the same thing oneself, that the first was socially proper.

Clearly, a story does much more than simply endorse a previous story. However, some utterances have only or primarily a meta-communicative, endorsing function, and it is such utterances that I will define more closely below.

Consider, as an initial example, this fragment from a committee meeting. The discussion is about job gradings, and *ten* represents a possible grading.

9.41   A: ... then you look at the one they've recommended for ten
        B: that's a good point Russ
        A: not very much there at all
        B: you're quite right yes

B aligns himself with A's utterances, accepting them into the discourse, supporting them as *a good point* and as *quite right*. A possible functional gloss for such utterances might be: "I wish to be associated with that utterance" or "I'd have said that if I'd thought of it."

Goffman has argued that the ways in which speakers support and endorse each others' talk is a very general organizational feature of conversation. He writes (1955), for example, 'mutual acceptance ... where everyone temporarily accepts everyone else's line ... seems to be a basic structural feature of interaction.' As with much of Goffman's work, these remarks are very suggestive, but he fails to specify exactly how ritual equilibrium is signalled in the details of actual talk. However, an analysis of discourse can study the ways in which talk is pursued 'with ritual care' for other conversationalists.

Endorsements are, then, a category of great potential sociological interest. Their function is not merely to convey propositional content, but to take up an alignment, to make a commitment to a position, to claim fellowship or form alliances. As Moerman (1973) says:

It seems impossible to 'just talk' ... without thereby also doing things such as: claiming fellowship, sharing superiority, enacting roles, insulting, forming alliances, etc.

If such notions of ritual support are developed, then a large and apparently disparate set of other observations can be brought together. Other closely related concepts are: social solidarity, as signalled for example by sociocentric sequences (e.g. *you know*) (Bernstein, 1971a); orientation and convergence between speakers, as signalled by lexico-referential repetition across different speakers (Sinclair and Coulthard, 1975); markers of involvement between speakers (McIntosh, 1963). If we then accept Bernstein's formulation that social solidarity amounts to putting the *we* above the *I*, then other research still is seen to be closely related. For example, Furlong (1976), Mishler (1972) and Torode (1976) have all proposed independently in studies of classroom interaction, that the use of *we* and *I* are important signals of social cohesion of distance between speakers. The work of R. Brown and Gilman (1960) on the use of pronouns of address is also closely related here.

Concepts such as alignment, convergence and endorsement are important for another reason. They deal directly with interaction and communication between speakers: that is, they deal directly with signals of what participants think they have communicated to each other, or with signals of when speakers think they are on the same wavelength (cf. chapter 3). This involves serving the meta-interactional function of accepting utterances into the ongoing discourse. Also, endorsements are a way in which mini-topics are established, sustained and defined for a speech event. What endorsements do is ratify or legitimate particular points, to help to ensure that remarks do not slip by unnoticed. To say *That's a point!* is explicitly to define a contribution as being relevant and worth talking about. In most written language, at least formally published articles and books, topics are given, often stated in advance, summarized or at least alluded to in titles, abstracts and initial paragraphs. In spoken interaction, however, topics are determined in advance only for some kinds of speech event, for example, committee meetings, seminars and lectures and even here the content of individual contributions is managed utterance by utterance. Dascal and Katriel (1979: 225) point out that there are different terms in English for speech events, according to whether the topic is perceived as well-defined. Discussions have well-defined topics, chats do not, and conversations are neutral in this respect. Thus it is odd to say: 'Our chat was very much to the point.' But in spoken interaction, topics do not remain constant: each initiation raises a new mini-topic and this has to be negotiated each time.

6   Acknowledge, accept and endorse

I now have to define more explicitly the form and function of endorsements. (Cf. Stubbs, 1974; Coulthard, 1981.)[2] Acknowledge,

[2] Section 6 of this chapter, and some material elsewhere in this book, develops work in Stubbs (1974). This work is extensively quoted without acknowledgement by Coulthard (1981: 24–5, 28–30).

accept and endorse are all metainteractional moves which accept a preceding utterance into the discourse, by minimally confirming that it has been heard, by more explicitly accepting it as relevant, or by more enthusiastically endorsing it. These moves form a cline, but can be distinguished as follows, both in terms of their function or semantic content, and also in terms of their formal exponents.

Acknowledge is the minimal purely metainteractional category of move, which does no more than indicate that an utterance has been heard and accepted into the stream of talk, and thus indicates continued auditory presence. Such an item often simply fits into the phonological rhythm of the discourse. It has no propositional content, and claims merely to have heard a preceding utterance. A functional gloss might be: "I am still listening." Its exponents are a closed class of items including *yeah*, *uhuh* and *mm*, with falling tone and mid or low pitch.

Accept is a slightly more committed category of move which claims understanding of the propositional content of the preceding utterance. A gloss might be "I understand what you have just said and this is news to me" (e.g. *Oh, I see*), or "I understand and this is no news" (e.g. *Yes, quite!*). However, it does not prove understanding, since a speaker may say *Oh, I see!* without having understood anything (cf. Sacks, 1967–72). Exponents are again a closed class of items, including *yeah*; *OK*; *yeah, I know*.

Endorse is a category which explicitly supports preceding utterances. It is a move which backs up, adds weight to, approves, upholds, chimes in with, ratifies or recognizes as relevant previous talk. Examples given above were *Yeah that's a point* and *You're quite right yes*. A possible gloss is: "I understand what you have said and think it is a good point." Such an utterance therefore both supports the propositional content of a preceding utterance, and also has its own propositional content. A test for this claim is that an endorsement could be given different paraphrases even out of context. The set of exponents cannot be a closed class, because of the surface syntactic variation possible, for example:

9.42   (that's) a (very) good/excellent point, (isn't it?)/(don't you think?)
9.43   I quite/entirely/absolutely agree
9.44   you're quite/absolutely right/correct

Nevertheless, it is possible to list several recognition criteria. The following list comprises groups of specific items which all occur in audio-recorded informal committees. Some items can occur either independently or as utterance prefaces:

(yes)
$\begin{cases} \text{that's right} \\ \text{you're quite right} \\ \text{that's a (good) point/thought} \\ \text{this is the point I was going to make} \\ \text{I think so too} \end{cases}$

Other items are utterance-initial:

(yes) (well)
$\begin{cases} \text{because} \dots \\ \text{I would (like to) have} \dots \\ \text{I reckon} \dots \\ \text{I was going to say} \dots \\ \text{I was thinking that} \dots \end{cases}$

Alternatively there may be a long item between *yes* and *because*:

(yes)
$\begin{cases} \text{partial repetition} \\ \text{sentence completion} \\ \text{sentence continuation} \end{cases}$ because $\begin{cases} \text{one of the above} \\ \text{items} \end{cases}$

Yes is optional, but usually occurs. *Yes* may come after the items listed, but usually occurs before. *Yes* on its own may endorse an utterance, but this could clearly be ambiguous and could be an acknowledge or accept. Whilst in principle the category of endorse is open-ended, in practice a small number of partly routinized forms are used for the majority of cases. The following realization statement would allow the majority of endorsements to be correctly identified:

(yes) (well)
$\begin{cases} \text{X right} \dots \\ \text{X point} \dots \\ \text{I} \dots \\ \text{because} \dots \\ \text{(repetition of part of preceding utterance)} \end{cases}$

where X = anything; and *right, point, I* and *because* are characteristic lexical items.

In conclusion, I append a few extracts of data to provide some examples of endorsements in the context of the utterance they endorse. I have chosen examples of exchanges which illustrate that speakers can endorse endorsements: either mutually, A and B engaging in a little mutually supportive ritual; or with different speakers endorsing one utterance.

9.45	A:	I think that's a nine	(1)
	B:	yes I think so too because ...	(2)

(2) endorses (1) as signalled by *yes*, plus lexical repetition, plus the explicit *I think so too*, plus *because*.

9.46	A:	looks a bit	(1)
	?:	e : r	(2)
	B:	I was going to say it looks a bit heavy doesn't it	(3)
	C:	⌈ the reason	(4)
	A:	it looks a bit ⌊ weird doesn't it	(5)

B endorses A, then A endorses B, i.e. (3) endorses (1) as marked by an explicit *I was going to say*, plus sentence completion, plus repetition. (5) endorses (3) as marked by repetition.

9.47	A:	... and if they don't like they er	(1)
	B:	they'll squeak	(2)
	A:	they know what they can do	(3)

(2) proposes a sentence-completion for (1), and (2) is then itself endorsed by (3) which is A's own sentence-completion.

9.48	A:	... already presented with a very complicated document – er	(1)
	B:	with a long history	(2)
	C:	with a long history th th this is the point and and it struck me	(3)

(2) endorses (1) by a sentence-continuation. (3) also thus endorses (1). But (3) also endorses (2) by repetition, plus an explicit *this is the point*.

9.49	A:	I can't remember the title now	(1)
	B:	supplier – progress field representative part sales rep	(2)
	C:	that's the one that	(3)
	B:	part sales rep ⌈ UK	(4)
	C:	⌊ I was thinking that – that's the	(5)
	D:	maybe that was the one you had in mind	(6)
	C:	that was the one that the guy came up to talk ⌈ about	(7)
	B:	⌊ that's right yeah	(8)

A: yeah – tha – yeah that's right sorry I'm – they did
       include in that part of their that's right   (9)
C: and they were reps   (10)

This extract illustrates how endorsements may continue over several utterances, in a kind of group think process, with participants explicitly trying to work out what others *have in mind* (6).

In summary, it is possible to define an exchange as comprising an initiation and those utterances which support its preconditions, presuppositions and so on (cf. chapters 6 and 7). There are various ways of supporting a preceding utterance, but one set of options is to produce an utterance whose function is purely to accept the preceding utterance into the discourse, and it is possible to define such utterances functionally, semantically and formally.

7   *Conclusion*

I have made two main points in this chapter. First, it is important to study how speakers signal the organization and illocutionary force of their utterances in overt ways. This aspect of discourse has tended to be neglected by much of speech act theory, which has largely relied on contrived and idealized data. Second, a study of such overt signals of discourse organization provides a precise and explicit way of studying topics of great sociological interest, including how discourse displays alignments between speakers, and how it signals social relationship through markers of mitigation.

10

Stir until the Plot Thickens: the Propositional Analysis of Text

This chapter analyses some features of a short story by Hemingway and bases a literary interpretation of the story on the analysis. This might seem rather a long way from the normal concerns of sociolinguistics, and from the analysis of spoken, interactive discourse discussed in the rest of this book. However, it is not adequate to separate analyses of spoken, written and literary discourse, and I will show that there are interpretative procedures, particularly concerned with the interpretation of ambiguous and indirect speech acts, which are common to both spoken and written literary language. In particular, it is obvious that story telling is common to both spoken and written language. (See also section 13.)

1   A method for investigating narrative structure

This chapter is about ways of studying the organization of stories or narratives, especially ways of investigating the concept of the plot of a story.

There are no well-developed methods for analysing narrative structure. I do not mean that no work at all has been done on analysing narratives, but that there is little consensus on how one might go about the analysis: no firm agreement even on what the units of a narrative might be. This chapter is therefore concerned with developing a method for doing such analyses and for working out the organization or plot of narratives. The chapter is therefore primarily methodological or procedural: hence the title – stir until the plot thickens.[1] We require recipes for making good plot summaries. And we also want to be able to specify ways to spoil the broth: that is, we want to be able to predict what will be regarded as deviant or poor plot summaries.

[1] I owe the title of the chapter and much of the original plot to Deirdre Burton.

The argument should be of interest at several different levels. At the most obvious level, it provides a close analysis of a particular literary text, a short story by Hemingway, and an interpretation of this text. It should be of more general interest to literary critics, since it provides a way of discussing certain kinds of ambiguity in texts, and a way of discussing what is and is not crucial to the interpretation of narratives. The argument should also be of interest to linguists, since ways of describing the semantic structure of texts are poorly understood, although of great importance to our understanding of how language is used. (Cf. section 14 for references to related work on the semantic organization of texts.) And it should also be of interest to teachers, since a common activity in much teaching or examining requires students to make summaries of different kinds of material. I will make some apparently abstruse points about semantics and the propositional structure of texts. I will then try to show that these points, are, after all, not as abstruse as they seem, and can illuminate some very common features of everyday story telling – not to mention telling lies! (The implications of this kind of work for teachers are set out at length in Stubbs, 1982 and in press.)

2 Literary competence

The basic argument is as follows. Competent readers of stories are able to identify the plot, distinguish the plot from background information, summarize the story, discuss the adequacy of such summaries, decide whether two summaries are equivalent, identify borderline cases, and so on. This ability is part of our literary competence, and the organization of plots or narrative structure must therefore, in principle, be analysable. This argument is put forward by Culler (1975: 205).

What we require therefore is a way of collecting evidence about this competence. The procedure which I adopted was as follows: I gave readers copies of *Cat in the Rain*, a short story of around a thousand words by Hemingway, with instructions to make two summaries of the plot of the story. The informants were schoolteachers and university students and lecturers, readers who could be expected to have the kind of competence which I wished to investigate. There would have been little point, at least initially, of giving the task to school pupils or foreign learners, who might not have the literary ability which I wanted to study. The exact instructions were:

> Read the story and summarize the plot. The summaries must be accurate – that is, other people should be willing to accept your summary as a fair summary. Make two summaries, one of less than 60 words and one of less than 25 words.

Note the following points about these instructions. First, the instructions are vague, but deliberately so, since the aim is to investigate informants' understanding of plots. More precise instructions, including, for example, some definition of plot, could have imposed my preconceived ideas on informants. Despite this vagueness, they appear to be entirely meaningful and precise to informants. They also appear to be interpreted in an almost identical fashion by informants, since the summaries which are produced are all very similar.

What appears to happen is therefore as follows. People respond to the ill-defined instruction in well-defined ways, and produce summaries. These summaries are people's models of the original story: simplified representations, idealizations which pick out essential points and ignore others. They are the products of interpretations of the story. (Cf. chapter 9, section 3.) Clearly there is no way of observing the process of interpretation itself: you cannot look inside people's heads. However, at least the products can give data for making inferences about the interpretation: especially if informants' summaries are all very similar, and therefore presumably the products of similar interpretative processes.

One reason for eliciting summaries was simply that I thought it might be easier to analyse the summaries than the original story, since they are shorter and presumably simpler! This hope may have been optimistic, but at least it generates ideas. The summaries can be compared with the original to see which points are retained and essential in some way. It can be seen whether any points are included in all or most summaries. And on this basis, it might be possible to construct an ideal, or at least a consensus summary: a model of the main features of informants' models. Comparative analysis is always a good way of producing ideas.

The complete text of *Cat in the Rain* is easily accessible and published in several places. (See Hemingway, 1925; the story is also reprinted in Stubbs, 1982.) It tells a superficially straightforward story of an American couple staying at a hotel in Italy. They are introduced in the first sentence of the story:

There were only two Americans stopping at the hotel.

The wife looks out of the window of their hotel room, and sees a cat sheltering from the rain under a table. She goes down to get the cat: the 'poor kitty' as she keeps referring to it throughout the rest of the story. On her way out, she passes the hotel-keeper, a dignified old man, for whom she feels a great liking. The maid accompanies her outside with an umbrella. They look for the cat, but it has gone. Back in the hotel room, the wife complains to her husband:

'I wanted it so much,' she said. 'I don't know why I wanted it so much. I wanted that poor kitty.'

She goes on to complain that she is tired of the way she looks, of her clothes, and of her way of life in general. The story ends as follows:

George was not listening. He was reading his book. His wife looked out of the window where the light had come on in the square.
   Someone knocked at the door.
   'Avanti,' George said. He looked up from his book.
   In the doorway stood the maid. She held a big tortoise-shell cat pressed tight against her and swung down against her body.
   'Excuse me,' she said, 'the padrone asked me to bring this for the Signora.'[2]

Here are four samples of shorter and longer summaries collected from informants.

(a)   A woman sees a cat in the rain and tries unsuccessfully to bring it indoors. But the owner of her hotel later sends her one.

[2] The ending is reprinted here as it appears in Hemingway, 1925 and subsequent editions. However, the second last sentence reads oddly, and this may be a misprint for: 'She held a big tortoise-shell cat pressed tight against her and *its tail* swung down against her body.' (Emphasis added.)

(b)   A woman, ignored by her husband, goes to search for someone to love. Her need is sensed, but not fully understood, by a foreign admirer.

(c)   An American and his wife are in a hotel and it is raining hard. Outside there is a cat crouched under a table. The wife sees it and goes to rescue it but it disappears. She returns to the room. She says she wants a cat. The maid knocks on the door holding one, a present from the hotel-keeper.

(d)   An American couple are staying at a hotel in Italy. The wife observes a cat outside, in the rain. She wants the cat. The hotel-keeper is interested and offers a maid and an umbrella. But the cat has gone. On her return she becomes distressed and longs for the cat. The maid then brings the cat.

3   *Propositions in stories*

Many of the summaries were committed to the truth of one or both of the following propositions. (Propositions are enclosed in double quotes, to distinguish them from sentences.)

10.1   "The couple are American."
10.2   "The hotel is in Italy."

The term *proposition* will be defined more carefully below. For the moment we can say that a summary is committed to the truth of 10.1 if it includes phrases such as:

10.3   The American couple.
10.4   An American and his wife.

Similarly a summary is committed to 10.2 if it includes phrases such as:

10.5   An Italian hotel.
10.6   The couple are in Italy ... in a hotel.

Consider first just two possibilities: that propositions 10.1 and/or 10.2 are conveyed: or that 10.1 and/or 10.2 are omitted, and that no position is therefore taken on their truth-value. The following distribution of the two propositions was found in a hundred summaries of 60 and 25 words:

	60 words		25 words	
	Included	*Omitted*	*Included*	*Omitted*
"The couple are American" (10.1)	95	5	48	52
"The hotel is in Italy" (10.2)	80	20	13	87

According to these figures, the fact that the couple are American appears to be seen as more important than the fact that the hotel is in Italy. Proposition 10.2 is frequently conveyed by the longer summaries, but it is one of the propositions to be regularly dropped in the shorter summaries. But proposition 10.1 is conveyed by almost all the longer summaries, and still by around half of the shorter summaries.

On reflection, the fact that the couple are American might not seem essential to the plot. It might be seen as central to the theme of the story (for example, the theme of marital discontent), to the atmosphere of a typical Hemingway story, and so on. But the fact makes no difference at all to the development of the narrative, in the sense that nothing in the action hinges on it. A proposition such as:

10.7   "The woman sees a cat."

is central to the plot: without it, there would be no story at all. However, the point is that the informants *did* systematically include proposition 10.1, and we are concerned with collecting data on what *they* regarded as being essential or peripheral.

Note one complicating factor here. The summaries were constructed according to a word-count limit. But it takes just as many words to say, for example, *a man and his wife* as to say *an American and his wife.* And several informants reported this as a factor in their choice of information to be included: if it is possible to include more information in the same number of words, then do so. Note that phrases such as *a couple* or *two Americans* are shorter than *an American and his wife*; but they are also more ambiguous: the fact that they are husband and wife is crucial to the story – at least, as we have noted, to the theme, if not strictly the plot.

So, the ingenuity involved in having to produce short summaries may distort their value as evidence of informants' literary competence. However, the proposition about the couple being American is arguably more important than simply being an artefact of the artificial word-limit. For example, it is conveyed by the opening sentence of the story. In addition, this opening sentence has a particular grammatical form which will be fully discussed below.

4   *The concepts of plot and summary*

Consider a few general points about the concepts of a summary and of a plot. First, a summary of a literary work of fiction (such as a novel, short story, play or poem) is not the same kind of object as a summary of a non-literary work (such as a textbook, academic article or factual newspaper article). The relationship between the summary and the original is different in each case. A summary of a poem is no longer a poem. And a summary of *Hamlet* is no longer *Hamlet*. The difference between a play and a summary of it probably accounts for the vaguely humorous quality of Lamb's *Tales from Shakespeare* (Lamb and Lamb, 1822), in which Lamb tells the story of the plays. Or consider Tom Stoppard's (1980) play *Dogg's Hamlet*, which presents two versions of *Hamlet*, as performed by a cast of schoolboys: a 'fifteen minute *Hamlet*', followed by an Encore where the original is reduced to a hilarious two pages of text performed at breakneck speed. These versions are not intended to be merely summaries or performances of *Hamlet*. However, a summary of the main points of an argument in a textbook *is* still an argument, and an abstract at the beginning of an article in an academic journal *is* the same kind of object as the original article.

Second, therefore, a summary of the plot of a work of imaginative literature may well have a superficial or trivial character. It is intuitively clear that Hemingway's story is not 'about' a woman fetching a cat out of the rain, although this is what most of the summaries report. This point is made of Lodge (1978):

> ... although *Cat in the Rain* is a narrative, and perfectly co-
> herent and intelligible as such, the narrative structure itself does
> not satisfy the reader's quest for meaning. This can be demon-
> strated by trying to make shorter and shorter summaries of the
> story. By the time you pare it down to, say, twenty-five words,
> you will find that in trying to preserve what is essential to the
> narrative – the quest for the cat, the disappointment, the reversal
> – you have had to discard what seems most essential to the

meaning of the text as a whole ... The action of *Cat in the Rain*, trivial in itself, brings into focus a rift or disorder in the relationship between husband and wife.

This is not to say that some works of imaginative fiction do not comprise something approaching pure plot. Certain kinds of folk tale and certain kinds of detective story may approach this. And this may be one reason why certain kinds of folk tale and myth have seemed particularly amenable to structuralist analysis (Propp, 1928). But the point shows immediately that the kind of analysis proposed in this chapter does not exhaust the literary possibilities of the text. This is rather obvious, but it is worth stating explicitly, since it is sometimes thought that linguists claim to provide complete or exhaustive analyses of the meaning of bits of language. This is, if anything, a rather gross misunderstanding, since, if a detailed linguistic analysis shows anything, it is that language is so amazingly complex that new levels of meaning can always be found in it. The whole linguistic approach, in fact, is to look for different levels of organization and meaning in language.

Third, *summary* or *plot* must be semantic concepts. This is so because two plot summaries could be equivalent and yet contain no sentences in common. A plot cannot therefore comprise syntactic units which consist of clauses or sentences. As I have already begun to indicate, it is probably best to regard plots as consisting of semantic units such as propositions. It is in principle conceivable that two summaries might be equivalent and yet have no words in common. Such summaries would clearly be difficult if not impossible to construct in practice, but equivalent propositions could in principle be constructed using synonyms for major lexical items. Thus the following two sentences have identical truth conditions in the context of the story:

10.8   The American lady goes to get the cat.
10.9   The wife sets off to fetch the kitty.

The possibility of two summaries not sharing vocabulary becomes remote, however, for the following interesting reason. Almost none of the summaries collected contained the word *kitty* although it is common in the original story: they all preferred the word *cat*. Text frequencies in Hemingway's story are *cat*, 13; *kitty*, 6; *gatto*, 1. Arguably, languages have a core vocabulary and a vocabulary of more peripheral items. Thus *cat* is a core word, whilst *kitty*, *pussy*, *feline* are non-core. Studying words used in summaries can provide one way of identifying this core vocabulary. I would predict that summaries will contain very low frequencies of non-core items, even if these occur in the original. Core vocabulary would, of course, have to be identified independently, in a different way, or the procedure would be circular. (Cf. Dixon, 1971; Hale, 1971.)

However, although a summary is a semantic unit, a summary is not a representation of the meaning of a text, since there is more meaning in the original than in the summary. Nor is the relation between original and summary purely linguistic, since it is possible to summarize non-linguistic events. Both these points are made by Morgan and Sellner (1980).

5   The semantic analysis of plots

In general, then, in discussing plots, we are dealing with semantic relationships between words, sentences and propositions. It might be easier to state some of the important relationships between two summaries, or between a summary and the original text, than to state the semantic structure of a text.

These relationships include synonymy, contradiction, presupposition and entailment. For example, suppose that two summaries convey the propositions:

10.10   "The hotel is in Italy." (= 10.2)
10.11   "The hotel is in Greece."

Then these two summaries would be *contradictory*. That is, one cannot assert the truth of both 10.10 and 10.11. To assert the truth of one involves the denial of the other. Alternatively, a summary might simply not mention where the hotel is: such a summary would therefore be compatible with both of the first two summaries, since it has no commitment one way or another to the truth-value of 10.10 or 10.11.

Or consider another example. A proposition such as:

10.12   "It is raining hard."

entails the proposition:

10.13   "It is raining."

That is, we cannot assert that 10.12 is true, without being committed to the truth of 10.13. But the entailment does not hold in the opposition direction: 10.13 does not entail 10.12.

6   *Propositions, entailments and presuppositions*

We are now at a point in the argument where we require a more systematic statement of what is meant by *proposition* and by various semantic relations which might hold between sentences and propositions. A proposition is part of the meaning of a sentence. More accurately, the meaning of a sentence may be represented as a set of propositions, and this set may be quite large (N. Smith and Wilson, 1979: 148–71). Each of the propositions has a truth-value: it may be true or false. Another informal way of defining a proposition is to say that it is what is expressed by a declarative sentence. But propositions are not the same as declarative sentences, since different sentences may express the same proposition. For example, in the context of the story, the two sentences:

10.14   She goes back to the room.
10.15   The wife goes back to the bedroom.

both commit us to the truth of the proposition which could be expressed informally as:

10.16   "The American woman returns to her hotel room."

That is, propositions are abstract representations of meaning, which ignore grammatical and lexical form.

Propositions may be related by entailment. Proposition A entails proposition B, if B follows logically from A. That is, if one asserts A, one is committed also to claiming the truth of B. A sentence will typically entail a large set of propositions, and some of these propositions will themselves be related by entailment. For example, the sentence:

10.17   An American woman tries unsuccessfully to bring a cat indoors.

entails:

10.18   "A woman tries to bring a cat indoors."

and 10.18 in turn entails:

10.19   "A woman tries to bring something indoors."

There are different kinds of proposition. The *presuppositions* of a sentence are necessary pre-conditions for the sentence being true or false (cf. section 15). The test for presuppositions is that they remain the same whether a sentence is positive or negative. For example, both sentences:

10.20   The American woman found the cat.
10.21   The American woman did not find the cat.

presuppose:

10.22   "The woman is American."

Presuppositions can be questioned. One might say:

10.23   She's not American: her husband is.

But 10.20 and 10.21 presuppose her being American. Presuppositions also remain constant if a sentence is made interrogative. So 10.22 is also presupposed by:

10.24   Did the American woman find the cat?

7   Existential presuppositions: or how to tell jokes

One type of presupposition is an *existential presupposition.* For example, 10.20, 10.21 and 10.24 all presuppose:

10.25   "There is an American woman."
10.26   "There is a cat."

If an existential presupposition is not fulfilled, then the original proposition has no truth value: the question of its being true or false does not arise. One might wish to interpret the story (although I would not) by arguing that the cat is a delusion of the wife: but the propositions of the story presuppose its existence. For example, it is semantically very odd to say:

10.27   *The American woman found (did not find) the cat, but there was no cat.

Such points may seem unnecessarily abstruse. But in fact the assertion of an existential proposition is a common and recognisable way of beginning a story or joke. Nash (1981) discusses examples which are common in the mythic, fictive domain, such as:

10.28   Once upon a time there were three bears.

Or consider examples such as:

10.29   There was a Scotsman, an Englishman and an Irishman ...

10.30 There were these two literary critics and they were stranded on a desert island...

The opening sentence of Hemingway's story also uses this form:

10.31 There were only two Americans stopping at the hotel.

These facts may account for so many informants conveying the proposition that "the couple are American" in their summaries, when this proposition is apparently not required for the development of events in the plot.

8   Co-reference: one cat or two?

Finally, there is a type of proposition which concerns identity of reference at different points in a text. I am not familiar with any standard term for this, but will use the term *co-referential propositions*. For example, suppose one has two sentences in a text:

10.32 An American and his wife are in a hotel. The wife sees a cat.

A normal interpretation would assume the proposition:

10.33 "It is the American's wife who sees the cat."

That is, we are dealing with matters of co-reference: it is the same wife that was mentioned before. In order to analyse such questions fully, we would require to study the various kinds of cohesion which a connected text may display; especially relationships of anaphora (Halliday and Hasan, 1976).

Again, such points are not of purely analytic interest, for a matter of co-reference is crucial to the whole point of Hemingway's story. The summaries I have collected are fairly evenly divided between three different propositions:

10.34 "The maid brings the same cat that the woman has seen."
10.35 "The maid brings a different cat."
10.36 "The maid brings a cat which may or may not be the same."

If we look at the end of Hemingway's story, then the third alternative appears to accord with the original: although this proposition 10.36 is not asserted. On the other hand, the second alternative accords with my understanding of the story: the *big tortoise-shell cat* which the maid brings does not sound like the *kitty* which the woman has gone to look for. This provides a precise way of stating the ambiguity at the crux of the story: 10.36 is, strictly speaking accurate, but 10.35 seems most likely.

9   Entailments and implicatures: or how to tell lies

We now have another puzzle, however – and this puzzle is of central importance to the interpretation of literature – concerned with this non-literal use of language. How is it that we can understand a proposition such as 10.35 which is neither asserted, nor presupposed, nor entailed by what is said? There are, of course, many meanings which are conveyed by almost any use of language, but which are neither stated in so many words, nor which follow logically from what is said. So, it is quite usual to say things such as: John implied X, but he didn't actually say as much. How is it, then, that we can convey messages which are not directly related to the linguistic content of sentences?

Note, first, a further ambiguity at the end of the story. When the maid knocks, the wife is looking out of the window, as she is the first time that she is mentioned in the story. It is George who calls *avanti* and who sees the cat. It may be that we are intended to understand the description of a *big tortoise-shell cat* as being solely his perception, and differing from his wife's perception. In any case, we do not know at the end of the story whether the wife has yet seen the cat or not, and we do not have her reaction.

Suppose, then, that we imagine questioning the wife some time later. We might say:

10.37   Question: Did you get the cat?
        Wife: I got a big tortoise-shell cat.

I think we would normally interpret such an answer as: "No, I didn't get the cat you are referring to"; although this is not asserted in so many words. Similarly, suppose we ask:

10.38   Question: Did you get the little kitty?
        Wife: I got a cat.

Again, I think the normal interpretation would be: "No, I got a different cat."

Before I discuss how such utterances get interpreted in this way, consider the following genuine conversational interchange from my field notes:

10.39 A: How many chocolate biscuits have you eaten?!   (1)
       B: Three.   (2)
       A: You've eaten the whole packet!   (3)
       B: Well, then I must have eaten three.   (4)

Assuming that the packet contained more than three biscuits, is (2) a lie? One definition of a lie is that it is an utterance intended to deceive. (Cf. Gardner, 1965: 36–7, for a detailed conceptual analysis of lying.) And there are many ways of using language to deceive, apart from making utterances which are literally false. The literal truth of a sentence is not sufficient for honesty, since, as we have seen, any sentence characteristically commits the speaker to a whole set of presupposed and entailed propositions. And, in addition, speakers may deceive by leaving things unsaid. Now, the proposition:

10.40 "I have eaten a whole packet of biscuits."

clearly entails, on the assumption of a normal packet:

10.41 "I have eaten three biscuits."

If 10.40 is true, then 10.41 is true. The reverse entailment clearly does not hold. So, 10.39(2) is literally true. But one does not normally answer questions by stating only an entailment of the expected answer. And this begins to provide an explanation of why (2) is misleading. We might say informally that (2) implies:

10.42 "B has eaten *only* three biscuits."

But (2) does not entail 10.42. The implication could be cancelled, for example, if B says:

10.43 I've eaten three biscuits – in fact, I've eaten more than three.

However, presuppositions and entailments cannot be cancelled in this way, hence the oddity of sentences such as:

10.44 *I've eaten three biscuits, but there were no biscuits.
10.45 *I've eaten three biscuits, but I've not eaten anything.

where 10.44 attempts to cancel an existential presupposition ("there were some biscuits"), and 10.45 attempts to cancel an entailment ("I've eaten something").

These tests therefore distinguish presuppositions and entailments on the one hand, from other kinds of propositions which may be conveyed by sentences. This distinction is drawn in the well-known paper by Grice (1975). He uses the term *implicature* to refer to the type of proposition which may be cancelled, and I will use this term here, to distinguish this notion from the term *implication* which is used loosely in many different ways in everyday English.

A comparable example was provided by a recent quiz programme in the radio series *Top of the Form*. One question asked was:

10.46   Henry VIII had two wives. True or false?

The question-master accepted the answer *False*, saying *Correct – he had six wives*. Now, of course,

10.47   "Henry VIII had six wives."

entails:

10.48   "Henry VIII had two wives."

But 10.48 would normally be taken to implicate:

10.49   "Henry VIII had *only* two wives."

No confusion was caused by the question: the schoolboy answering the question got the answer right, having interpreted the question in the way it was obviously intended.

10   *Maxims of quantity*

We have not yet quite succeeded in explaining why in 10.39 (2) is a lie: that is, intentionally misleading, although it is literally true. To do this we need to invoke the Maxims of Quantity which are formulated by Grice (1975: 45):

> Make your contribution as informative as is required (for the current purposes of the exchange). Do not make your contribution more informative than is required.

On any reasonable interpretation, 10.39(1) is demanding to know the total number of biscuits eaten, and (2) therefore deliberately violates a Maxim of Quantity. What we are concerned with here, then, is the difference between what is said and what is implicated (but not entailed); and with rather general conventions which govern the normal conduct of conversation. For example, we expect speakers to tell us what we want to know and not deliberately to mislead us.

I therefore have little sympathy with the argument put forward by the Professor of English, that he was not lying when he was stopped by a flag-seller, and said:

10.50 I've been stopped already.

This was true, but nevertheless misleading and deliberately so; since in context, 10.50 implicates "and I have already contributed to your charity". That is also a genuine example, by the way!

11 *Implicatures*

Back then to the cat, or cats. What is at issue is giving readers just the amount of information they require, no more and no less. We have already seen that Hemingway fails to assert either that it is the same cat, or a different one, and this already weakens his commitment to the truth of both these propositions. My interpretation is therefore that Hemingway implicates that it is not the same cat. He does this by inserting information which is otherwise irrelevant: that the maid brings *a big tortoise-shell cat*. Informally, we might say that there is no reason to mention what kind of cat it is, unless this is significant, and unless we are expected to draw our own conclusions. But being an implicature, it could be cancelled, by saying, for example:

10.51 The big tortoise-shell cat didn't look like the kitty the wife had seen – but it was.

We are dealing therefore with a kind of deception. Hemingway's story is deliberately ambiguous: he intends, as we might say, to keep his readers guessing. Such Maxims of Quantity are, notice, particularly relevant in literature, where every detail may be expected to have potential significance for the interpretation. This has nothing to do with the language used, but with the expectations with which readers approach literary texts.

This is another reason why the kind of analysis I am discussing could never be expected to provide a complete analysis of a literary text. It is also a reason why the analysis could not be automatic or 'objective' in any simplistic way. The kind of analysis we do always has to be carried out against a background of knowledge which will include the conventions of various literary genres.

However, there is no point in being over-modest, since we have made some progress. We now have a yet more precise way of talking about the ambiguity at the end of the story. A characteristic of implicatures is that they can be cancelled: They may be denied without logical contradiction. (They are a relatively safe way to tell lies, since they *can* be denied!) They are therefore essentially ambiguous. So we might represent the end of the story as follows, to show the relation between asserted and implicated propositions:

1   "The wife says she wants a cat, and the padrone sends her one."
2   "But it doesn't look like the cat she saw."

Where 1 implicates that her wish is fulfilled, but 2 cancels this implicature.

3   "But it is – she was deluded about what she thought she saw through the window."

Where 2 implicates that it was a different cat, but 3 cancels this implicature, and allows a different interpretation of the story. We can continue with this game more or less indefinitely:

4   "But she is delighted with the cat anyway – it suggests that the padrone understands something of her longings."
5   "But he is just catering for the whim of a guest."
6   "But the woman is a special guest and has a special rapport with the padrone."
7   "But not all that special."

12 *Summary*

I have argued that literary competence involves the ability to understand several different kinds of semantic relationship: between a text and a summary of it; between different summaries; between sentences and different kinds of proposition conveyed by them; and between what is said and what is implied. These distinctions give more precise insight into some aspects of literary fiction, since a traditional concern of literary criticism is the ambiguity and multiple meanings of literary texts, and how meanings may be conveyed without having to be stated in so many words. It therefore also gives some insight into the conventions involved in interpreting fictional texts, and how they differ from factual reports.

My discussion of *Cat in the Rain* has been deliberately overbuilt. It may be felt that we do not need to go to such lengths to explain what is, after all, a very short and simple story, although I hope I have shown that the complexity involved even here is considerable, and is easy to underestimate. However, the payoff would come if the concepts are more widely applicable. I have already shown how the analysis can be of general interest to literary critics and linguists, since it touches on questions of the ambiguity and semantic organization of texts.

13   The sociolinguistic analysis of literary language

As I admitted at the beginning of this chapter, the analysis of literary texts may seem a long way from the normal concerns of socio-linguistics. I have already shown that there are processes of interpreta-tion which are applicable to both written and spoken language, and that literature may exploit implicatures just as casual conversation may do. However, it would be useful to mention other reasons why the sociolinguistic analysis of discourse should not ignore literary texts.

One major tradition within sociolinguistics, the ethnography of communication (Hymes, 1962) developed directly from work on poetics and stylistics (Jakobson, 1960). (Cf. chapter 3, section 6.) This tradition provides standard arguments for regarding stylistics as a branch of sociolinguistics and of the study of language in use in natural contexts. However, there are other arguments specifically related to my concerns in this book.

There are some obvious differences between spoken and written language, some quite fundamental (Stubbs, 1980). On the other hand, many features of discourse organization operate equally in both spoken and written language: lexical and syntactic cohesion, propositional development, implicature, and so on.

Literature is obviously not merely a function of language, on a par with other functions such as describing, denying, arguing, accusing and the like. Nor are literary and non-literary stylistics entirely analogous. Literature is not analogous to other types of text which provide data for non-literary stylistics: for example, advertise-ments, school textbooks, menus and technical manuals. On the other hand, literary language is not something freakish and entirely special. Only the over-concentration of much stylistics on authors such as

e. e. cummings and James Joyce might give this impression. Literary language makes a sometimes specialized use of the normal patterns of language. As Sinclair (1981) argues, literature exploits the latent patterns in everyday language, in particular ways. Latent patterns are patterns which can be avoided, but are there to be exploited for various effects (in both literary and non-literary language). Simple examples are alliteration and syntactic parallelism between sentences. In any case, the question of how similar literary and non-literary language are is an empirical question, and I have pointed out some similarities in this chapter.

It might be thought that written language is not interactive, and that this constitutes an essential difference from conversational language. This is true only if discourse is seen merely as the realization of sequences of propositions which could be represented in the predicate and propositional calculus: semantic content plus logical relations. However, anything else is interactive. That is, any devices for presenting the semantic content are interactive, since they design discourse for its hearers or readers. Such devices include the use of main versus subordinate clauses, focusing and topicalization, and anaphora. Spoken monologues are therefore similarly interactive. (Cf. Roe, 1977, and Tadros, 1980 on such interactive features of academic textbooks.)

Another prima facie difference is that unplanned spoken language (cf. chapter 2, section 8) is constructed in real time, whereas written language is generally produced and edited at leisure. There are very strong conventions against allowing the real time pressures on written composition to intrude on the finished written product. For example, readers of books generally have no way of telling whether the chapters were written in the same order as they are printed; and cross-references cover long distances both backwards and forwards. A study of spoken language must therefore take into account its nature as process, although many studies treat it as product. For this reason, I have insisted on the predictive power of the structural frame in conversational exchanges (cf. chapter 5). It is reasonable, however, to treat highly edited written texts partly as product, since this is how they are intended to be perceived. From the point of view of a reader (at least when reading a text for the first time), however, reading is a psycholinguistic guessing game (F. Smith, 1973), and the process of comprehension is similar to the comprehension of spoken language. The correct generalization appears to be that the linear nature of written discourse can sometimes be partly overcome; but both speakers and hearers are much more closely constrained by the linear nature of spoken language (Sinclair, 1980).

Linde and Labov (1975) have argued that narratives are a basic discourse form, from which other discourse organizations are derived. On the other hand, narratives are untypical of many written texts, in that they are intended to be heard or read in the order that they are presented. This relates narratives to spoken language in general: hearers have to follow the linear sequence of presentation of speakers. However, many written texts are intended to be skimmed in search of information, and not necessarily in the order of presentation.

However, comparable work has been done on both literary and spoken narratives. The best known work on the macro-structure of literary texts is by Propp (1928) and Todorov (1969), and on the macro-structure of spoken narratives by Labov and Waletsky (1967) and Labov (1972d). This work takes a 'top-down' approach: proposing an overall structure for narratives of the type: abstract, orientation, complicating action, evaluation, result, coda (Labov, 1972d). (Cf. chapter 2, section 7.)

The distinctions between spoken, written and literary discourse are therefore partly artificial and have been partly exaggerated by different academic traditions, including literary criticism and linguistics. Any general theory of discourse will have to take into account as wide a variety of discourse as possible.

14 *Propositional analysis*

Work within a cognitive psychological tradition has, on the other hand, followed a 'bottom-up' approach: analysing texts into constituent propositions. Much of this work has been concerned with informants' ability to recall the semantic content of texts, which is defined as a network of propositions. Often this investigation involves the experimental manipulation of texts: for example, by moving key propositions to different positions within the text, by asserting propositions explicitly or conveying them implicitly, and so on. (See Van Dijk and Kintsch, 1978; Mandler and Johnson, 1977, for reviews of this enormous literature.)

The study reported in this chapter is comparable in some ways to this work on text-recall, though mainly in its methodology, rather than in its cognitive psychological concerns. It would be useful, therefore, to mention some limitations of such work on propositional analysis in general. Although the concept of proposition is intuitively appealing, no one has yet managed to define propositions in such a way that a definitive listing of the constituent propositions of a text may be drawn up. Typically, there is a reasonable agreement between coders, but no entirely replicable list. Even if such a list could be arrived at, it would be inordinately complex for a text of any realistic length. This problem is central for any textual analysis. A formal analysis of any complete text of more than a few hundred words is so complex that probably no one would ever want to read it. Interesting analyses are therefore inevitably selective, and the basis of the selection is usually inexplicit. Hence stylistics has concentrated on short poems rather than novels. Also, being a bottom-up analysis, a propositional analysis is not predictive. Micro propositional analyses therefore require to be combined with macro structural analyses.

15   *Presuppositions*

In addition to these problems in rigorously listing the constituent propositions of a text, there are problems over the relation between different types of proposition. In this chapter, my definition of the terms *proposition, entailment* and *presupposition* has been necessarily brief, but precise enough for the present argument. Fuller discussions can be found in several introductory textbooks (e.g. Lyons, 1977; N. Smith and Wilson, 1979). In addition, I have used concepts which are currently disputed by semantic and pragmatic theory. This is a standard problem in analysing texts: one inevitably applies to texts analytic categories which are questioned by theory. For example, I have simply taken for granted that presuppositions should be distinguished from entailments, although this has been questioned (e.g. by Kempson, 1975, 1977; D. Wilson, 1975.) I have, then, deliberately ignored various arguments which are put forward within semantics. This is partly on grounds of expediency: no analysis of texts would ever get done otherwise. However, I want also to defend this distinction, since it bears on two important issues: how much weight should be given to discourse facts in establishing syntactic and semantic and semantic categories; and how much weight should be given to speakers' own perceptions of the functions of language?

No one would argue, I presume, that such intuitions, about discourse and about everyday functions of language, should be entirely ignored, or that they should be accepted without question. However, just which intuitions should be retained and how much weight should be given to them, in the face of other kinds of data, is a question which is not often asked, much less answered.

A central problem in modern semantic theory concerns the concept of presupposition, where there is considerable debate over whether this intuitively appealing concept can be accommodated within a traditional two-valued truth-conditional semantics by being reduced to the concept of entailment; or whether it requires setting up a new kind of three-valued logic. Confronted with the classic example:

10.52   The King of France is bald.

the commonsense, users' reaction would probably be, not that the sentence is false (as one would have to say within a two-valued logic); but that there is something strange about the sentence, since its existential presupposition ("There is a King of France") fails. In other words, it is this presupposition which is false, whereas the assertion is void or inoperative. This commonsense reaction leads to a three-valued logic, in which such statements may be said to be neither true, nor false, but third-valued or truth-valueless.

The term *presupposition* is used in many different senses in the literature, including semantic and pragmatic senses. But the sense above is arguably the central one: in which a presupposition is defined as a proposition which remains constant under negation and interrogation. (Cf. section 6.) Thus 10.52 and also 10.53 and 10.54:

10.53   The King of France is not bald.
10.54   Is the King of France bald?

are all said to presuppose:

10.55   "There is a King of France."

And, centrally to my argument here, this also corresponds to the intuitive, pre-theoretical sense of the term, where a speaker might say in reaction to 10.52, 10.53 or 10.54:

10.56   But you are presupposing that there is a King of France.

However, this concept of presupposition, which seems both intuitively appealing and clear (there are clear tests for it), appears problematic under more careful examination. Second, one has to decide whether this is sufficient justification for abandoning the concept altogether.

There are many recent discussions of the main facts at issue. A succinct statement is by Kempson (1977: ch. 9), and for convenience I will restrict my comments to her types of example.

The most commonly cited test for presupposition is constancy under negation, and this predicts therefore that positive and negative sentences behave symmetrically in this respect. However, this is not always the case, as in these wh-questions:

10.57 What did John do?
10.58 What did John not do?

Further, the behaviour of positive and negative compound sentences which contain a factive verb in the matrix sentence appears asymmetrical. The problem arises with sentences containing a verb such as *regret*; that is, a factive verb which entails the truth of the proposition in the embedded sentence. Thus 10.59 entails 10.60:

10.59 Edwin regrets that it is raining.
10.60 "It is raining."

However, Kempson argues (p. 146) that sentences such as 10.61 are contradictory, whereas 10.62 is not:

10.61 *Edwin regrets that the King of France is bald, but there is no King of France.
10.62 Edwin doesn't regret that the King of France is bald, because there is no King of France.

Kempson makes several points about possible interpretations of 10.62. She argues that it depends on an interpretation of the first clause which is 'not normal', since the first clause would normally presuppose the existence of the King of France. However, she then admits the possibility of its being quite normal, if it is used to deny a preceding utterance such as:

10.63 Edwin regrets that the King of France is bald.

But she later (p. 153) argues that this special denial use of negation is not clearly distinct from the normal use of negation. The presuppositional analysis, she argues, assumes that negative sentences are ambiguous between natural and special denial senses (p. 147), and she questions the validity of this distinction. (Cf. chapter 6, section 5.) She appears therefore to admit the possibility of intuitive distinctions between the functions of utterances in discourse, but then argues that these intuitions are unclear and to be disregarded.

Kempson also considers (p. 150) sentences such as:

10.64   John is married and he beats his wife.

The second clause on its own presupposes:

10.65   "John has a wife" or "John is married".

However, this proposition is not presupposed, but asserted, by the first clause. Therefore, argues Kempson, the whole sentence does not presuppose what the second clause does, therefore the presuppositional analysis is contradictory. However, Kempson fails to consider why one should ever use a sentence such as 10.64. One obvious use is in an exchange such as:

10.66   A: Married men are kinder than bachelors.
         B: Well, John is married and he beats his wife.

She fails to consider in what discourse circumstances speakers may state the obvious, or assert what might normally be presupposed. One discourse function is to establish common ground for a point in an argument, and to provide the basis for a topic–comment structure.

The situation, in summary, appears to be as follows: Kempson admits (a) that the presuppositional analysis is intuitively appealing, (b) that it is supported for simple sentences, and (c) that negative sentences may have a characteristic use in denying a preceding utterance in a discourse sequence. Nevertheless, she prefers the entailment analysis because it provides a single explanation for both simple and complex sentences. Yet, the entailment analysis appears to provide a less satisfying analysis for the simple sentences, and an analysis which contradicts the user's pretheoretical understanding of the issue. In addition, the complex sentences on which the argument rests appear artificially contrived, especially when they are considered largely outside of discourse contexts in which they can be seen to have particular speech act functions: it is well known that sentences which are anomalous from a logico-semantic point of view (for example, tautologies and contradictions of various kinds) are nevertheless used in conversation. Thus, Kempson appears to undervalue both users' intuitions about the phenomena and also the discourse uses of the utterances which she is discussing. The question of how much significance should be attached to such phenomena appears to be largely a question of faith: I agree with the details of Kempson's arguments, but disagree with the general conclusions which she draws from them.

11

Collecting Conversational Data: Notes on Sociolinguistic Methodology

In earlier chapters I have discussed several different ways of collecting and analysing data for discourse analysis. In this chapter I will develop these points in more detail, and at a more advanced level. The general approach to collecting conversational data which I will recommend is to collect and analyse transcripts of conversational data (cf. chapter 2), supplemented by observations collected by ethnographic observation (cf. chapter 3), but also to combine different methods of data collection, both naturalistic and experimental, which have different advantages and limitations (cf. chapter 7). This final chapter therefore provides practical advice for readers who intend to go and do discourse analysis, but also reminds them of various theoretical chasms in the enterprise.

Changes in the concept of what constitutes good data have led, over the past hundred years, to major reorientations in linguistic theory and in our conception of the nature of language. Such a change has again been taking place since the early 1970s as great problems have become apparent in the Chomskyan concept of introspective data. As attention has begun to shift to naturally occurring conversational data, corresponding changes have also occurred in our ideas about the relation between syntax, semantics and discourse.

Labov (1972c: 97), points out the sudden shift in attitudes to data and to data-collection which differentiated Chomskyan from Bloomfieldian linguistics:

> Less than twenty years divide us from the time when the study of methods was the reigning passion of American linguistics; yet the status of *methodology* has fallen so fast and so far that it now lies in that outer, extra-linguistic darkness where we have cast speculation on the origin of language and articles about slang.

With Labov's elegantly written paper (1972c) on this topic, questions of sociolinguistic methodology and the associated theory of data-collection have regained respectability. In this chapter, I discuss the kinds of issue that Labov raises, particularly with respect to data for discourse analysis, and also some aspects of the theory of data-collection with which Labov does not deal.

Linguists, and social scientists in general, are, with a few exceptions, strangely coy about discussing in print the kind of problems that are involved in collecting and analysing data. Some perhaps do not wish to admit that they have problems with basic research tasks: What do I say to my informants? How much data do I need? My thinking is in a rut: how can I get some new ideas? Others possibly do not see such basic research tasks (collecting, transcribing, coding and comparing data) as in any way problematic or of interest. Alternatively, for many linguists at least, it may just be that methodological questions have been out of fashion since Chomsky reacted strongly against the emphasis on fieldwork and procedures in American linguistics from the 1920s to the 1950s. In this paper I will try to combine discussion of some aspects of the theory of data-collection in sociolinguistics with discussion of some of the practical, day-to-day problems of sociolinguistic research on conversation. Along with Labov (1972c), other work which includes very useful discussion of sociolinguistic methodology, with particular relevance to discourse analysis is: Burton (1980: ch. 5), Labov (1975a,b), Milroy (1980: chs. 2 and 3), Wolfson (1976), and several of the articles in Adelman, ed. (1981).

1   The lack of accepted procedures in discourse analysis

There is, then, a lack of recognized and accepted procedures for collecting, presenting and analysing conversational data. Paradoxically, many papers on spoken interaction do not attempt to analyse and present data on verbal behaviour which has been systematically, in whatever way, collected, recorded or observed in specific, naturally occurring social situations. This is not the place to discuss in detail the failure of the social sciences, until relatively recently, to provide descriptive theory for everyday behaviour. But for striking, and very different, examples of well-known papers on social inter-action which present no data, see Goffman (1955), Hymes (1962) and Bernstein (1971a). For the present, we can simply ask, with Alice, 'What is the use of a book without pictures or conversation?' (Carroll, 1865/1966: 11).

Consequently, the more problematic aspects of data-collection are often not discussed. When it is made clear what data do support an analysis, these sometimes turn out to be very far from observed spoken interaction. One example is Hymes' (1966) ethnographic account of three speech events in Wishram Chinook culture, which is explicitly based on Hymes' re-interpretation of Spier and Sapir's interpretation (memory ethnography) of events which were not otherwise recorded. Yet it is precisely this problematic relationship between data and analysis, via interpretation, which must be one central topic of study for sociolinguistics. Hymes is the first to emphasize that the analyses which he proposes in the ethnography of communication are at the level of general cultural patterns of speech behaviour, and not analyses of specific interactions. He is concerned with proposing a general schema or heuristic framework which would be of help to a researcher in the field, rather than with providing a model for analysing data on spoken interaction. I would propose, however, as a principle for sociolinguistics, that any analysis of speech behaviour will ultimately stand or fall on its success in coming to grips with audio-recordings of what speakers actually say to each other in specific, naturally occurring social settings.

When there are few accepted procedures of analysis, as in research on spoken interaction, it is particularly important to keep the reader in clear view of precisely what data the analysis has been based on. Labov (1972c) insists that readers should be able to check the data and proposes that more tapes and transcripts should be published. Loman (1967) has simply published transcripts of conversations in an American Negro dialect, without analysis. However, whilst the publication of such data is useful, the ideal is the publication of appropriate data plus analysis. Sinclair and Coulthard (1975), in their study of classroom language, have also argued for the need to give the reader a clear idea of how the data have been handled when there is no well-defined and established methodology. Alongside general descriptive theory of classroom language, they publish some 50 pages of coded transcripts of teacher–pupil talk. The ethno-methodologists have recently been particularly scrupulous, as part of their general theoretical stance, about quoting the small fragments of data on which their analyses of conversation are based, and have discussed at length certain aspects of the problematic nature of the relation between such data and theory. Some of the most important articles which contain transcribed conversational data plus analysis are by Sacks (1967–72), Schegloff and Sacks (1973), Schegloff (1968, 1972), Jefferson (1972, 1973), and Turner (1970, 1972). Many more such studies have appeared more recently.

2   *Labov and sociolinguistic methodology*

Broadly speaking, Labov has done two types of sociolinguistic study: survey-style work on language variation in a speech community, focusing primarily on phonological and grammatical variables (Labov, 1972a); and, more recently, work on conversational analysis and the organization of speech events (e.g. 1972b) and Labov and Fanshel (1977). But many of his principles apply to both types of study. Labov is concerned with methods of observing speech as social action, and of gathering empirical data to choose between competing theories of language in use. His most important point may simply be his encouragement to other linguists to ignore various self-imposed restrictions on twentieth century linguistics, and to emphasize: that it is possible to observe directly linguistic variation; that speakers' feelings about language are accessible; and that linguistics should use non-linguistic data to explain linguistic variation.

Labov makes clear various principles of sociolinguistic study. These principles are based mainly on the premises that there are no single-style speakers, and that speech elicited in any situation of observation will inevitably be more formal than the speaker's most casual style. He gives advice on controlling interview situations to elicit different styles of language from formal to casual. And he proposes supplementing interviews by collecting data from tests, elicitations, experiments, observations and different types of recordings. The most condensed statement of these principles and practical methods is Labov (1972c), which brings together principles developed over his previous empirical studies. These principles are primarily concerned with giving the linguist access to the *vernacular*, which Labov defines as that variety of language which is least self-conscious: which is unmonitored and has least attention paid to it. The vernacular therefore provides an essential baseline for the study of language variation. However, as well as being arguably the most important variety for linguists to describe, it is also the most difficult to observe, and it is with these problems of observation that I am mainly concerned in this chapter.

3   *Practical problems*

With reference to very practical problems, Labov is again in the forefront, reassuring researchers by emphasizing as genuine such problems as: Where should the microphone go, and how can the best quality recordings be obtained? What does the field worker actually say to his informants when he comes face-to-face with them? He says (1972c: 111) that he is often asked questions such as: 'Under what pretext do you speak to these people?'

The recording problem is especially difficult in public places such as schools, with large numbers of speakers involved, echoing corridors, bells, bare floors and walls, no curtains, and scuffling feet. A compromise solution which I have adopted in studies of classroom language (cf. chapter 3) is to tape-record small groups comprising a teacher with up to half-a-dozen pupils; and to take observational notes in traditional sized classes as a check on the type of speech recorded. In a comparable study, Sinclair and Coulthard (1975) also tape-recorded small groups of pupils with a teacher; they made no check by observational methods, but analysed a few tapes of whole classes recorded by others. In recording small groups, I have found that a cassette tape-recorder with an omnidirectional microphone, placed on the teacher's desk or worn by him as a lavalière microphone, is adequate for a very clear recording of the teacher and understandable recordings of pupils, even of foreign speakers.

The other main practical problem in conversational analysis is the amount of time needed for transcription, which is of course only a preliminary to coding or other types of analysis. Transcription is an enormously lengthy business, and in itself cuts down the amount of data that can reasonably be analysed. A discussion lasting 50–60 minutes takes up about 30 pages of transcript, typed double spaced. Transcription time varies enormously depending on the quality and complexity of the recording, but it could take a minimum of 20 hours to transcribe such a discussion down to word level and hesitation phenomena, and correspondingly much longer to transcribe for intonation or phonetically. This is about the time quoted also by Stern (1969: 164). Pittenger et al. (1960) say that it took 25–30 hours to transcribe the five minutes of interview they use in their book, that is, down to narrow phonetic transcription. Birdwhistell gives even longer transcription times for dealing with kinesic data. He claims (1970: 12) to have reduced transcription time from about 100 hours per second to less than one hour per second.

However, the amounts of data which are necessary or useful for studies on spoken interaction is a theoretical question, to which I now turn.

4   *How much data?*

Different amounts of data such as audio-recordings or notes, are needed for different purposes. More data are needed to compare different groups of speakers in situations, for example, than to isolate characteristic features of a discourse variety as such. Birdwhistell (1961), who is interested in the system underlying people's knowledge of how to behave in public, stresses the sheer repetitiousness of human behaviour. He claims to have isolated basic patterns of behaviour in 20-second stretches of film. Talking of patterns of language-use according to social-class stratification, Labov (1972a) claims that patterns emerge from samples of only 25 speakers, and that results are possible with only five speakers in each cell, and five to ten samples of each linguistic variable from each speaker. To study independent variables which correlate with linguistic behaviour, such as age and ethnic groups, Labov estimates that a larger sample of about 80 speakers is required. To study sociolinguistic variation, it may not be necessary, then, to analyse statistically the speech of large numbers of informants. Sankoff (1972) finds that in studies of complex speech communities, a well-chosen sample of 50 to 150 speakers can represent the whole range of variation existing within that community. Le Page (1975) argues, however, that such numbers are too low. The notion of a sample being well or intelligently chosen introduces implicitly the concept of theoretical sampling, which I develop below.

There are many striking examples of how very general theory may result from study of small amounts of data. In spite of the criticisms which Labov (1975a,b) makes about Chomsky having recourse to his own intuitions in producing data, Chomsky has certainly shown that advances in linguistics do not necessarily come from poring over vast amounts of data, but can also result from analysing fragments in great detail. Chomsky has proposed various linguistic universals almost entirely on the basis of a small subset of the sentences of English. He can be faulted insofar as his claims should be tested on languages other than English in order to be empirically corroborated, and such corroboration on a wide range of non-Indo-European languages is now a central aim of Chomskyan linguistics. However, he cannot be faulted insofar as his primary aim is to generate formal linguistic theory, and to make refutable claims about formal constraints on syntax.

Similarly, in discourse analysis, Sacks has isolated highly general mechanisms, such as membership categorization device and adjacency pair, by analysing conversational exchanges of only a few utterances in length (Sacks, 1967–72) or by over-analysing a sequence of just two sentences (Sacks, 1972). Other illustrations that very general descriptive statements can emerge from a close analysis of small amounts of conversational data are Goffman's (1971) analysis of supportive and remedial interchanges, and Schegloff (1968) on the first five seconds of telephone calls.

The argument that research on spoken interaction is not necessarily advanced through the accumulation by data-mongering of vast amounts of undigested facts, brings us again to the concept of theoretical sampling, discussed below.

5   Theoretical biases in recording

As well as the practical problems concerned with obtaining good quality audio-recordings, recording also raises important theoretical problems. The main problem is usually referred to as the observer's paradox. Ideally we want to know how people use language when they are not being observed. When speakers know they are being observed, their language shifts towards more formal styles, probably rather erratically, as not everything in language is under equal conscious control, and as speakers probably go through cycles of half forgetting they are being recorded. So the most casual language is the most difficult to observe. The language which linguists would most like to be able to record is the language which is most susceptible to contamination by observation.

With modern audio-recording equipment, there is, of course, no difficulty in recording speakers clandestinely, in many face-to-face situations or on the telephone. Some researchers have ethical objections to clandestine recordings; others adopt a compromise solution of recording without the speakers' knowledge and then telling them afterwards (e.g. Crystal and Davy, 1975). However, suppose one decides to record people with their knowledge, what solutions are there, if any, to the effect of the recording on the speakers? In many cases, the recording may have to be with the speaker's consent in any case: for example, if recording teachers, doctors, magistrates, or official meetings of different kinds.

One argument, put forward by Wolfson (1976), is that there is no such thing as natural speech in any absolute sense. All language changes to be appropriate to the situation. All there is to study, then, is what people regard as appropriate in different situations. In any case, in all social situations, we are aware of being monitored to some extent by others present: being monitored by a tape-recorder and researcher is therefore just a particular example of this. This type of argument usefully points out that the hunt for pure, natural or authentic data is a chimera. On the other hand, we may be investigating how people speak when they are uncomfortable. Being permanently recorded and studied is not a normal situation for most people: and those for whom it is an everyday occurrence (including celebrities, radio personalities, courtroom lawyers) develop special verbal strategies to deal with it. There is always the suspicion that in extraordinary situations people produce extraordinary language.

One research strategy is proposed by J. Wilson (in prep.). He argues that since speakers will inevitably be affected by the recording, one should deliberately study such effects: what he calls tape-affected speech. Examples would include direct references to the recording equipment or uncharacteristically polite usages, or the opposite – deliberately obscene references, for example, where speakers are showing that they do not care what is recorded. This suggestion is useful, insofar as it warns researchers what to beware of in recordings. On the other hand, we want to know about normal language, not about such artificially produced anomalies.

It is regularly proposed that speakers grow accustomed to being recorded, and that tape-affected speech decreases with time. One can, therefore, record speakers over some hours or days, and either edit out tape-affected sections, or simply discard earlier data. Although this principle seems very plausible, there appear to be no studies which have tested its validity. A similarly plausible but not well-tested claim is that if people are recorded in self-selected groups, then the pressures of interacting in a group will override the influence of the tape-recorder. Labov (1972b) claims that recording Negro youths in their peer groups decreased the attention they paid to their speech. On the other hand, he was recording gangs of boys who might have gone out of their way to display their group solidarity to the observer. A different version of this argument is used by Milroy (1980) who recorded natural social groups in working class areas of Belfast. She herself became a natural member of the groups, with a socially recognized role. Despite the fact that she was known by some members to be making tape-recordings, she was not seen as a researcher, but as a 'friend of a friend'. Having been introduced initially into the group by someone who knew her interests, these interests were not always seen as relevant, and not necessarily mentioned in introducing her to other members. She could, therefore, observe the group while not being defined as an observer. In other words, she found a way of being present herself without breaking the interactional norms of the group. She also claims that people get used to recording equipment, and that the effect of recording could not last for the long periods during which she recorded.

Slightly different arguments are used by S. Harris (1980). She recorded interaction in Magistrates' courts in an English city. She argues that the defendants were under considerable stress, in a situation where their personal lives and finances were being discussed: this would override the effect of being recorded. In addition, no one bothered to explain to the defendants the purpose of the recording. Observers of various kinds were normal in the court, and since no one consulted the defendants for their permission to record, they regarded it as a normal part of courtroom procedure.

Another possibility is to leave the tape-recorder with the speakers and to allow them to record themselves when they wish. At least the researcher is not also present, observing in person. Cheshire (1978) used this technique in a study of adolescents in peer groups in an adventure playground. It is worthwhile emphasizing that cassette tape-recorders are now entirely familiar to most adolescents, and for this reason alone may affect their language less than some years ago.

This general availability of and familiarity with audio-recording equipment can be exploited in other ways, and make it very easy to record certain types of data. For example, many radio and television discussion programmes are now much less formal than previously, and frequently involve unrehearsed participation of members of the public. (Goffman, 1981: 197ff discusses the use of radio data in some detail.) It is now standard to transmit live and unrehearsed commentary on topical events (although it is often not obvious just what is being transmitted live and unedited, and this should be checked). For example, recent editions of the British radio panel discussion *Any Questions* have been disrupted by hecklers in the audience, and provided fascinating data on argumentative and abusive language. The very common format of radio phone-in programmes provides good comparisons of the interactional style of members of the public versus more practised media personalities. Finally, it is now common to interview speakers who have been witnesses to news events, often crimes or tragedies, or who have been participants in riots and the like. In some cases, the pressure of emotions involved may partly cancel out the self-consciousness in front of the microphone. (Researchers should, however, check on the copyright regulations in different countries before indiscriminately recording material from radio or television.)

A major source of data has been available to British researchers since 1979, now that parliamentary proceedings in the House of Commons, House of Lords and Select Committees are broadcast on BBC radio. Such radio transmissions can also be compared with the official version of the debates which appear in Hansard, to study ways in which spontaneous spoken language is converted into a written record. (See below on secretarial practices.) As far as I know, this source of data has not yet been used by discourse analysts. (Some discourse analysis has been done on the Nixon Watergate tapes, see Lerman, 1980.)

These are some answers which are often given to the objection that it is impossible to record natural language. However, it is obvious that they are only very partial solutions. It is clearly possible to alter the effect which recording has on people. For example, one could produce very different behaviour by setting up a film camera in a shopping street, with three different signs on the camera on three consecutive days, say: 'BBC Television Outside Broadcasts', 'Nottinghamshire County Constabulary' and 'University of Nottingham Project on Crowd Behaviour'. In extreme cases, observation itself may generate artificial behaviour. And, although the effects may be controlled, it is never possible to guarantee that there are no effects. This, after all, is precisely what is meant by the observer's *paradox*: you cannot observe people when they are not being observed.

6   Theoretical biases in transcription

It is also obvious that transcription poses not only practical, but theoretical problems. It is not a mechanical procedure, which can be left unproblematically to a research assistant, as is often done. Abercrombie (1954) emphasizes how the process of transcribing tape-recordings embodies 'an initial classification and even theorizing about the raw material'. Birdwhistell (1970: 13) discusses briefly how skilled secretaries who are asked to do close transcriptions of tape-recorded conversation make about one 'mistake' every five words. Unfortunately, Birdwhistell does not make clear precisely what he means by 'mistakes', but such data on how audio-recordings are tidied up to bring them into line with conventions of written language, would provide valuable secondary evidence concerning how people hear and interpret conversation. In recent work I have had practical experience of the disagreements which can arise within a group of linguists working together on the same tape-recorded data, over what constitutes a correct transcription at word level. Much more discussion and dispute is normal over such features as intonation, tone-group boundaries and timing of interruptions. Experimental data is available on how even trained phoneticians using the Trager–Smith system of intonation-transcription use their understanding of meaning in order to do what might appear superficially to be the mechanical task of transcribing intonation contours (Lieberman, 1965). Only someone who has regularly worked with audio-recorded conversational data, even with good, clear recordings knows the tricks his ears can play: how whole words can simply not be heard even after repeated listening, how overlaps are similarly not heard, and how one person can sometimes transcribe at first hearing a phrase that a colleague has failed to make sense of after hearing it 50 of 100 times on a loop-repeater. Such auditory hallucinations are real problems, both practically and theoretically.

A most important point is that much of the complexity of spoken conversation is evident only in close *written* transcriptions: it is typically not evident to the participants themselves. I am thinking of such frequent conversational complexities as: false starts, hesitations, self-corrections, ungrammatical and unfinished sentences, overlapping utterances, and so on. Conversation *looks* odd, incoherent and broken when seen in the written medium – but it does not *sound* odd to those taking part in it. (Cf. chapter 2.) This is not to say that the complexity is an artefact of changing the medium of transmission, but that listeners listen selectively to conversation. They do not hear many of the overlaps, false starts, hesitations, and so on. The presentation of spoken interaction in the form of a transcription has, therefore, an estrangement effect. We can *see* that conversation is not so self-evidently coherent as we might have thought, but that the coherence is achieved through interpretation. The problem is then: how does talk which appears superficially to be casual, incomplete, incoherent or defective nevertheless produce an impression of order from its participants? How can we explain that conversation which is evidently, to the eye, full of stops, starts and stammers, nevertheless sounds coherent? A close transcription of spoken conversation can reveal even to the unbeliever ways in which the perceived order of the social world is but an elaborate illusion, constructed by interpretation.

Note, however, that it is possible to stand this formulation of the theoretical importance of mere transcription on its head. For a close transcription can reveal types of very detailed conversational order at levels at which conversationalists would never suspect any. Such intense organization has been especially the topic of Sacks *et al.* (in the articles quoted in section 1).

This leads, however, to one other danger in transcriptions which it is worthwhile spelling out. In much published work on conversation, particularly by the ethnomethodologists (e.g. Sacks *et al.*), transcriptions show great detail. Conventions have been developed to show simultaneous, overlapping and contiguous utterances, lengthened syllables, stressed syllables, voice quality, and the like. (See Schenkein, ed., 1978: 11–16, who brings together such notational conventions.) There is a danger that such conventions are a kind of folk phonetics, marking, for example, stress and intonation in an *ad hoc* way, without reference to any theory of phonology.

There is also a danger that such transcriptions, purporting to show fine details of conversations, may be perceptually unreal. Thus Schenkein (ed., 1978: 11) writes that Jefferson has attempted to develop such a system of notational conventions 'to produce a reader's transcript – one that will look to the eye how it sounds to the ear'. This is surely impossible. By changing the medium, from aural to visual, one changes also what is perceived. Moreover, casual conversation is characterized precisely by phonological obscurities: elisions, consonant cluster simplifications, and so on. Comprehension is a sampling procedure, in which a lot of the phonetic details do not matter. A very general danger of discourse analysis is that it focuses unwarranted attention on details of interaction which had no reality for the conversationalists at the time. As is well known, there is in any case no single correct transcription for a given utterance. A broad transcription and different narrow transcriptions can select different features for representation, depending on the purpose of the transcription. There is no solution to such problems: no method of transcription which is appropriate for all studies of discourse. In this book, I have sometimes provided a transcription showing speaker-overlaps and some phonological obscurity when such features were relevant. In other data, I have standardized orthography where such features seem irrelevant to the point at issue. The important point is to be clear that such decisions are theoretical and take for granted interpretations and analyses of the data.

7   Field notes

These problems of how data are pre-interpreted by apparently routine research tasks such as transcription, are seen even more acutely with respect to field notes on speech behaviour. The analysis does not begin when the researcher writes about what he has written in the field. In making notes in the field, he is already interpreting, analysing and making choices about what to record and what to miss out. These choices themselves draw upon the communicative competence which is the very topic of study. Suppose, for example, that a study of classroom language is based on observational notes on teacher–pupil talk taken in classrooms. (Cf. chapter 3.) Assuming that the researcher has successfully gathered examples of typical teacher-talk, what knowledge did he draw on in the classroom to enable him to do this? This knowledge, about how good examples of teacher-talk can be recognized, is precisely one topic of study. Such notes cannot be treated as a mere resource, to be analysed later in the quiet of one's office. They already embody one type of analysis. Labov (1972f) states the problem as follows:

> There are many acts of perceiving, remembering, selecting, interpreting, and translating, which lie between the data and the linguist's report, and these are almost all implicit in such papers.

8   Theoretical sampling

Concepts of sampling traditionally involve the notion of randomness. The researcher dips into a population at random, on the assumption that a large enough sample will show the whole range of behaviour he wants to study. However, it is very difficult, if not impossible, to get a theoretically random sample. To take a very simple example, the pin-and-telephone-book method will produce not a random sample, but a sample biased towards those people in middle and upper income groups, who have telephones; although the resulting sample may well be negligibly biased, for practical purposes, on criteria other than social class (unless you hold that social class correlates with everything!). Similar biases creep into more sophisticated methods. In any case, as we have seen above, there are particular difficulties in collecting uncontaminated data on natural language.

Realizing the ultimate impossibility of entirely random samples, what more usually happens is that the researcher makes a compromise, such as dividing up the population into theoretical categories, such as social class groups, and then dips into each category. For example, in well-known British work on children's language development, Wells and his colleagues (e.g. G. Wells and Montgomery, 1981) used the following technique to collect samples of spontaneous language from children who had previously been selected from different family backgrounds. Recordings were made by means of a radio-microphone, worn by the child, and linked to a tape-recorder programmed to record 24 ninety-second samples at 20-minute intervals throughout the day. This technique has several advantages. The language is presumably natural and spontaneous, insofar as no researcher is present, and neither the child nor others in the child's home know exactly when the tape-recorder is switched on. But it also has disadvantages. Only the words are recorded, and the researcher cannot observe the context: this was partly resolved by playing the tape back to the mother and asking her to recall activities which were taking place. Also it might be questioned whether 90-second samples were long enough to analyse discourse sequences. Certainly recorded fragments will start and end at random, with no relation to the structure of the interaction.

There is, however, an alternative to trying to obtain a random sample. This is to be deliberate and explicit about choosing a sample which will give special insights into whatever one wants to study. This is essentially the concept of theoretical sampling, proposed by Glaser and Strauss (1967). It involves seeking out people and situations which are likely to be particularly revealing or fruitful with respect to the phenomena in which one is interested. It is a way of gathering suggestive and rich data, in as pure a form as possible, and with as little time wasted as possible. The researcher chooses groups of situations that will help to generate to the fullest extent the properties of his theoretical categories. Parlett and Hamilton (1972) combine the concept of theoretical sampling with progressive focusing, which is theoretical sampling within theoretical sampling, and similar to the concept of a tapered corpus (Samarin, 1969: 70). Progressive focusing also implies a flexible methodology which allows new information to redefine and clarify emerging problems as the investigation unfolds. Problems are not predefined from the outset of the investigation: when this is allowed to happen, the methodological tail has wagged the dog. Glaser and Strauss (1967) put forward these recommendations within the general argument that anyone can provide a dust heap of facts, but only the social scientist can provide the theory that makes sense of them. They claim also that concepts that are generated by, or grounded in, the data collected by theoretical sampling will typically be more understandable to sociologists and laymen alike, than much grand sociological theory which has often no explicit links with data.

The notion of theoretical sampling is present, in an elementary form, in Labov's suggestion (1972c: 118) that: 'the future study of language in context will depend heavily upon the development of means of *enriching the data* of natural conversation' (emphasis added). Labov is concerned primarily with eliciting rare grammatical forms, but the point holds good in studies of language functions and discourse analysis. Labov details various interview situations which will elicit different style of speech along a casual–formal continuum, but does not specify any techniques for enriching the data as such, outside interview situations, or for choosing suggestive naturally occurring situations. His ingenious techniques such as spot questions in stores to elicit answers of, say, *fourth floor* (to study pronunciation of post-vocalic consonants) are quick ways of collecting data for a specific hypothesis, not ways of enriching data.

As an example of one way in which the concept of theoretical sampling may be applied, consider its use in the study of classroom talk presented in chapter 3. My main interest in this study was in ways in which teachers organize or control the conversational situation in the classroom; and one problem was, therefore, to collect rich data on this use of language. The tape-recorded data used in the study came mainly from traditional classroom lessons, in which native English-speaking teachers were teaching English as a foreign language to French children. All the talk was in English, and I was particularly concerned with analysing the teachers' language. This highly selective choice of data was made via the concept of theoretical sampling, which was used in two main ways. The main socio-linguistic concern of the study was to isolate ways in which one speaker may control or organize the development of discourse. Teaching situations are a good place to start looking for such types of organization in talk, since teachers themselves are explicitly concerned with how to organize the material they present verbally to their pupils. Teachers are also professionally interested in organizing other aspects of the communication system in the classroom. They are concerned with: getting and keeping their pupils' attention; getting them to contribute to the lesson when appropriate and to keep quiet when appropriate; checking on whether their pupils understand the point of the lesson; and with clarifying what they think their pupils have not understood. Therefore, taking the teaching situation as an example of a speech event is itself an example of theoretical sampling. It supposes that the particularly asymmetrical power relations within most classrooms will provide rich data on the range of ways in which one speaker may control the development of discourse. Second, tape-recorded data collected in a French–English teaching situation highlight certain peculiarities of the communication situation in the classroom as follows. A native speaking to foreigners is likely to be conscious of having to make an effort to make sure he is 'getting across' to his hearers. But this problem probably only exaggerates the essentially similar problem faced by any teacher: how can he check up on whether his pupils understand what he is trying to teach them? In other words, to ask a teacher to teach foreign pupils arguably does not present him with essentially different problems (in terms, at least, of monitoring understanding), but only with more acute problems of the same kind. The idea of theoretical sampling was therefore applied here to reveal a form of behaviour which might otherwise be difficult to study in its full range, by setting up a situation which would generate a wide range of this behaviour. In case it be thought, however, that such a cross-cultural teaching situation is too odd to be of much relevance to normal teaching, the tape-recorded data were supported by observation of teacher-talk during periods of classroom observation in traditional English lessons in a Scottish secondary school. Rich data generated by theoretical sampling can be used to develop concepts which can then be applied to, or checked against, more normal situations.

In a comparable way, S. Harris (1980), in her study of discourse in Magistrates' courts, argues that the social situation is one which by its very nature produces a large number of questions, directives and threats from the magistrate to the defendant. The situation, therefore, provides very rich data on the possible realizations of such speech acts. Harris also argues that the enormous repetitiveness of the data provides a good check that the data are being correctly interpreted by the analyst. In everyday casual conversation, there is a flood of meanings conveyed, often very elliptically, and the corresponding danger that utterances will be misinterpreted by an outsider. However, the arrears and maintenance courts which she recorded provide a natural control over the propositional content of what is said. The content is very predictable, the basic proposition which is continually conveyed by all magistrates to all defendants being, "If you don't pay, you will go to prison." With the propositional content held constant, it is possible to study the relation between this content and the range of surface syntactic and lexical forms which may realize it.

The basic point of theoretical sampling is, therefore, that all data are biased in some way, but that these biases may be systematically exploited.

9 *Triangulation*

It is a matter of everyday commonsense, as well as of police methods and the theory of social sciences, that accounts of an event should be cross-checked against other independent accounts or evidence gathered by a variety of methods. The term *triangulation* is used in different ways, but essentially it refers to collecting and comparing different perspectives on a situation. Thus survey data might be checked against ethnographic observations, and more generally quantitative data might be checked against qualitative reports, and vice versa. An important part of Glaser and Strauss' (1967) argument is that any method may be good for generating ideas, and that a combination is probably best. Webb *et al.* (1966) similarly argue the need for combining different methods of research in the social sciences, first since this provides a means of cross-validation, and second since no measure ever taps a single, isolated, pure parameter. So far, in this chapter I have argued precisely that all measures are theoretically complex, since they always involve the researcher's interpretations. Cicourel (1973: 124) also uses the term, in a theoretically more loaded way, emphasizing that however much we triangulate, the result will always be indefinite:

> I use the expression 'indefinite triangulation' to suggest that every procedure that seems to 'lock in' evidence, thus to claim a level of adequacy, can itself be subjected to the same sort of analysis that will in turn produce yet another indefinite arrangement of new particulars or a rearrangement of previously established particulars in 'authoritative', 'final', 'formal' accounts.

Thus different kinds of evidence may be combined, but the account will always depend on the reader filling in knowledge, and will never be finally validated.

The procedures of triangulation used by Adelman (1981) emphasize that there is potentially no end to the collecting and comparing of accounts. He is interested in how teachers and pupils interpret each other in the classroom, although he does not do any detailed linguistic analysis of his data. He recorded classroom lessons, on audio-tape, in tape-slide sequences, and in other forms. Selected extracts were played back to pupils involved, and they were asked for their accounts and interpretations. These accounts, also recorded, were played back to the teacher, who interprets the pupils' comments. Lesson and accounts were transcribed and extracts derived from the same incident were juxtaposed. This is one possible sequence of comparing different perspectives: clearly, there are others, and clearly there is no point at which the comparison has ended.

One major idea behind the concept of triangulation is, therefore, that the analyst's account should be compared with participants' accounts. There is a tenuous thread in sociological method which admits participants' own interpretations of events as valid data. A classic, early paper which suggests the value of taking an actor at his word, is C. Wright Mills' (1940) work on vocabularies of motive. The analysis of participants' accounts of events continues in work by Scott and Lyman (1968), Harré and Secord (1972) and in the work of the symbolic interactionists and the ethnomethodologists. Linguists, on the other hand, have tended to dismiss users' accounts of their own behaviour or attitudes to language as haphazard, unreliable and naive. I have argued in detail elsewhere (Stubbs, 1981) that linguists should pay more attention to what speakers have to say about their own language.

However, more generally, triangulation can refer to combining different kinds of data. It has become fairly frequent for papers on sociolinguistics to insist that different methods be combined in research. For example, Hymes (1962) insists that it is meaningless to study language-use, language functions and attitudes to language as though they were separate, and that different methods are required to study this complex of behaviour and belief. Similarly, Labov's (1972c: 102) principle of convergence in linguistic methodology is that 'the value of new data for confirming and interpreting old data is directly proportional to the differences in the methods used to gather it.' Labov's own macro-level, survey-style studies on patterns of social class stratification and language variation link data on the use of phonological and grammatical variables, gathered in interview situations and partly checked by unsystematic observation in natural situations, and data on subjective evaluations of language, gathered by artificially constructed tests. (In the subjective reaction test subjects are asked to rate tape-recorded speakers in terms of occupational suitability. And the index of linguistic insecurity requires subjects to choose which of two socially significant pronunciations or words is 'correct' and which they themselves use. The measure of linguistic insecurity is the number of items on which their judgements differ between correctness and reported self-usage.) He shows that complementary patterns emerge from different sets of data. His analysis of a speech event (Labov, 1972e, on sounding or exchanges of ritual insults in American Negro culture) links data on the grammatical forms and sequencing of 'sounds', with inferences as to their function, and with a discussion of participants' own evaluations and explicit discussion of the 'sounds'. The links made are not, however, discussed by Labov as in any way problematic.

Within recent Chomskyan linguistics, there has been an extreme narrowing of focus, and an extreme reliance on one type of introspective data. However, other linguists have always resisted this artificial narrowing of data. For example, Quirk has always, in his work, combined meticulous observation, use of a corpus of data, personal intuitions, elicitation of intuitions, and other experimental methods (e.g. Quirk and Greenbaum, 1970). The most important point is that all methods of data-collection have sources of error: one should, therefore, combine methods which have different biases.

In a study of classroom discourse Willes (1980; 1981) points out that participant observation and recording are not enough to investigate pupils' communicative competence, since a pupil may be competent, but silent. She therefore uses also experimental, elicitation techniques to investigate the linguistic competence of such children. And in a study of classroom discourse in West Australian schools, Malcolm (1979) combines different kinds of data: audio-recordings of teacher–pupil dialogue, together with associated observations and coding; interviews with teachers and Aborigines; and interpretations of the classroom recordings by Aboriginal aides. He thus combines different kinds of data, and uses the kind of participants' interpretations proposed by Adelman.

Labov, in a quote cited above, warns about the indefinite string of interpretation which always lies between data and analysis. And yet in the principle of convergence, also cited above, he appears to hold that triangulation provides a solution to the problem. In parts of his methodological statements, Labov argues (1972c: 68) for 'the possibility of being right' in producing theories of language-use, putting forward this argument with reference to Popper's principles concerning the nature of scientific explanation. The article ends with this sentence, which refers to the principle of convergence:

Data from a variety of distinct sources and methods, properly *interpreted* [emphasis added], can be used to converge on *right* answers to hard questions.

Labov is clearly arguing for a 'God's truth' view that language, as a system in use, has a structure that is 'out there' and which the linguist has to work out. For an equally extreme God's truth statement, compare the final sentences of Labov (1972f):

... the kind of solutions offered to problems ... are deeply embedded in the data. It is reasonable to believe that they are more than constructions of the analyst – they are properties of language itself.

He is implicitly opposing the 'hocus-pocus' view that the structure is, at least partly, a product of the linguist's interpretative analysis. But Labov's position appears contradictory when he talks within one sentence of interpretations and of right answers, since to emphasize the interpretative work on which the analysis depends, is to emphasize that the analysis is essentially and unavoidably a researcher's product. He is, in any case, misrepresenting Popper, who argues for the relativity of basic statements in science, and that we can never know if we are right:

Theories are ... *never* empirically verifiable.... The empirical basis of objective science has nothing 'absolute' about it. Science does not rest upon solid bedrock. The bold structure of its theories rises, as it were, above a swamp. (Popper, 1959: 40, 111, emphasis in original; Labov's references are also to Popper, 1959.)

For equally unequivocal statements from Popper, see: 'There can be no ultimate statements in science' (1959: 47); 'Science ... can never claim to have attained truth or even a substitute for it such as probability' (1959: 278); '... every scientific statement must remain tentative forever' (1959: 280); etc.

Much recent linguistics has ignored actually occurring language data, rejecting these as mere performance. Discourse analysis cannot ignore actual occurrences, but it would be a similar mistake to restrict study to actual occurrences, without using other data: intuitive and experimental, and participants' as well as analysts' accounts, in order to converge on a well corroborated descriptive statement. However, as Cicourel (cited above) emphasizes, such triangulation will remain indefinite.

10   *The problem of perception*

One final and very important justification for a form of theoretical sampling, and also for triangulating on the data by deliberately collecting different perspectives on them, is the problem of perception. There are two distinct problems in research on social interaction. One is to describe it: what are the appropriate descriptive categories? But the first problem is to see what is going on: how can we learn to notice what we normally take for granted? This is a general problem of research strategies. What is the researcher to do when confronted with what has been called the 'bloomin', buzzin' confusion' of any normal social setting? Even so perceptive a commentator on conversation as Harvey Sacks admits to having spent over a year working on a particular piece of data before he noted a central feature of its construction which was obvious once pointed out (see Sacks, lecture 3, Spring 1970, April 16). Much writing on social interaction has stopped short with a kind of awe that it shows such detailed complexity at all levels, including paralinguistic (intonation, accent, etc.), kinesic (body motion), proxemic (body position), as well as different linguistic levels. Pittenger *et al.* (1960) is an early study of spoken interaction, using audio-recorded data from the first five minutes of a psychiatric interview. The study shows great sensitivity to the extreme complexity of what is going on, but this does not lead to any significant generalization about the functions of different items of communicative behaviour. The analysis, as the authors admit, is entirely at the ideographic level of what is particular and unique. Lenneberg (1962) puts this neatly and ironically in a review of the book: 'Microscopic interview analysis... is a new tool for its users. Its resolving power seems to be excellent. Let us hope, now that we can discover something with it.' A commonly expressed overall conclusion is that in human communicative behaviour, 'nothing never happens' or that 'anything anyone ever says is true' (quoted by Pittenger *et al.*, 1960: 234). Such paradoxical statements reveal disquieting truths. A teacher inevitably communicates something to his pupils the moment he walks into the class-room – by his style of speech, his accent, his tone of voice, his gestures, his facial expression, and by whether he sits stolidly behind his desk or walks up the passage and puts his arm around a pupil's shoulder. Members of a society do interpretative work on the smallest and most fleeting fragments of behaviour. However, in another sense, such paradoxical statements are unhelpful. There is no direct way to investigate such complexity of behaviour. If a researcher wants a fruitful strategy, it does not help simply to emphasize how skilfully we all manipulate and interpret information coming and going simultaneously on many channels. Too much happens too fast for the researcher to take account of it and describe it directly. It is all too easy to collect data on speech behaviour – all one needs is a tape-recorder. But such data are too rich to be useful, unless one has also a way of focusing on the features of communication which are relevant. An undiscriminating gaze down the microscope will generally tell the researcher nothing. What events reveal depends on the nature of our questions. The 'seen but unnoticed' expectancies (Garfinkel, 1967: 36) which govern the smooth ongoing of verbal interaction are even more difficult to make visible in their relevant details than other taken-for-granted aspects of everyday life in society. Language is even closer to us than other social routines, implicated as it is in the development of our cognitive and self-regulative processes, as well as being part and parcel of our everyday social interaction. The researcher therefore needs some estrangement device to enable him to step back and observe what is going on in situations of face-to-face verbal communication.

The linguist–researcher is typically a native member of the society whose behaviour he is trying to describe, but, as such, he pre-interprets the behaviour just as other native members do. He understands what he sees, even before he has a chance to record it. On the other hand, there is no reason why the linguist–researcher should be afraid to use his intuitive knowledge of the system of communicative behaviour in order to work out its structure. Indeed, there is, in principle, no way of inducing the systematic significance of fragments of behaviour, without making use of the tacit knowledge of the system held by a native or near-native member. It would be impossible to set up an automatic procedure which would allow one to induce the rules for appropriate speech behaviour in a given speech community, without the privileged access to the meaning of the speech held only by someone with intuitive knowledge of the system.

Different people react differently to such demonstrations of the complexity of everyday behaviour. Some infer, quite wrongly I believe, that complexity means chaos, that there is no pattern to be found, and that interaction is 'natural'. Such an attitude is unhelp- ful. In order to show that there is no pattern in something, one would have to have tried and rejected every possible pattern: an impossible task, in practice and also in theory. Others infer that complexity cannot be handled and therefore has to be controlled by artificial experimental procedures: this may lead them to studying artificial instead of natural behaviour. I believe that both of these reactions are unnecessary. But the problem remains: how do we manage to see patterns in taken-for-granted behaviour which is awesomely more complex than we generally realize? A well-known reaction to this problem is Garfinkel's, who discusses ways of making visible the 'seen but unnoticed' expectancies (1967: 36) of social interaction. He proposes (1967: 38) techniques 'as aids to a sluggish imagination' which 'produce reflections through which the strange- ness of an obstinately familiar world can be detected'. And several of his estrangement techniques are well known, particularly those involving his penchant for deliberately disrupting social scenes: 'procedurally it is my preference to start with familiar scenes and see what can be done to make trouble' (1967: 38). It is not necessary, however, to disrupt behaviour artificially: a technique in common use amongst linguists is to focus on situations in which something is naturally going wrong. For example, Laver (1970) discusses evidence about the neural control system from hesitations, language disorders, and the like. Campbell and Wales (1970) discuss errors in language acquisition as evidence of ways in which children organize experience through language. Fry (1970) uses error-correction in normal speech as evidence for multi-level planning and reception of speech. Marshall (1970) summarizes evidence from some pathological speech disturbances. A classic study from another field, based on the same principle, is, of course, Freud's *The Psychopathology of Everyday Life* (1901) which discusses the deep determinants of slips of the tongue, forgetting of proper names, and so on, to argue that 'the unconscious does not lie'.

Ferguson has developed in great detail the value of studying deviant production and comprehension, in his work on the simplified registers of the kind which speakers of different languages use in interacting with babies, foreigners, deaf people, mentally retarded people, animals, and so on. (Ferguson, 1977, provides one useful summary statement.) He argues for the value of studying language produced where there are perceived difficulties in communication.

And he argues that users have views of what it is psycholinguistically easy to process. Such varieties as baby-talk and foreigner-talk are not peripheral deviations from normal language, but display universal tendencies in linguistic simplification, which are also observable in pidginization.

One way of breaching the researcher's expectancies is to have him concentrate on the causes, forms and effects of miscommunication. Rather than attempt to capture directly how people communicate, the researcher can concentrate on the problematic aspects of communication situations – points, for example, at which the communication typically breaks down or encounters difficulties. By looking at what happens when people fail to get the message across, at why this happens and at what speakers do in order to reinstate the normal smooth flow of interaction, one can gain insight into the routine structures of behaviour.

Even in everyday conversation, moments of miscommunication arise more frequently than is often realized. But there is a general rule in our society that demands that interaction proceed at a smooth flow: silences are often considered embarrassing and disagreements must normally be mitigated. So speakers immediately counteract departures from the smooth ongoing of normal face-to-face interaction by making (if necessary, violent) attempts to restore the ritual equilibrium (Goffman, 1955). Normally, vigorous attempts are not necessary, since a constantly self-regulating mechanism generally operates during situations of talk – a delicately set thermostat which keeps the communication system simmering at the desired temperature. Gaffes and faux pas are only allowed to run their disastrous or farcical course on the stage. Participants in a conversation or discussion typically combine to minimize misunderstandings as soon as they appear on the horizon, by constantly monitoring their own language, reading between the lines of other speakers' speech and by keeping an eye on the system itself. But think of common expressions in English to do with communication going wrong and with people failing to pick up communicative cues: 'a nod's as good as a wink to a blind horse', 'he doesn't know when he's not wanted', 'he didn't get the message' and 'he can't take a hint'. All these idioms point to the need to do constant interpretative work on the attitudes underlying the overt message – the need to continually 'read between the lines'. (Milroy, in press, discusses theoretical and practical reasons for studying miscommunications.)

However, these systems-management mechanisms are brought into action so fast that they are not easily visible except in problematic situations which force the speakers to take more explicit and vigorous correcting manoeuvres than usual. As well as those situations listed above, problematic situations which reveal more clearly the kind of strategy which speakers have for keeping in touch with each other include: talking to a blind person, or talking to someone on the telephone (no visual feedback); situations of cross-cultural communication; most situations involving someone met for the first time; teaching. I am suggesting, therefore, that it is a fruitful research strategy to look at ways in which speakers compensate for difficulties inherent in the communication system. For people in social situations have not only ways of maintaining equilibrium, they also have systematic ways of dealing with problematic situations when they arise. What kind of instructions are available to speakers who find themselves in problematic situations? What kind of competence can be imputed to them? What are the limits on this kind of ability? How do teachers compensate for the particularly bad communication conditions which characterize the typical classroom?

One source of data on communication with the hard of hearing or the visually handicapped is radio programmes. A recent edition of the BBC radio programme *In Touch*, for the blind and partially sighted, discussed listeners' letters on the problem they have of attracting the attention of personnel in shops, and the problems they have when normally sighted people try to engage them in a social encounter before, say, helping them across the street. The discussion focused on what cues could be substituted for the normal nonverbal cues routinely used to initiate conversation with another person, and therefore revealed aspects of conversation which are problematic for the blind, but taken-for-granted by sighted people. As Bird-whistell (1970: 112) warns, however, it would be simplistic to believe that the study of the deaf and the blind will somehow isolate communicative behaviours and make them easy to study. Such studies give a different, but not a simplified, perspective. Similarly, Cicourel (1973) and Cicourel and Boese (1972) study native signers amongst the deaf for the insights this gives into oral language: they too emphasize the complexity of signing as a fully developed natural language. H. G. Wells' (1904) short story, *The Country of the Blind*, is a fascinating example of the sociological insights which can result even from a fictional account of a problematic communication situation.

Another procedure for focusing on problematic discourse is discussed at length by Burton (1980), who compares natural conversation with dialogue in the theatre. She concentrates in particular on the Theatre of the Absurd, on the grounds that it sets out explicitly to make problematic our commonsense understanding of everyday conversation. Much modern theatre in general is set explicitly within the tradition of alienation (Verfremdungseffekte), developed at length by Brecht, and aims to get audiences to think about what they take for granted as everyday reality, rather than sinking comfortably into a purportedly realistic genre of literature.

All these various methodological procedures, then, are ways of making strange what we normally do not perceive, because we take it for granted as competent conversationalists. The basic concept is that of using alienation or estrangement devices, to focus the attention on what is usually not noticed. As I implied above, simply the facts of recording and transcribing conversational data are themselves valuable estrangement techniques. Most people have simply never examined discourse objectively, in the way that is made possible by such methods. On the one hand, such records reify the process. On the other hand, by turning a dialogue into a reified product, this makes available a type of data which leads to the perception of unnoticed phenomena. The discipline of making a detailed transcription forces the transcriber to listen over and over again to features of discourse which otherwise remain hidden. All methodological procedures have inherent dangers, but their inadequacies can often also be exploited.

11   An illustration

As a concrete footnote to a rather abstract methodological chapter, consider the following short conversational exchange, from my field notes, as a piece of data which illustrates some of the things that I have been discussing: namely, a problem in communication, a moment of miscommunication, and a long string of interpretative work collapsed into a very short interchange, including two re-interpretations of one remark.

The situation is a small conversational group within a party on an evening during a research conference. C is doing imitations of people. He does a peculiar walk. No one recognizes it. Finally I recognize it as Groucho Marx. C redoes his walk, and the exchange goes:

MS: Very good. Ten out of ten. Full marks.   (1)

C: (Pause. No reaction.)   (2)
      (Suddenly.) You've almost got it.   (3)
MS: I HAVE got it.   (4)
C: Ah!   (5)

I start with a problem of how to communicate to C that I have recognized the walk without telling the others the answer. I must not only tell C that I know the answer (he might think I was bluffing), but show him that I know. Within this short exchange at least the following interpretations were performed and solutions to problems found.

(a)   I find a play on words: Marx/marks.

(b)   I find a context in which to apply this play on words by apparently using the comment *Full marks* to praise the walk as a good walk, funny in itself perhaps.

(c)   But I have another problem. If I say *Full marks* on its own, this may not be understood out of context: i.e. I am aware of a possible misunderstanding. One source of trouble might be that some people could mishear it as a name, since that is what they are expecting at this point. If they mishear it as the name *Marx,* my play on words would have misfired. So I construct a context which sets up hearers to hear it as I intend, by saying: *Very Good, Ten out of ten . . . .*

(d)   I expect C to hear both senses, since I know that he knows the name, and I expect him to bring this knowledge to bear on interpreting my utterance.

(e)   C does not react – he does not understand my joke. He interprets my remarks as the others would, as applying unambiguously to a description of the walk.

(f)   At (3) C *re*interprets what I have said. He sees the play on words that I have made, but does not realize that I made it consciously. C now tells me the joke that I have just told him! Presumably he does this as a clue to me and others. He gives me a puzzle to solve, not realizing that I have already constructed that puzzle and given it to him.

(g)   At (4) I show him that I am aware of the joke. i.e. I solve a new problem: for after (3) I still have to tell C that I recognize the walk. If I say nothing now, my joke is wasted, and doubly – for I now have the chance of a joke at C's expense: that he has told my own joke, on top of my original play on words.

(h)   C *re*interprets my remark (1) for the second time, and then tells me that he has 'got the point' and that he now 'knows what I am talking about'. Note that he inevitably sees both jokes together: he could not see one without the other. He sees my original joke, plus his joke misfiring, plus my topping his attempted joke, plus that we both see all this. At the end of the sequence, he can see the sense of the whole sequence, which he has not seen during it. For C, the sense of what is going on or what is being talked about emerges and changes during the exchange. The meaning which unfolds is also negotiated: expressed informally, I refuse to let C get away with the interpretation of my original remark which (I suppose) he forms.

Obviously this exchange is not typical. We are not always required to solve plays on words. But we do routinely perform long strings of interpretations, collapsed in short and rapid conversational exchanges. Such examples demonstrate the complexity of interpretation of which conversationalists are technically capable. Ways in which jokes are used spontaneously in everyday conversation can provide many insights into the routine structures of interaction. But their complex social functions, (for example, in social control or in breaching taboo topics) have hardly been studied. Analyses of jokes have on the whole been psychological. For papers which do discuss how jokes are used in social settings, see Torode (1976) and Walker and Adelman (1976).

However, the point of the example is that it is not typical, but illuminative: it shows up sharply what might be less clear in more mundane exchanges. It is a short theoretical sample based explicitly on a problem of communication and miscommunication. I have commented on this exchange only by showing particular examples of some of the interpretations which were probably made, in order to argue that other interpretative work could also have been involved in the exchange.

Having shown this analysis, precisely as it appears here, to C, I received these comments from him which can be used to triangulate on the quoted data:

You need...my cultural expectations...(The incident) was a surprise – it was not in my expectations for how you would be thinking and talking...As you point out, I did not realize that you had not got the answer but had capped it with a pun... But the bit left out is the way my strong cultural expectations of you prevented the *meaning* of what you said being understood by me. If the remark had come from X or Y I probably would have got the point.

A central topic for sociolinguistic study is ways in which more general and formalized statements can be made about this kind of interpretative work which is routinely performed on connected discourse. Without such interpretations, discourse is not connected.

12 Conclusions

As L. Hudson (1966: 29) writes, 'In practice, scientific research is frequently a muddled, piratical affair, and we do no service to anyone by pretending otherwise.' I have argued in this chapter that finding patterns in the passing social scene involves particular practical problems. I have also argued that such practical problems are irremediably involved in theoretical questions, when the topic of research is how people interpret social behaviour.

Published papers in sociolinguistics, and in the social sciences in general, rarely give glimpses of the methodological troubles of their authors. Books appear tidily packaged, as this one is, between introductions and conclusions, and provided with titles, section headings, references, cross-references, footnotes, and quotes from eminent scholars. Behind such books lie the untidy aspects of research: informants who never turned up, drawers full of collected but unused (unusable?) data, and days spent writing chapters on methodology to put off collecting data and analysing it.

Further Reading

Students using this book as a textbook may find helpful the following suggestions for further reading. The books listed are representative of a wide range of approaches to analysing discourse which I have not been able to discuss in detail. Their level of difficulty should make them accessible to students who have read this book.

Burton, D. (1980) *Dialogue and Discourse: A Sociolinguistic Approach to Modern Drama Dialogue and Naturally Occurring Conversation.* London, Routledge & Kegan Paul.

A comparison of natural conversation and theatrical dialogue, including an analysis of short plays by Pinter and Ionesco. Based on the Birmingham approach to discourse analysis discussed in chapter 7 above. ·

Crystal, D. and Davy, D. (1975) *Advanced Conversational English.* London, Longman.

Actually intended as a textbook for English as a foreign language. But a useful source of data, containing transcriptions of conversations, and also some commentary on features of conversational English.

De Beaugrande, R. and Dressler, W. (1981) *An Introduction to Textlinguistics.* London, Longman.

A useful summary of work by Van Dijk, Kintsch, Petöfi, and others with many references to their original work. Rather abstract overall.

Edmondson, W. (1981) *Spoken Discourse: A Model for Analysis.* London, Longman.

Useful discussion of the relation between speech act theory and discourse analysis. All the data are hypothetical or simulated.

Ervin-Tripp, S. and Mitchell-Kernan, C., eds. (1977) *Child Discourse.* New York, Academic Press.

Several important analyses of child–adult and child–child discourse.

Goffman, E. (1981) *Forms of Talk.* Philadelphia, University of Pennsylvania Press. Oxford, Blackwell.

A micro-sociological approach to discourse. Chapter 1 is especially relevant to my discussion of exchange structure in chapters 6 and 7.

Labov, W. and Fanshel, D. (1977) *Therapeutic Discourse: Psychotherapy as Conversation.* New York, Academic Press.

A detailed analysis of a psychotherapeutic interview. And a general discussion of central principles of discourse analysis.

McCawley, J. D. (1981) *Everything that Linguists Have Always Wanted to Know about Logic but were Ashamed to Ask.* Chicago, University of Chicago Press. Oxford, Blackwell.

Clear discussions of propositional and predicate logic, and chapters on speech acts, implicatures and presuppositions.

Saville-Troike, M. (1982) *The Ethnography of Communication: An Introduction.* Oxford, Blackwell. Baltimore, University Park Press.

A clear summary of findings about spoken communication in many different cultures.

The following collections of readings also contain important work. Students may find the articles in these books rather more difficult: Cole, ed., 1978; 1981; Cole and Morgan, eds., 1975; Dressler, ed., 1977; Joshi *et al.*, eds., 1981; Schenkein, ed., 1978; Werth, ed., 1981.

References

Abercrombie, D. 1954. The recording of dialect material. In *Studies in Phonetics and Linguistics.* London: Oxford University Press, 108–13.

Adelman, C., ed. 1981. *Uttering, Muttering.* London: Grant McIntyre.

Adelman, C. 1981. On first hearing. In Adelman, ed., 78–97.

Algeo, J. 1978. What consonant clusters are possible? *Word*, 29, 3, 206–24.

Ardener, E., ed. 1971. *Social Anthropology and Language.* London: Tavistock.

Argyle, M. 1969. *Social Interaction.* London: Methuen.

Atkinson, M. and Griffiths, P. 1973. Here's here's, there's, here and there. *Edinburgh Working Papers in Linguistics*, 3, 29–73.

Atkinson, P. 1981. Inspecting classroom talk. In Adelman, ed., 98–113.

Auerbach, E. 1946. *Mimesis.* Princeton: University Press.

Austin, J. L. 1958. Performative-constative. In Searle, ed., 1971, 13–22.

Austin, J. L. 1961. Performative utterances. In Austin, 1961.

Austin, J. L. 1961. *Philosophical Papers*, ed. J. O. Urmson and G. J. Warnock. 2nd edn, 1970. London: Clarendon.

Austin, J. L. 1962. *How to Do Things with Words*, ed. J. O. Urmson. London: Oxford University Press.

Bald, W.-D. 1980. Some functions of *yes* and *no* in conversation. In Greenbaum *et al.*, eds., 178–91.

Bar-Hillel, Y. 1954. Indexical expressions. *Mind*, 63, 359–76.

Bar-Hillel, Y. 1970. Communication and argumentation in pragmatic languages. In B. Visentini *et al.*, eds., *Linguaggi nella Società e nella Tecnica.* Milan: Edizioni di Comunità, 269–84.

Bar-Hillel, Y., ed. 1971. *Pragmatics of Natural Languages.* Dordrecht: Reidel.

Barnes, D., Britton, J. and Rosen, H. 1969. *Language, the Learner and the School*. Harmondsworth: Penguin.

Bartlett, F. C. 1932. *Remembering*. London: Cambridge University Press.

Bates, E. 1976. *Language in Context: the Acquisition of Pragmatics*. New York: Academic Press.

Baumert, M. 1977. Classification of English question–answer structure. *Journal of Pragmatics*, 1, 1, 85–92.

Belnap, N. D. 1977. A useful four-valued logic. In M. Dunn and G. Epstein, eds., *Modern Uses of Multiple-Valued Logic*. Dordrecht: Reidel.

Bennett, J. 1976. *Linguistic Behaviour*. London: Cambridge University Press.

Bernstein, B. B. 1971a. *Class, Codes and Control*, vol. 1. London: Routledge & Kegan Paul.

Bernstein, B. B. 1971b. On the classification and framing of educational knowledge. In M. F. D. Young, ed., *Knowledge and Control*. London: Collier Macmillan, 47–69.

Berry, M. 1980a. They're all out of step except our Johnny: a discussion of motivation (or the lack of it) in systemic linguistics. Unpublished paper read to Seventh Systemic Workshop, Sheffield.

Berry, M. 1980b. Systemic linguistics and discourse analysis. a multi-layered approach to exchange structure (Part 2). University of Nottingham, Mimeo.

Berry, M. 1981a. Systemic linguistics and discourse analysis: a multi-layered approach to exchange structure. In Coulthard and Montgomery, eds., 120–45.

Berry, M. 1981b. Polarity, ellipticity and propositional development, their relevance to the well-formedness of an exchange. *Nottingham Linguistic Circular*, 10, 1, 36–63.

Birdwhistell, R. L. 1961. Paralanguage twenty-five years after Sapir. In Laver and Hutcheson, eds., 1972, 82–100.

Birdwhistell, R. L. 1970. *Kinesics and Context*. Philadelphia: University of Pennsylvania Press. Also Harmondsworth: Penguin.

Bleiberg, S. and Churchill, L. 1975. Notes on confrontation in conversation. *Journal of Psycholinguistic Research*, 4, 3, 273–8.

Bloomfield, L. 1933. *Language*. New York: Henry Holt.

Brazil, D. 1975. *Discourse Intonation*. Discourse Analysis Monographs, 1, University of Birmingham, English Language Research. Mimeo.

Brazil, D. 1981. Discourse analysis as linguistics: a response to Hammersley. In French and McLure, eds., 59–72.

Brazil, D., Coulthard, M. and Johns, K. 1980. *Discourse Intonation and Language Teaching.* London: Longman.

Bright, W., ed. 1966. *Sociolinguistics.* The Hague: Mouton.

Brown, G. 1977. *Listening to Spoken English.* London: Longman.

Brown, G., Currie, K. and Kenworthy, J. 1980. *Questions of Intonation.* London: Croom Helm.

Brown, R. 1980. The role of the listener's expectations in speaker recognition. *Work in Progress,* 13, 72–8.

Brown, R. and Gilman, A. 1960. The pronouns of power and solidarity. In Sebeok, ed., 253–77.

Bruner, J. S. 1975. The ontogenesis of speech acts. *Journal of Child Language,* 2, 1–19.

Bublitz, W. 1978. *Ausdrucksweisen der Sprechereinstellung im Deutschen und Englischen.* Tübingen: Niemeyer.

Bublitz, W. 1980. Conducive yes–no questions in English. Paper 70, Series 12, University of Trier, Linguistic Agency.

Bühler, K. 1934. *Sprachtheorie.* Jena: Fischer. Reprinted Stuttgart: Fisher, 1965.

Burton, D. 1978. *Dialogue and Discourse.* Unpublished Ph.D. thesis, University of Birmingham.

Burton, D. 1980. *Dialogue and Discourse.* London: Routledge & Kegan Paul.

Burton, D. 1981a. The sociolinguistic analysis of spoken discourse. In French and MacLure, eds., 21–46.

Burton, D. 1981b. Analysing spoken discourse. In Coulthard and Montgomery, eds., 61–81.

Butler, C. S. 1982. *The Directive Function of the English Modals.* Unpublished PhD. thesis, University of Nottingham.

Butler, C. S. in press. Communicative function and semantics. In Halliday and Fawcett, eds.

Campbell, R. and Wales, R. 1970. The study of language acquisition. In Lyons, ed., 242–60.

Carroll, L. 1865. *Alice's Adventures in Wonderland.* London: Macmillan, 1966.

Carter, R. A. 1979. *Towards a Theory of Discourse Stylistics.* Unpublished Ph.D. thesis, University of Birmingham.

Cazden, C., John, V. and Hymes, D., eds. 1972. *Functions of Language in the Classroom.* New York: Teachers College Press.

Chafe, W. L. 1974. Language and consciousness. *Language,* 50, 111–33.

Cheshire, J. 1978. Present tense verbs in Reading English. In Trudgill, ed., 52–68.

Chesterton, G. K. 1929. The Green Man. In *The Scandal of Father Brown.* London: Cassell. Also Harmondsworth: Penguin, 1978.

Chomsky, N. 1965. *Aspects of the Theory of Syntax.* Cambridge, Mass.: MIT Press.

Cicourel, A. 1973. *Cognitive Sociology.* Harmondsworth: Penguin.

Cicourel, A. and Boese, R. J. 1972. Sign language acquisition and the teaching of deaf children. In Cazden *et al.*, eds., 32–62.

Clarke, D. D. 1975. The use and recognition of sequential structure in dialogue. *British Journal of Social and Clinical Psychology,* 14, 333–9.

Cohen, L. J. 1974. Do illocutionary forces exist? *Philosophical Quarterly,* 14. Also in K. T. Fann, ed., *Symposium on J. L. Austin.* London: Routledge & Kegan Paul, 420–44.

Cole, P., ed. 1978. *Syntax and Semantics,* vol. 9, *Pragmatics.* New York: Academic Press.

Cole, P., ed. 1981. *Radical Pragmatics.* New York: Academic Press.

Cole, P. and Morgan, J. L., eds. 1975. *Syntax and Semantics,* vol. 3, *Speech Acts.* New York: Academic Press.

Coulmas, F. 1979. On the sociolinguistic relevance of routine formulae. *Journal of Pragmatics,* 3, 3/4, 239–66.

Coulthard, M. 1977. *An Introduction to Discourse Analysis.* London: Longman.

Coulthard, M. 1981. Developing the description. In Coulthard and Montgomery, eds., 13–30.

Coulthard, M. and Ashby, M. C. 1975. Talking with the doctor. *Journal of Communication,* 25, 3, 240–7.

Coulthard, M. and Brazil, D. 1981. Exchange structure. In Coulthard and Montgomery, eds., 82–106.

Coulthard, M. and Montgomery, M., eds. 1981. *Studies in Discourse Analysis.* London: Routledge & Kegan Paul.

Creider, C. A. 1979. On the explanation of transformations. In Givón, ed., 3–22.

Crystal, D. 1980. Neglected grammatical factors in conversational English. In Greenbaum *et al.*, eds., 153–66.

Crystal, D. and Davy, D. 1969. *Investigating English Style.* London: Longman.

Crystal, D. and Davy, D., 1975. *Advanced Conversational English.* London: Longman.

Culler, J. 1975. *Structuralist Poetics.* London, Routledge & Kegan Paul.

Dahl, R. 1970. The great automatic grammatizator. In *Someone Like You.* Harmondsworth: Penguin, 190–209.

Dalton, P. and Hardcastle, W. D. 1977. *Disorders of Fluency*. London: Edward Arnold.

Danes, F. 1968. Some thoughts on the semantic structure of the sentence. *Lingua*, 21, 55–9.

Dascal, M. and Katriel, T. 1979. Digressions: a study in conversational coherence. *Poetics and the Theory of Literature*, 4, 203–32.

Davison, A. 1975. Indirect speech acts and what to do with them. In Cole and Morgan, eds., 143–86.

Dixon, R. M. W. 1971. A method of semantic description. In Steinberg and Jakobovits, eds., 436–71.

Douglas, J., ed. 1970. *Understanding Everyday Life*. New York: Aldine.

Downes, W. 1977. The imperative and pragmatics. *Journal of Linguistics*, 13, 77–97.

Dressler, W. V., ed. 1978. *Current Trends in Textlinguistics*. Berlin: De Gruyter.

Duncan, S., Jr. 1972. Some signals and rules for taking speaking turns in conversations. *Journal of Personality and Social Psychology*, 23, 2, 283–92.

Edmondson, W. 1981. *Spoken Discourse*. London: Longman.

Egli, U. and Schleichert, H. 1976. A bibliography on the theory of questions and answers. *Linguistische Berichte*, 41, 105–28.

Ervin-Tripp, S. 1976. Is Sybil there? The structure of some American English directives. *Language in Society*, 5, 25–66.

Ervin-Tripp, S. and Mitchell-Kernan, C., eds. 1977. *Child Discourse*. New York: Academic Press.

Ferguson, C. A. 1975. Towards a characterization of English foreigner talk. *Anthropological Linguistics*, 17, 1–14.

Ferguson, C. A. 1977. Baby talk as a simplified register. In Snow and Ferguson, eds., 209–36.

Ficht, H. 1978. Supplement to a bibliography on the theory of questions and answers. *Linguistische Berichte*, 55, 92–114.

Firth, J. R. 1935. The technique of semantics. In *Papers in Linguistics 1934–51*, London: Oxford University Press, 1957, 7–33.

Fishman, J. A. 1971. *Sociolinguistics. A Brief Introduction*. Rowley, Mass.: Newbury House.

Flanders, N. 1970. *Analysing Teaching Behaviour*. London: Addison-Wesley.

Franck, D. 1979. Speech act and conversational move. *Journal of Pragmatics*, 3, 5, 461–6.

Fraser, B. 1975. Warning and threatening. *Centrum*, 3, 2, 169–80.

Frayn, M. 1965. *The Tin Men*. London: Collins.

French, P. and MacLure, M., eds. 1981. *Adult–Child Conversation.* London: Croom Helm.

Freud, S. 1901. *The Psychopathology of Everyday Life.* London: Benn, 1972.

Fries, C. 1952. *The Structure of English.* New York: Harcourt Brace. Also London: Longman, 1957.

Fry, D. B. 1970. Speech recognition and perception. In Lyons, ed., 29–52.

Furlong, V. 1976. Interaction sets in the classroom. In Stubbs and Delamont, eds., 23–44.

Gardner, M. 1965. *Mathematical Puzzles and Diversions.* Harmondsworth: Penguin.

Garfinkel, H. 1967. *Studies in Ethnomethodology.* Englewood Cliffs, New Jersey: Prentice Hall.

Garfinkel, H. and Sacks, H. 1970. On formal structures of practical action. In J. McKinney and E. Tiryakian, eds., *Theoretical Sociology.* New York: Appleton-Century-Crofts, 337–66.

Gazdar, G. 1974. Dialogue reconstruction: an experimental method. Unpublished paper.

Gazdar, G. 1979. Class, 'codes' and conversation. *Linguistics*, 17, 314, 199–211.

Gazdar, G. 1979. *Pragmatics.* New York: Academic Press.

Gazdar, G. 1980. Pragmatics and logical form. *Journal of Pragmatics*, 4, 1–13.

Gellner, E. 1959. *Words and Things.* London: Gollancz.

Givón, T. 1978. Negation in language: pragmatics, function, ontology. In Cole, ed., 69–112.

Givón, T. 1979. From discourse to syntax: grammar as a processing strategy. In Givón, ed., 81–112.

Givón, T., ed. 1979. *Syntax and Semantics*, vol. 12, *Discourse and Syntax.* New York: Academic Press.

Glaser, B. G. and Strauss, A. L. 1967. *The Discovery of Grounded Theory.* New York: Weidenfeld & Nicolson.

Godard, D. 1977. Same setting, different norms: phone-call beginnings in France and the United States. *Language in Society*, 6, 209–19.

Goffman, E. 1955. On face-work: an analysis of ritual elements in social interaction. In Laver and Hutcheson, eds., 1972, 319–46.

Goffman, E. 1964. The neglected situation. *American Anthropologist*, 66, 6 ,2, 133–6.

Goffman, E. 1971. *Relations in Public.* Harmondsworth: Penguin.

Goffman, E. 1981. *Forms of Talk.* Oxford: Blackwell.

Goodenough, W. 1964. Cultural anthropology and linguistics. In Hymes, ed., 36–9.

Greenbaum, S., ed. 1974. *Acceptability in Language*. The Hague: Mouton.

Greenbaum, S., Leech, G. and Svartvik, J., eds. 1980. *Studies in English Linguistics for Randolph Quirk*. London: Longman.

Grice, H. 1975. Logic and conversation. In Cole and Morgan, eds., 41–58.

Grimes, J. E. 1972. *The Thread of Discourse*. The Hague: Mouton.

Gumperz, J. J. and Hymes, D., eds. 1972. *Directions in Sociolinguistics*. New York: Holt, Rinehart & Winston.

Gunter, R. 1974. *Sentences in Dialog*. Columbia, S. Carolina: Hornbeam Press.

Haberland, H. and Mey, L. 1977. Editorial: pragmatics and linguistics. *Journal of Pragmatics*, 1, 1, 1–12.

Haiman, J. 1978. Conditionals are topics. *Language*, 54, 564–89.

Hale, K. 1971. A note on the Walbiri tradition of antonymy. In Steinberg and Jakobovits, eds., 472–82.

Halliday, M. A. K. 1970. Language structure and language function. In Lyons, ed., 140–65.

Halliday, M. A. K. 1978. *Language as Social Semiotic*. London: Edward Arnold.

Halliday, M. A. K. and Fawcett, R. P., eds. in press. *New Developments in Systemic Linguistics*. London: Batsford.

Halliday, M. A. K. and Hasan, R. 1976. *Cohesion in English*. London: Longman.

Hancher, M. 1979. The classification of co-operative illocutionary acts. *Language in Society*, 8, 1, 1–14.

Harré, R. and Secord, P. R. 1972. *The Explanation of Social Behaviour*. Oxford: Blackwell.

Harris, S. 1980. *Language Interaction in Magistrates' Courts*. Unpublished Ph.D. thesis, University of Nottingham.

Harris, Z. S. 1952. Discourse analysis. *Language*, 28, 1–30, 474–94.

Hemingway, E. 1925. Cat in the rain. In *In Our Time*. New York: Boni & Liveright. New York: Scribner, 1955. Reprinted in *The Essential Hemingway*. London: Jonathan Cape, 1947. Also Harmondsworth: Penguin, 1964; London: Granada, 1977.

Hinde, R. A., ed. 1972. *Non-Verbal Communication*. London: Cambridge University Press.

Hockett, C. F. 1968. *The State of the Art*. The Hague: Mouton.

Hoenigswald, H. M. 1966. A proposal for the study of folk-linguistics. In Bright, ed., 16–19.

Hoey, M. 1979. *Signalling in Discourse.* Discourse Analysis Monographs, 6, University of Birmingham, English Language Research, Mimeo.

Hoey, M. in prep. *On the Surface of Discourse.* London: Allen & Unwin.

Hofstadter, D. 1979. *Gödel, Escher, Bach: An Eternal Golden Braid.* London: Harvester. Also Harmondsworth: Penguin, 1980.

Hoyle, F. 1966. *October the First is Too Late.* London: Heinemann. Harmondsworth: Penguin, 1968.

Hudson, L. 1966. *Contrary Imaginations.* London: Methuen. Harmondsworth: Penguin.

Hudson, R. A. 1975. The meaning of questions. *Language,* 51, 1–31.

Hudson, R. A. 1976. *Arguments for a Non-Transformational Grammar.* Chicago: University of Chicago Press.

Hymes, D. 1962. The ethnography of speaking. In J. Fishman, ed., *Readings in the Sociology of Language.* The Hague: Mouton, 1968, 99–138.

Hymes, D., ed. 1964. *Language in Culture and Society.* New York: Harper & Row.

Hymes, D. 1966. The types of linguistic relativity (with examples from Amerindian ethnography). In Bright, ed., 114–57.

Hymes, D. 1972. Models of the interaction of language and social life. In Gumperz and Hymes, eds., 35–71.

Jackson, P. W. 1968. *Life in Classrooms.* New York: Holt, Rinehart & Winston.

Jakobson, R. 1960. Closing statement: linguistics and poetics. In Sebeok, ed., 350–77.

Jefferson, G. 1972. Side sequences. In Sudnow, ed., 294–338.

Jefferson, G. 1973. A case of precision timing in ordinary conversation. *Semiotica,* 9, 1, 47–96.

Jespersen, O. 1933. *Essentials of English Grammar.* London: Allen & Unwin.

Joshi, A. K., Webber, B. L. and Sag, I. A., eds. 1981. *Elements of Discourse Understanding.* London: Cambridge University Press.

Karttunen, L. 1976. *Discourse referents.* In McCawley, ed., 363–85.

Keller, E. 1979. Gambits: conversational strategy signals. *Journal of Pragmatics,* 3, 3/4, 219–38.

Kempson, R. M. 1975. *Presupposition and the Delimitation of Semantics.* London: Cambridge University Press.

Kempson, R. M. 1977. *Semantic Theory.* London: Cambridge University Press.

Key, M. R. 1975. *Paralanguage and Kinesics.* Metuchen, N. J.: Scarecrow.

Krakowian, B. & Corder, S. P. 1978. Polish foreigner talk. *Work in Progress*, 11, 78-86. University of Edinburgh, Department of Linguistics.

Kress, G. R. 1977. Tense as modality. *UEA Papers in Linguistics*, 5, 40-52.

Kuno, S. 1978. Generative discourse analysis in America. In Dressler, ed., 275-94.

Labov, W. 1966. On the grammaticality of everyday speech. Paper presented to the LSA Annual Meeting, New York.

Labov, W. 1971. The notion of system in creole languages. In D. Hymes, ed., *Pidginization and Creolization of Languages.* London: Cambridge University Press, 447-72.

Labov, W. 1972a. *Sociolinguistic Patterns.* Philadelphia: University of Pennsylvania Press.

Labov, W. 1972b. *Language in the Inner City.* Philadelphia: University of Pennsylvania Press.

Labov, W. 1972c. Some principles of linguistic methodology. *Language in Society*, 1, 1, 97-120.

Labov, W. 1972d. The transformation of experience in narrative syntax. In Labov, 1972a, 354-96.

Labov, W. 1972e. Rules for ritual insults. In Sudnow, ed., 120-69, 434.

Labov, W. 1972f. The study of language in its social context. Revised version in Labov 1972a, 183-259. First published, 1970.

Labov, W. 1975a. Empirical foundations of linguistic theory. In Austerlitz, ed., *The Scope of American Linguistics.* Lisse: Peter de Ridde, 77-134.

Labov, W. 1975b. *What is a Linguistic Fact?* Lisse: Peter de Ridde. (Same as Labov, 1975a.)

Labov, W. 1978. Crossing the gulf between sociology and linguistics. *The American Sociologist*, 13, 2, 93-103.

Labov, W. and Fanshel, D. 1977. *Therapeutic Discourse.* New York: Academic Press.

Labov, W. and Waletsky, J. 1967. Narrative analysis. In J. Helm, ed., *Essays on the Verbal and Visual Arts.* Seattle: University of Washington Press, 12-44.

Lakoff, G. 1971. Presupposition and relative well-formedness. In Steinberg and Jakobovits, eds., 329-40.

Lakoff, G. and Johnson, M. 1981. *Metaphors We Live By.* Chicago: University of Chicago Press.

Lakoff, R. 1972. Language in context. *Language*, 48, 907-27.

258   REFERENCES

Lakoff, R. 1973. Questionable answers and answerable questions. In B. Kachru, *et al.*, ed., *Papers in Linguistics in Honor of Henry and Reneé Kahane*. Urbana: University of Illinois.

Lamb, C. and Lamb, M. 1822. *Tales from Shakespeare*, 4th edn, London: Godwin.

Langacker, R. W. 1974. Movement rules in functional perspective. *Language*, 50, 630–64.

Laver, J. 1970. The production of speech. In Lyons, ed., 53–76.

Laver, J. 1974. Communicative functions in phatic communion. *Work in Progress*, 7, 1–18. Department of Linguistics, University of Edinburgh.

Laver, J. and Hutcheson, S., eds. 1972. *Face-to-Face Communication*. Harmondsworth: Penguin.

Le Carré, J. 1979. *Smiley's People*. London: Hodder & Stoughton.

Leeson, R. 1975. *Fluency and Language Teaching*. London: Longman.

Lenneberg, E. 1962. Review of Pittenger *et al. The First Five Minutes. Language*, 38, 1, 69–73.

Le Page, R. B. 1975. Projection, focusing, diffusion, or steps towards a sociolinguistic theory of language. Mimeo. University of York.

Lerman, C. L. 1980. *A Sociolinguistic Study of Political Discourse: The Nixon White House Conversations*. Unpublished Ph.D. thesis, University of Cambridge.

Lieberman, R. 1965. On the acoustic basis of the perception of intonation by linguists. *Word*, 21, 40–54. Reprinted in Oldfield and Marshall, eds., 1968, 107–22.

Linde, C. and Labov, W. 1975. Spatial networks as a site for the study of language and thought. *Language*, 51, 924–39.

Lodge, D. 1978. Literary symbolism and Hemingway's 'Cat in the Rain'. Unpublished, University of Birmingham.

Loman, B. 1967. *Conversations in a Negro American Dialect*. Washington D.C.: Center for Applied Linguistics.

Longacre, R. 1976. *An Anatomy of Speech Notions*. Lisse: de Ridder.

Longacre, R. 1978. Why we need a vertical revolution in linguistics. In W. Wölch and P. L. Garvin, eds., *The Fifth LACUS Forum 1978*. Columbia, S. Carolina: Hornbeam Press.

Lycan, W. G. 1977. Conversation, politeness and interruption. *Papers in Linguistics*, Champaign, Illinois, 10, 1/2, 23–53.

Lyons, J. 1968. *Introduction to Theoretical Linguistics*. London: Cambridge University Press.

Lyons, J., ed. 1970. *New Horizons in Linguistics.* Harmondsworth: Penguin.

Lyons, J. 1977. *Semantics*, vols. 1 and 2. London: Cambridge University Press.

Malcolm, I. 1979. *Classroom Communication and the Aboriginal Child: A Sociolinguistic Investigation in Western Australian Primary Schools.* Unpublished PhD. thesis, University of Western Australia.

Malinowski, B. 1923. The problem of meaning in primitive languages. In Ogden and Richards, eds., 296–346.

Mandelbrot, B. 1965. Information theory and psycho-linguistics. In B. B. Wolman and E. Nagel, eds., *Scientific Psychology.* New York: Basic Books.

Mandler, J. M. and Johnson, N. S. 1977. Remembrance of things parsed: story structure and recall. *Cognitive Psychology*, 9, 111–51.

Marshall, J. C. 1970. The biology of communication in man and animals. In Lyons, ed., 229–41.

Martin, J. R. 1981. How many speech acts? *UEA Papers in Linguistics*, 14–15, 52–77.

McCawley, J. D., ed. 1976. *Syntax and Semantics*, vol. 7, *Notes from the Linguistic Underground.* New York: Academic Press.

McCawley, J. D. 1981. *Everything that Linguists have Always Wanted to Know about Logic but were Ashamed to Ask.* Chicago: University of Chicago Press. Also Oxford: Blackwell.

McIntosh, A. 1963. Language and style. In J. Pride and J. Homes, eds., *Sociolinguistics.* Harmondsworth: Penguin.

McTear, M. F. 1979. Review of Labov and Fanshel 1977. *Nottingham Linguistic Circular*, 8, 1, 60–67.

McTear, M. F. 1980. The pragmatics of *because*. Ulster Polytechnic, Mimeo.

Mehan, H. 1979. The competent student. *Working Papers in Sociolinguistics.* Austin, Texas, 61, 1–34.

Mills, C. W. 1940. Situated actions and vocabularies of motive. *American Sociological Review*, 5, 904–13.

Milroy, L. 1980. *Language and Social Networks.* Oxford: Blackwell.

Milroy, L. in press. Comprehension and context: successful communication and communicative breakdown. In Trudgill, ed., in press.

Mishler, E. G. 1972. Implications of teacher-strategies for language and cognition. In Cazden *et al.*, eds., 267–98.

Mishler, E. G. 1975. Studies in dialogue and discourse: an exponential law of successive questioning. *Language in Society*, 4, 31–51.

Moerman, M. 1973. The use of precedent in natural conversation. *Semiotica*, 9, 3, 193–218.

Mohan, B. A. 1974. Do sequencing rules exist? *Semiotica*, 12, 75–96.

Montgomery, M. 1977. *The Structure of Lectures*. Unpublished MA thesis, University of Birmingham.

Morgan, J. L. 1978. Two types of convention in indirect speech acts. In Cole, ed., 261–80.

Morgan, J. L. and Sellner, M. B. 1980. Discourse and linguistic theory. In Spiro *et al.*, eds., 165–199.

Morreal, J. 1979. The evidential use of *because*. *Papers in Linguistics*, 12, 1/2, 231–8.

Munitz, M. K. and Unger, P. D., eds. 1974. *Semantics and Philosophy*. New York: New York University Press.

Myers, T., ed. 1979. *The Development of Conversation and Discourse*. Edinburgh: Edinburgh University Press.

Nash, W. 1981. Openings and preconditions: a note on narrative. *Nottingham Linguistic Circular*, 10, 1, 64–71.

Newmeyer, F. J. 1980. *Linguistic Theory in America*. New York: Academic Press.

Ochs, E. 1979. Planned and unplanned discourse. In Givón, ed., 51–80.

Ochs Keenan, E. 1977. Making it last: repetition in children's discourse. In Ervin-Tripp and Mitchell-Kernan, eds., 125–38.

Ochs Keenan, E. and Schieffelin, B. 1976. Topic as a discourse notion. In C. Li, ed., *Subject and Topic*. New York: Academic Press.

Ogden, C. K. and Richards, I. A. 1923. *The Meaning of Meaning*. London: Routledge & Kegan Paul.

Oldfield, R. C. and Marshall, J. C., eds. 1968. *Language*. Harmondsworth: Penguin.

Opie, I. and Opie, P. 1959. *The Lore and Language of Schoolchildren*. London: Oxford University Press.

Owen, M. 1981. Conversational units and the use of 'well'. In Werth, ed., 99–116.

Palmer, F. 1974. *The English Verb*. London: Longman.

Palmer, F. 1976. *Semantics*. London: Cambridge University Press.

Parlett, M. and Hamilton, D. 1972. Evaluation as illumination. Occasional Paper 9, Centre for Research in the Educational Sciences, University of Edinburgh. Mimeo.

Pittenger, R. E., Hockett, C. F. and Danehy, J. J. 1960. *The First Five Minutes: A Sample of Microscopic Interview Analysis*. New York: Ithaca.

Pomerantz, A. 1975. *Second Assessments: A Study of Some Features of Agreements/Disagreements*. Unpublished Ph.D. thesis, University of California, Irvine.

Popper, K. R. 1959. *The Logic of Scientific Discovery*. London: Hutchinson.

Pride, J. B. 1971. Customs and cases of verbal behaviour. In Ardener, ed., 95–117.

Priestley, J. B. 1946. *Bright Day*. London: Heinemann.

Prince, E. F. 1978. A comparison of wh-clefts and it-clefts in discourse. *Language*, 54, 883–906.

Propp, V. 1928. *Morphology of the Folktale*, trans. L. Scott. Bloomington: Indiana University Press.

Quirk, R. and Greenbaum, S. 1970. *Elicitation Experiments in English*. London: Longman.

Quirk, R., Greenbaum, S., Leech, G. and Svartvik, J. 1972. *A Grammar of Contemporary English*. London: Longman.

Quirk, R. and Svartvik, J. 1966. *Investigating Linguistic Acceptability*. The Hague: Mouton.

Radford, A. 1979. The functional basis of transformations. *Transactions of the Philological Society*, 1979, 1–42.

Richardson, K. 1978. *Worthing Teachers' Centre: A Case Study in Discourse Analysis*. Unpublished M.A. thesis, University of Birmingham.

Robinson, W. P. and Rackstraw, S. J. 1972. *A Question of Answers*, 2 vols. London: Routledge & Kegan Paul.

Roe, 1977. *The Notion of Difficulty in Scientific Text*. Unpublished Ph.D. thesis, University of Birmingham.

Ross, R. 1975. Where to do things with words. In Cole and Morgan, eds., 233–56.

Sacks, H. 1967–72. *Unpublished Lecture Notes*. University of California.

Sacks, H. 1972. On the analysability of stories by children. In Gumperz and Hymes, eds., 329–45.

Sacks, H., Schegloff, E. and Jefferson, G. 1974. A simplest systematics for the organization of turn-taking for conversation. *Language*, 50, 696–735.

Sadock, J. 1974. *Towards a Linguistic Theory of Speech Acts*. New York, Academic Press.

Samarin, W. 1969. *Field Linguistics*. New York: Holt, Rinehart & Winston.

Sankoff, G. 1972. A quantitative paradigm for the study of communicative competence. Paper presented to Texas Conference on the Ethnography of Speaking.

Saville-Troike, M. 1982. *The Ethnography of Communication.* Oxford: Blackwell.

Schegloff, E. A. 1968. Sequencing in conversational openings. *American Anthropologist,* 70, 1075–95.

Schegloff, E. A. 1972. Notes on a conversational practice: formulating place. In Sudnow, ed., 75–119.

Schegloff, E. A. 1979. The relevance of repair to syntax-for-conversation. In Givón, ed., 261–86.

Schegloff, E. A., Jefferson, G. and Sacks, H. 1977. The preference for self-correction in the organization of repair in conversation. *Language,* 53, 2, 361–82.

Schegloff, E. A. and Sacks, H. 1973. Opening up closings. *Semiotica,* 8, 289–327.

Schenkein, J., ed. 1978. *Studies in the Organization of Conversational Interaction.* New York: Academic Press.

Schmerling, S. F. 1975. Asymmetric conjunction and rules of conversation. In Cole and Morgan, eds., 211–32.

Scott, M. B. and Lyman, S. M. 1968. Accounts. *American Sociological Review,* 33, 46–62.

Searle, J. R. 1969. *Speech Acts.* London: Cambridge University Press.

Searle, J. R., ed. 1971. *The Philosophy of Language.* London: Oxford University Press.

Searle, J. R. 1975a. Indirect speech acts. In Cole and Morgan, eds., 59–82.

Searle, J. R. 1975b. The logical status of fictional discourse. *New Literary History,* 6, 2, 319–32.

Searle, J. R. 1976. A classification of illocutionary acts. *Language in Society,* 5, 1–23.

Sebeok, T., ed. 1960. *Style in Language.* Cambridge, Mass.: MIT Press.

Sinclair, J. McH. 1966. Indescribable English. Unpublished Inaugural Lecture, University of Birmingham.

Sinclair, J. McH. 1972. *A Course in Spoken English: Grammar.* London: Oxford University Press.

Sinclair, J. McH. 1980. Discourse in relation to language structure and semiotics. In Greenbaum *et al.,* eds., 110–24.

Sinclair, J. McH. 1981. Planes of discourse in literature. University of Birmingham, Mimeo.

Sinclair, J. McH., Forsyth, I. J., Coulthard, M. and Ashby, M. C. 1972. *The English Used by Teachers and Pupils.* Mimeo, University of Birmingham, Report to SSRC.

Sinclair, J. McH. and Coulthard, M. 1975. *Towards an Analysis of Discourse.* London: Oxford University Press.

Smith, F. 1973. *Psycholinguistics and Reading.* London: Holt, Rinehart & Winston.

Smith, N. & Wilson, D. 1979. *Modern Linguistics: The Results of Chomsky's Revolution.* Harmondsworth: Penguin.

Snow, C. E. and Ferguson, C. A., eds. 1977. *Talking to Children.* London: Cambridge University Press.

Snyder, B. 1971. *The Hidden Curriculum.* New York: Knopf.

Sperber, D. & Wilson, D. 1981. Irony and the use-mention distinction. In P. Cole, ed., 295–318.

Spiro, R. J., Bruce, B. C. and Brewer, W. F., eds. 1980. *Theoretical Issues in Reading Comprehension.* New Jersey: Lawrence Erlbaum.

Stalnaker, R. 1974. Pragmatic presuppositions. In Munitz and Unger, eds., 197–214.

Steinberg, D. D. and Jakobovits, L. A., eds. 1971. *Semantics.* London: Cambridge University Press.

Stern, H. H. 1969. *Languages and the Young School Child.* London: Oxford University Press.

Stoppard, T. 1980. *Dogg's Hamlet, Cahoot's Macbeth.* London: Faber.

Strang, B. M. H. 1962. *Modern English Structure.* London: Arnold.

Strawson, P. F. 1964. Intention and convention in speech acts. *Philosophical Review*, 73, 439–60. Also in Searle, ed. 1971.

Strunk, W. Jr. and White, E. B. 1979. *The Elements of Style*, 3rd edn. New York: MacMillan.

Stubbs, M. 1973. Some structural complexities of talk in meetings. *Working Papers in Discourse Analysis*, 5. University of Birmingham, Mimeo.

Stubbs, M. 1974. The discourse structure of informal committee talk. Mimeo. English Language Research, University of Birmingham.

Stubbs, M. 1976. *Language, Schools and Classrooms.* London: Methuen.

Stubbs, M. 1980. *Language and Literacy.* London: Routledge & Kegan Paul.

Stubbs, M. 1981. Analysts and users: different models of language. Paper read to Applied Linguistics Colloquium, Berne, June 1981.

Stubbs, M. 1982. Stir until the plot thickens. In R. A. Carter and D. Burton, eds., *Literary Text and Language Study.* London: Edward Arnold, 56–85.

Stubbs, M. in press. Applied discourse analysis and educational linguistics. In Trudgill, ed., in press.

Stubbs, M. and Delamont, S., eds. 1976. *Explorations in Classroom Observation.* London: Wiley.

Stubbs, M. and Robinson, B. 1979. Analysing classroom language. In M. Stubbs, B. Robinson and S. Twite, *Observing Classroom Language*, Block 5, PE232. Milton Keynes: Open University Press.

Sudnow, D., ed. 1972. *Studies in Social Interaction.* New York: Free Press.

Svartvik, J. 1980. *Well* in conversation. In Greenbaum *et al.*, eds., 167–77.

Tadros, A. 1980. Prediction in economics text. *ELR Journal* (= English Language Research), 1, 42–59. (University of Birmingham, Mimeo.)

Todorov, T. 1969. *Grammaire du Décaméron.* The Hague: Mouton.

Torode, B. 1976. Teachers' talk and classroom discipline. In Stubbs and Delamont, eds., 173–92.

Trudgill, P., ed. 1978. *Sociolinguistic Patterns in British English.* London: Edward Arnold.

Trudgill, P., ed. in press. *Applied Sociolinguistics.* London: Academic Press.

Turner, R. 1970. Words, utterances and activities. In Douglas, ed., 165–87.

Turner, R. 1972. Some formal properties of therapy talk. In Sudnow, ed., 367–96.

Turner, R., ed. 1974. *Ethnomethodology.* Harmondsworth: Penguin.

Van Dijk, T. A. 1972. *Some Aspects of Text Grammars.* The Hague: Mouton.

Van Dijk, T. A. 1977. *Text and Context.* London: Longman.

Van Dijk, T. A. 1979. Pragmatic connectives. *Journal of Pragmatics*, 3, 5, 447–57.

Van Dijk, T. A. and Kintsch, W. 1978. Cognitive psychology and discourse: recalling and summarising stories. In Dressler, ed., 61–80.

Walker, R. and Adelman, C. 1976. Strawberries. In Stubbs & Delamont, eds., 133–50.

Webb, E. J., Campbell, D. T., Schwartz, R. D. and Sechrest, L. 1966. *Unobtrusive Measures.* New York: Rand McNally.

Wells, G. 1981. Describing children's linguistic development at home and at school. In Adelman, ed., 134–62.

Wells, G. *et al*. 1979. The development of discourse: a report of work in progress. University of Bristol, Mimeo.

Wells, G. & Montgomery, M. 1981. Adult–child interaction at home and at school. In French and MacLure, eds., 210–43.

Wells, H. G. 1904. 'The Country of the Blind'. In *Selected Short Stories*. Harmondsworth: Penguin, 1958.

Werth, P., ed. 1981. *Conversation and Discourse*. London: Croom Helm.

Widdowson, H. G. 1979a. Rules and procedures in discourse analysis. In Myers, ed., 61–71.

Widdowson, H. G. 1979b. *Explorations in Applied Linguistics*. London: Oxford University Press.

Willes, M. 1980. *Children into Pupils: a Study in the Development of Sociolinguistic Competence*. Unpublished Ph.D. thesis, University of Birmingham.

Willes, M. 1981. Learning to take part in classroom interaction. In French and MacLure, eds., 73–90.

Wilson, D. 1975. *Presupposition and Non-Truth-Conditional Semantics*. London: Academic Press.

Wilson, J. in prep. Ph.D. thesis. Queen's University, Belfast.

Winograd, T. 1972. *Understanding Natural Language*. New York: Academic Press.

Wolfson, N. 1976. Speech events and natural speech. *Language in Society*, 5, 2, 189–209.

Wolfson, N. 1979. The conversational historical present alteration. *Language*, 55, 1, 168–82.

Wooton, A. J. in press. The management of grantings and rejections by parents in request sequences. *Semiotica*.

Name Index

Subject Index

A-, B-, AB-events, 118–20; *see also* Shared knowledge
Accept, 189ff
Acknowledgement, 22, 30, 119, 189ff
Actions, utterances as, 1–4, 147–8; *see also* Speech acts
Active versus passive sentences, 124–5
Adjacency pairs, 131–2, 224
Adverbs (adverbials): problems in analysis, 67, 70ff, 179–80; sentence adverbs, 70–1, 180; time and place, 107
Alienation devices, *see* Estrangement devices
Alignments, 187ff, 193
Audio-recording, 222, 224–7, 238–9

Certainty of information, marking of, 77, 80–1, 120–2
Challenges, 149–50, 165ff, 172–4
Closed classes, 75, 107, 139, 190
Coding schemes, 50ff, 61–2, 64
Coherence in discourse, 9, 15, 59, 63, 85, 102, 123–4, 126–7, 130, 138, 141ff, 147, 169ff, 179ff, 187, 228
Cohesion, 9, 92, 107, 126–7, 143, 147, 151, 169, 184, 205, 211; lexical, 22–3, 26–8
Communicative stress, 36, 54, 47, 226
Competence, 85; communicative, 5, 102, 159, 230. 236; grammatical, 121; literary, 195–6, 210
Comprehensive coverage of data, 61–2
Constatives, 150, 152
Continuous classification (preclassification), 96, 105, 107, 109, 135–6
Control over discourse, 43–4. 48, 50ff, 56, 60, 134, 160–1, 184, 232–3
Conversational analysis, *see* Ethnomethodology

Co-ordinating conjunctions, 66, 77ff
Core vocabulary, 201–2
Corrigibility, 90–2, 125

Deceptive language, 206ff, 209ff
Definition of the situation, 60
Deniability, 174
Discourse acts, *see* Speech acts
Discourse analysis, definition of, 1, 9, 13
Disjunction markers, 69, 167–8
Distributional constraints, 71–2, 86; distributional tests, 71ff; *see also* Syntagmatic organization

Ellipsis, 105, 109, 111–12, 135, 142–3, 165, 167, 179, 233
Endorsements, 22, 30, 187ff
Entailments, logical, 79, 85, 97, 125, 202ff, 206ff, 214ff
Estrangement devices, 20, 239–43
Ethnography of communication, 8, 12, 40ff, 46–7, 63, 67, 211, 218, 220
Ethnomethodology, 10, 12, 152, 229, 235; *see also* Jefferson, Sacks, Schegloff, Schenkein, Turner in name index
Exchange: definition of, 28–9, 104, 109–10, 129, 131, 133, 135, 139, 143, 193; IRF, 29, 131–3, 137, 145–6; structure, 24, 28–9, 128ff, 131ff; *see also* Adjacency pair
Expansions, 142–3
Expectations, *see* Predictive structure
Experimental data, uses of, 92, 121, 129, 144–6, 159, 161, 195ff, 213, 218, 221, 236, 240

Feedback, 22–3, 30; *see also* Exchange, IRF